MOURNING
HAS
BROKEN

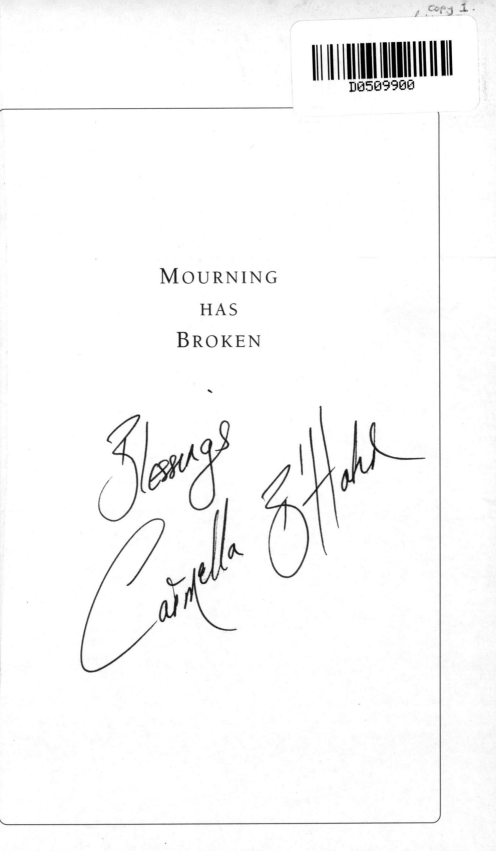

Blessings

Carmella B. Hahn

by the same author
BENJAYA'S GIFTS
(with M'haletta B'Hahn)

Carmella B'Hahn

MOURNING

HAS

BROKEN

Learning from the Wisdom of Adversity

CRUCIBLE

Published by
Crucible Publishers
Norton St Philip, Bath BA2 7LN, UK
www.cruciblepublishers.com

First published 2002
Reprinted 2002

ISBN 1-902733-05-3

Set in 11/12½pt Berkeley
Book design by Two Can, Bath
Cover design David Cowell & Two Can
Front cover photograph by M'haletta B'Hahn
Author's photo by Oliver Thomas

Printed in Great Britain by
Creative Print and Design Group

This book is dedicated
to
my mother,
M'haletta,
in gratitude for the
transformational times we have shared

and
to all those seeking to
"peace" themselves back together

FOREWORD
by Rachel Naomi Remen, M.D.

Often wisdom gets passed through the ages by storytelling. However, in the rush of 21st century life few of us find the time to tell our stories or listen to the stories of others. We turn to "experts" to tell us how to live, not realizing what life has already taught us and the people around us about how to live well. We may need to reclaim the art of listening to each other so that stories can work their magic of strengthening us and weaving us together as family and community once again.

Mourning Has Broken offers us the experience of listening deeply to the life stories of others and sharing the wisdom of those who have discovered their real strength through their wounds and found ways to live a good life even though it may not be an easy life. My grandfather, an orthodox rabbi, blessed me and strengthened me with the gift of his many stories. Although he has been gone for almost 60 years his stories strengthen me still.

Wrestling with the Angel

Almost the last story that my grandfather told me was about a man called Jacob who had been attacked in the night as he slept alone by the bank of a river. He had been traveling, and when he had stopped to make his meal and settle down to sleep, the place had seemed safe enough. But it was not so. He awakened to find himself gripped by muscular arms and pinned to the ground. It was so dark that he could not see his enemy, but he could feel his power. Gathering all his strength, he began to struggle to be free.

"Was it a nightmare, Grandpa?" I said hopefully. I often suffered from nightmares back then and had to sleep with a nightlight on. I moved closer to my grandfather and took his hand. "No, Neshume-le," he answered, "it was quite real but it happened a long time ago. Jacob could hear his attacker's breath, he could feel the cloth of his garments, he could even smell him. Jacob was a very strong man, but even using all of his strength he could not free himself and he could not pin his enemy down either. They were evenly matched and they rolled on the ground and struggled fiercely."

"How long did they struggle, Grandpa?" I asked with some anxiety. "A long, long time, Neshume-le," he replied, "but the darkness does not last forever. Eventually it was dawn and as the light came, Jacob saw that he had been wrestling with an angel."

I was astonished. "A real angel, Grandpa?" I said. "With wings?"

"I don't know if he had wings, Neshume-le, but he was definitely an angel," he told me. "With the coming of the light, the angel let go of Jacob and tried to leave, but Jacob held him fast. 'Let me go,' the angel told Jacob, 'The Light has come.' But Jacob said, 'I will not let you go until you bless me.' The angel struggled hard, for he wanted badly to escape, but Jacob held him close. And so the angel gave him his blessing."

I was very relieved. "Did he leave then, Grandpa? Is that the end?" I asked. "Yes," my grandfather said, "but Jacob's leg was hurt in the struggle. Before the angel left, he touched him on the place where he was hurt." This was something I could understand; often my mother did this, too. "To help it get better, Grandpa?" I asked. But my grandfather shook his head. "I do not think so, Neshume-le. He touched it to remind Jacob of it. Jacob carried it all the rest of his life. It was his place of remembering."

I was very puzzled by this story. How could it be that one might confuse an angel with an enemy? But Grandfather said this was the sort of thing that happened all the time. "Even so," he told me, "it is not the most important part of the story. The most important part of the story is that everything has its blessing."

In the year before he died, my grandfather told me this story several times. Eight or nine years afterward, in the middle of the night, the disease I have lived with for more than 45 years declared itself in the most dramatic way imaginable. I had a massive internal hemorrhage. There was no warning at all. I was in a coma and hospitalized for months. The darkness and the struggle lasted for many years afterward.

Looking back on it, I have wondered if my grandfather, old and close to the time of his death, had not left me with this story as a compass. It is a puzzling story, a story about the nature of blessings and the nature of enemies. How tempting to let the enemy go, and flee. To put the struggle behind you as quickly as possible and get on with your life. Life might be easier then but far less genuine. Perhaps the wisdom lies in engaging the life you have been given as fully and courageously as possible and not letting go until you find the unknown blessing that is in everything.

from *My Grandfather's Blessings* by Rachel Naomi Remen, M.D.

Thank You

This five-year journey of creating *Mourning Has Broken* has been laced with such extraordinary support that I have often wept in gratitude.

Each and every interviewee has graciously gifted his or her time and precious story for the good of others. Thank you.

My friend and self-appointed "agent", Linda Lantieri, with whom I share a deep sacred quest, has not wavered in her practical and emotional generosity. Among the countless opportunities she brought into my life was the opening of the door to the Fetzer Community of Scholars and Fellows whose circle of wisdom has had a profound impact on me and ultimately the content of this book. Thank you.

The financial support from Eileen Rockefeller-Growald, the Lifebridge Foundation, and Margie Baldwin and Elaine Seiler of the Marion Foundation has not only given me the material necessities for such a project and the freedom to fly where I was bidden to conduct the interviews, but also has given me the much needed moral support of the statement "We believe in you." Thank you.

My parents, Derek and M'haletta, with support from other family members, have tirelessly ferried me to and from Birmingham airport and fed and housed me on passing through in various states of jet-lag from the Atlantic crossing. And my ex-husband, Abel B'Hahn, who I still consider as family, has retained an unceasing commitment to support me with the childcare needed for our son, Asher, in the long labor of birthing this book. Thank you.

My Devon community of friends, especially my extraordinary women's group, have provided me with a vital web of loving connection to emerge into when I took breaks from the long hours in solitary confinement. Thank you.

Robin Campbell of Crucible Publishers recognized the worth of this book and with a glad heart took on the final task of bringing it to print and to find its market in the world. Thank you.

And finally, again, I would like to thank the life-force that came through me but is not from me. Without it my mourning would probably still not have broken and this book would not exist.

Acknowledgements

The author and publishers acknowledge permission to reproduce from the following works:

"Wrestling with the Angel", from *My Grandfather's Blessings* by Rachel Remen, M.D., copyright © 2000 by Rachel Naomi Remen, M.D.
Used by permission of Riverhead Books, an imprint of Penguin Putnam, Inc.

"Wrestling with the Angel", from *My Grandfather's Blessings* by Rachel Remen, M.D., reprinted by permission of HarperCollins Publishers Ltd.
© Rachel Naomi Remen, M.D., 2000

The Phoenix Factor - Surviving and Growing though Personal Crisis
by Karl Slaikeu and Steve Lawhead. Copyright © 1985 by Karl Slaikeu and Steve Lawhead. Reprinted by permission of Houghton Mifflin Company.
All rights reserved.

Waking the Tiger, Healing Trauma, by Peter Levine, (North Atlantic Books, 1997)

Journeys of Transformation
(One By One, Inc., P.O.Box 1709, Brookline, Ma 02446, USA).

Excerpted from *The Book of Awakening* by Mark Nepo,
copyright © 2000 by Mark Nepo, by permission of Conari Press.

The Journal of Jungian Theory and Practice, Fall 2001, vol. 3,
NY, C.G. Jung Institute of New York.

CONTENTS

INTRODUCTION

Mourning Has Broken has a life of its own, and firstly I want to honor that life. It is as if I am the mother of this book-child, a child who, in Kahlil Gibran's words from *The Prophet*, has come through me, but is not from me. Writing this book has meant catching a seed of an idea and then listening... listening... listening to how it wanted to manifest, before guiding it in that direction.

It is a book woven with deeply personal stories about transformation through adversity – dark nights that awaken to a new kind of morning. Written for anyone, like myself, with wounds that need healing, the stories offer the chance to walk a while in the moccasins of others through their roughest terrain... and out the other side. It is a voyage of discovery, inspiring new perspectives on traumatic events and offering practical keys to effective living. I have gathered healing stories by interviewing people of diverse backgrounds and ethnic roots, with different spiritual and religious influences, and with very different challenges as their teachers. I hope I have produced a global map book of the territory of transition. Its many pages offer a variety of routes to explore. It is also a workbook, the questions and reflections at the end of each section offering a guided journey of personal transformation.

The process I used in these interviews is similar to what is called a "formative evaluation" in the world of research. I was seeking to discover the perceptions of specific individuals regarding their life experience and to see if common themes might emerge across interviews. The interviews, which usually lasted for at least an hour and a half, were taped and transcribed. Certain questions were asked consistently, such as: What exactly did you endure in your time of crisis? What pulled you through? What sustains you now? How have you gained from this experience? What would you say to anyone else in crisis?

I have chosen to keep the stories as whole as possible because I want to model a way of learning that takes note of the bigger picture rather than following the more common way of reducing our offerings to bite-sized pieces. By including more of the picture, rather than seeing events as isolated incidents, the amazing wealth of learning present in each person's life tapestry is revealed.

The interviews focused on the "how" of each person's experience rather than the end result. I wanted to understand the dynamics of "breaking through mourning." There were of course multiple ways of interpreting what I heard, and so my intention with each of those interviewed was to gain insight into what meaning the experience had for that person.

As I read and analyzed each interview, I started to highlight statements that described essential elements of the healing process of my storyteller. I noticed that there seemed to be repeated predictable patterns emerging from the raw material. This process of evaluation is comparable to the "grounded theory" approach – a term coined by researchers Strauss and Corbin.[1] The researcher lets the process of the interview take them where the interviewee goes and the "theory" or explanation emerges from the investigation. Themes such as: the existence of a bigger picture, the need to trust, to share pain, to reassess what is important in life, to claim the gifts of the challenge, and to connect to our common humanity, arose time and again. This helped me group the interviews and settle in on the themes, which eventually became the eight keys to handling adversity, which I have used as section titles in the book.

The names of these eight keys are: Find the Bigger Picture, Trust and Surrender Control, Share Your Pain and Choose Life, Reassess Relationships, Identify and Release Life-long Patterns, Cultivate Compassion: Silence the Judge, Reclaim Your Heart and Spirit, and Find the Hidden Gifts.

What I thought would be my last interview for this book was conducted on that fateful day that will go down in history – September 11, 2001. It was an uncharacteristically frenetic morning. My new tape recorder batteries suddenly went flat, and my clip-on microphone that was working well at 8am stopped functioning by 10am. There was agitation in the air and my storyteller and I were both perturbed. At 3pm English time all hell broke loose. Flying terrorists had made their horrifying mark, and countless people were joining the sea of those who have experienced traumatic shock, soon to be followed by the painful process of mourning a monumental loss. My heart broke... again, and then, into that chasm of grief filtered a ray of gratitude as I realized the absolute perfection of the timing and title of *Mourning Has Broken*. With the instant shredding of our sense of safety in the West and the rising need for positive news and tools for healing, perhaps the message of this book would have more chance of being truly heard.

I observed carefully both my own response and the reaction of people and nations across the globe and it became evident that these same themes were emerging en masse as if this macrocosmic global event held the microcosm of each individual story in this book and many of the lessons therein. This I have captured in the final section entitled Gathering the Keys – From the Ashes of September 11.

I believe I was born in a state of mourning. Even my skin color was blue. On a dark, freezing day in 1958 I entered the world in a small semi-detached house in the middle of England, and as far back as my memories stretch, I recall a deep well of sadness within me. It has been an uphill struggle to break out of my shady hiding place into the light of the world. My parents were not the cause. No one knew why my world was such a sad and silent one. "Autism" was the only label to be found for my condition, but it did not stick for long.

I was like a delicate wild flower seed in the dark earth, wanting to hide safely in my shell rather than facing the danger and pain of negotiating the hazards en route to my unknown destination. The unknown terrified me, but nature had its way and I began to grow, hitting rocks and obstacles to which others seemed oblivious. My child-mind concluded that if others were not being crushed by the same rocks as me, then I must be a weedy misfit. Why was my nervous system being battered by life's trivial happenings when others needed a hurricane to bend them? I didn't manage to utter a word in public until I was six. Obtaining the salt at the dinner table or getting permission to go to the toilet during class was a major source of trauma for me.

My mother was my saving grace. Without attempting to mold me, with the skill of a seasoned midwife, she listened carefully to how I wanted to manifest and then guided me into being. Now, in adulthood, having at last broken through the earth, I can see countless types of flowers, and realize that every one has fought for its survival. We have all had different soils, rocks, worms, bogs and tin cans to negotiate on our way to the sun. Some of us grow fast, some slow. Some, like cacti in the desert, were born with an innate knowledge of surviving our habitat, while others, blown by strong winds, struggle to adapt and live through shocking hardships on the path.

The title of this book, *Mourning Has Broken*, describes how I feel now about life 44 years after my blue birth, and several years after facing a boulder on my path that threatened to crush me with its horrific weight. It was because I survived this weight and flourished that I felt compelled to connect with others who have experienced great hardships to discover and disseminate the wisdom they have gained from their wounds.

If I had to sum up in one word what fires me most in life it would be "transition." For over two decades now I have been observing with fascination the new emerging paradigms. In that time I have connected to thousands of people in the process of conscious personal transition, and it has not escaped my attention that the speed and depth of challenge and change have increased immeasurably.

Some will say that they see no evidence of positive change, and that from their standpoint, meaningless living, depression, negativity and evil are on the increase. It is my belief that "evil" (the opposite of live) has always been in existence and is rising from the underground at this time for all to see. It is "out there" happening in real life and yet it is also like a great mirror reflecting what we don't want to see – our own veiled violent tendencies. It is calling us to deal with darkness responsibly. I feel grateful also to have encountered in increasing intensity the side of life that is light and that enables me to balance my experience of those darkening shadows and to believe that love does have the power to conquer fear and hatred.

The following piece, edited from "Wisdom of the Elders" which is put out by the Hopi Nation, has spread at lightning speed around the globe. It obviously strikes an important chord, and it describes my experience perfectly:

To my fellow swimmers,

There is a river now flowing very fast. It is so great and swift that there are those who are afraid. They will try to hold on to the shore. They will feel as if they are being torn apart and will suffer greatly. Know the river has its destination. The elders say that we must let go of the shore, push off into the middle of the river, keep our eyes open and our heads above the water.

And I say, see who is in there with you and celebrate.

At this time in history we are to take nothing personally, least of all ourselves. For the moment that we do, our spiritual growth and journey comes to a halt.

The time of the lone wolf is over. Gather yourselves!
Banish the word struggle from your attitude and your vocabulary.

All that we do now must be done in a sacred manner and in celebration.

WE ARE THE ONES WE'VE BEEN WAITING FOR

It is my belief that we all need to improve our fitness on all levels *now* so that when we find ourselves in the rapids, as we surely will, we have the resilience required to swim with the powerful current. It is a current that has the potential to sweep us towards a global tide of positive change in human consciousness.

My simple, personal analogy of this wave of change is in terms of sight. Humanity is moving from the two-eyed viewpoint to single vision; from separation consciousness to an awareness of our ultimate unity. The two-eyed perspective, that is familiar to us all, is from within the body and its five senses and perceives itself as a three-dimensional being, separate from all living things. With this two-eyed sight we both see and experience the polarities in life, continuing to be a victim to the ups and downs of living and categorizing them as good or bad, right or wrong, triumph or tragedy.

Those with single vision experience themselves as multi-dimensional beings. They make use of extra senses which enable them to perceive life from a wider perspective; experiencing it as one great tapestry, a unified system in which each thread has an effect on the whole picture and is equally valuable, whatever its color and texture. When we have single vision we speak a language of the heart and spirit together with the head, and we trust and accept the process of life, knowing ourselves to be the weavers of our own pattern.

Over the years my passionate quest to perfect my single vision has drawn me into the sphere of countless truth seekers and I have become aware of the vastness of the global network of those who live their lives by inner laws. They are committed to the inner voice that calls for integrity and leads them along the fastest route of grace toward experiencing their natural state of wholeness. External events may temporarily shake and shock their senses but ultimately they draw upon a core of safety from within.

In my previous book, *Benjaya's Gifts*,[2] I told my own story of the extraordinary birth and shocking death of my five-year-old son and the legacy of learning from these experiences (which I will reveal throughout this book as it connects to the healing keys). Reading my story opened the door for others in pain to communicate with me and I found myself in the privileged position of being invited into the deepest, most wounded places in people, because they knew I would understand. In hearing these out-pourings, I became aware that the way in which people relate to challenge and transitions in life clearly shows their whole mental, emotional, physical and spiritual modus operandi. What an opportunity I would have then to learn more of this paradigm shift in human consciousness if I invited the right kind of people to share their personal transition stories with me.

Eagerly, I sought out individuals who have made strides in the direction of single vision, so that their tales of how they embraced traumatic events in their lives could be used to expand our understanding of new ways of thinking and relating to life; ways which substantially diminish pain and conflict, raise the spirits and nourish the healing process. I say, "made strides" because I am aware that each of the interviewees is still in process. God has not finished with any of us yet! I imagined that from the combined insights of my storytellers, a blueprint would be created of who we really are beneath our conditioning, and what we are capable of becoming.

My way of relating to life uses all that crosses my path as a reflection of my inner life. As Native Americans do, I pay particular attention to the wildlife that enters my day. I'm telling you this because this particular day, as I was writing the above, a pheasant sat outside the window, calling, screeching for attention. I was drawn to go outside and follow the pheasant, which was by now leaping in feathery bursts down the steep lane outside my cottage. It flew away and I was left standing there, transported by the beauty of this Devon countryside. My eyes became riveted on the forest that clothes the nearby valley, which was shimmering in the sun and wind.

This magnificent spectacle of nature offered a reflection of my desires for this book: one forest body created by the synthesis of individual trees in a myriad of shades, shapes, and colors – each weathered by the elements in their own unique way. I saw the importance of both the light and shadows being voiced in this book and had a sense that synergy – an energy or result greater than the sum of its parts – would be released. My intention is for

Mourning Has Broken to facilitate down-to-earth, yet transformational, healing.

There was more. I continued my silent walk, keeping my eyes loosely aware of the possible gifts of nature. They alighted on a tiny pale triangle in the grass, so I went to investigate. I pulled on the tip and out came a small, perfect pheasant's feather. Thank you, I thought, but what *is* the pheasant's message? I was aware of a thought passing through of how lovely it would be to find a larger feather, followed quickly by a reminder to simply appreciate the one I had been given. And so I was deep in gratitude looking at the feather when my feet compelled me to stop walking. Perplexed, I looked down, and there, right in front of my shiny boots, was a large, beautiful pheasant's feather. I cried and hurried home.

There, with a sense of urgency, I looked up the meaning of the pheasant in my *Animal Speak* dictionary of animal, bird, and reptile symbolism.[3] This is what I read: "Anyone with a pheasant totem who has badger feathers (with striped tapered markings like a badger) would do well to study the characteristics of the badger itself." Clutching my badger feathers with nervous fingers, I looked up "badger":

> *The badger is tied to the mystery of the "word" – especially the magic of storytelling... It is time to tell a new story about yourself and your life...*
>
> *"I would ask you to remember only this one thing," said Badger. "The stories people tell have a way of taking care of them. If stories come to you, care for them. And learn to give them away where they are needed. Sometimes a person needs a story more than food to stay alive. That is why we put these stories in each other's memory. This is how people care for themselves."*

This incident totally reinforced my belief in the healing power of stories; not only in the listening, but also the telling. In giving and receiving our life experiences we connect, we network, we weave the human tapestry into a sense of community that prevents the numbing pain of separation.

I have come to use the term "Osmotic Learning" to describe the conscious process of absorbing useful messages from stories – imprinting our souls – thereby accelerating the rate of personal transformation. I firmly believe that it is possible to imprint ourselves so deeply with an understanding of certain life lessons that we will no longer need to draw events toward us that teach those lessons. Of course we are all absorbing and being imprinted in every living moment. But what true transformation requires is purposeful opening to repeatedly absorb positive messages about how to break through to a more effective way of living.

I live with a conviction of the existence of a reality beyond the physical in which love and thoughts traverse time and space. I firmly believe that by listening respectfully and compassionately with an open mind to the storytellers' gifts, we will affect their lives positively, just as if we were a close friend fully present at the time of the sharing. Best selling author, Rachel Naomi Remen M.D., believes this as well. In her moving book, *Kitchen Table Wisdom*, also filled with stories, she says, "Stories allow us to see something familiar through new eyes. We become in that moment a guest in someone else's life, and together with them sit at the feet of their teacher."

I sat with my vision and intention for this book for a while with no notion of how I would manifest the people, the time or the money required. From the beginning I carried an absolute certainty that *Mourning Has Broken* would happen, and into that certainty, out of the blue, walked the woman who held the "how" piece of the puzzle.

Her name is Linda Lantieri, a New Yorker with Italian and German blood who is often taken for a Native American. I met her at my mother's Holistic Center in England in the summer of 1997, where she was staying on retreat from her intense work as an internationally known peace educator in schools. In our first conversation I found myself describing this book-to-be, which was greeted with instant excitement and a statement of her desire to support me to actualize it. She revealed that she is dedicated to connecting the conventional world of institutions with those who are developing new paradigms and visions, thereby helping to give the sacred its rightful place in the world. Her prolific contacts were generously laid at my disposal and her home was offered as a venue for interviews.

I have a deep sense of gratitude about this auspicious meeting, and recently recalled being told long ago by an intuitive friend that I would be meeting a powerful person from abroad who would help me manifest my life's work. It is as if some bigger intelligence holds the whole picture, and we both answered the call to play our parts in the script. Also, everyone I asked to interview (except some of those affected by September 11 who were not quite ready) responded quickly and positively, generously giving their stories for the good of others. They each voiced their gratitude at being given the opportunity to share, as it offered them another level of healing, adding a little more meaning and purpose to their ordeals.

It was very important to me how the interviews were conducted, and whatever the venue, whether it was a functional hotel bedroom, a college staff room, or Linda's lovely New York apartment, I set about creating a safe atmosphere conducive to sharing from the heart. I asked for inner guidance before each interview to help me create a safe, held space for each person. Of course, I had an advantage over some interviewers in that my "subjects" knew that I had faced my own nightmare. That knowledge alone was a powerful key to opening the door and letting me into their wounded places. An unspoken recognition and shared compassion speedily cemented the rapport.

Some of the storytellers found themselves sitting upon a very special quilt to unfold their stories. In 1995 Linda Lantieri was given an award in the Black Hills of South Dakota to honor her work with youth and conflict resolution. It is called "The Spirit of Crazy Horse Award" and, in a ceremony, recipients are given a Native American Star Quilt, made by the Lakota people over many months in a state of prayer.

I'll paint an image for you, especially seeing as the native quilt will also feature in one of the coming stories. Linda's quilt is the size of a double bed, and the star, which seems to pulsate as you look at it, consists of over a hundred diamond shapes in turquoise, green, red, and black, sewn together onto a background of white. Linda was told that with the award comes access to the spirit of Crazy Horse – a famous chief of the Oglala Sioux (also called the Lakota) who was said to be invincible in battle; protected by advice given in a vision. And so I spread this spirit on the floor to support those who came.

Although I did my best to create a sacred space for every storyteller, the sharings that took place in Linda's apartment had an added dimension because I had more resources at hand. I invited these storytellers to wander around the apartment and, without much application of the conscious mind, to choose three objects, the first to represent the trauma, the second to symbolize their present state of being, and the third to reflect their intent for the future. This proved to be a profound exercise, creating an outer reflection of their transformational journey. The collection of objects, placed in the center of the quilted star, became a temporary altar that inevitably called for alteration by the end of the story. Usually, at the beginning the objects were separate, sometimes in a row, without close relationship with each other. But then a need would arise to integrate the trauma symbol with the others so that it became accepted and held in a more holistic relationship.

I remember the moment when Janet, who had chosen a cactus as symbolic of herself in trauma, realized that the spikes were not nature gone wrong; they grew that way for a useful purpose. It was then, with a sigh of relief, that she moved her symbol, which had much nourishment hidden in its protective body, to join the lion and the lamb – her newfound combination of strength and gentleness. Between the lines, then, some of these stories have another level of movement in terms of healing taking place, which remains in the private domain of the individuals.

In listening to the stories, it soon became apparent that the keys – although appearing from the wisdom learned through adversity – resound with ancient truths that open the door to more effective living, whatever our circumstances. Having said this, although we have all experienced adversity to some degree and can apply all these keys to our everyday living, there is some information I believe it is necessary to impart to those who have been specifically affected by trauma or who have an interest in its effects.[4] This information will also help us to gain more from the stories themselves when we begin.

The *World English Dictionary* definition of adversity is "extremely unfavorable hardship and suffering" whereas trauma is defined, by renowned author and child psychiatrist, Dr. James Garbarino, as "arising from coming face to face with extreme danger and uncontrollable terror at the same time."[5] This danger can be acute or chronic and followed by Post Traumatic Stress Disorder (PTSD) which includes possible flashbacks, emotional detachment, attempts to avoid memories, hyper-arousal, and sometimes guilt about surviving when others have not. *Mourning Has Broken* contains stories of recovery from both adversity and trauma.

Resilience, or the ability to break through rather than break down, is actually a balancing act between "risk factors" and "protective opportunities." Most of the traumatic events experienced by the people I interviewed definitely increased the odds on them sustaining permanent harm. However, the research informs us that it was these people's internal resources and external assets that made all the difference to how they were able to cope. What makes someone break down from adversity is rarely caused by the reaction to a single traumatic event. It is the building up of several harmful risks without an equal number of inner and outer resources to counteract those risks that can break us.

James Garbarino tells us for example that "Children are resilient, but they do have their limits. Children suffer when the number of strikes against them increases to three or four or more – particularly when the hazards accumulate without compensatory building of favorable factors."[6] He uses the analogy of juggling tennis balls: you can learn to juggle two or even three but make it four and you drop them all unless someone teaches you more advanced juggling. The good news from the research is that it is possible to increase our protective opportunities if we know what those are. This was the case with those I interviewed. They were able to prevent their coping capacity from being overwhelmed and were able to bounce back as well as to avoid long term negative effects from their traumatic circumstances. In fact, the most current research on resilience points to the fact that specific negative influence in someone's life does not necessarily mean that there will be a negative outcome.

Some of my interviewees survived their difficult circumstances with secondary scars, even though they had broken through to a process of transformation and regeneration. Although they avoided the obvious risks often caused by trauma, some had to deal with other wounds – struggles with self-esteem issues or fear of intimacy.

The resilience literature makes an important distinction between coping and thriving. Human beings are adaptable and as a result we can tolerate or cope with a lot. However, in order to thrive in the face of adversity, some important elements are needed. The work of Losel and Bliesener[7] outlines seven components that contribute to thriving and resilience:

PERSONAL ANCHORS – Stable positive emotional relationships present in one's life.

COGNITIVE COMPETENCE – Having the intellectual capacity to analyze one's social environment and to be able to avoid self-defeating strategies for coping.

GAINING A TRACK RECORD OF SUCCESS – This enhances one's belief that one is capable of succeeding when another challenge comes our way.

ACTIVE COPING STRATEGIES – When one tries to actively master the challenge and does something rather than passively reacting, resilience is increased.

A POSITIVE TEMPERAMENT – This mostly inborn trait helps one to seek out and attract useful people and to draw them in for support.

THE SOCIAL CLIMATE – How open and supportive the climate is at home and in the other institutions with which one is connected.

ADDITIONAL SUPPORT – Access to a wider community beyond one's close circle.

As you enter the lives of those I interviewed, you will see some of these conditions very present. Add these together with the eight keys and the personal kernels of wisdom from each storyteller and you have a lot of ways to open the door to healing. Each story in this book has a different cadence and note, and the impact of the messages will be different for everyone. I encourage you to let the stories speak to you personally and to shed light on your own particular challenges.

In reading stories such as this it is natural that your own grief will be triggered – maybe even grief you didn't know you had will emerge. This is a healthy response and needs to be dealt with appropriately. I suggest space is given to any rising feelings, including the more joyous ones. Recognize their existence and allow them to move through rather than "swallowing" them in the rush to finish the story. Remember that all the storytellers will lead you to their place of resolution by the story's end. You might also need a way to positively resource yourself if you become engulfed in an intense emotional reaction at any point. Right now would be a good time to find an exceptionally positive memory, a time when you felt safe and good about yourself and life. Remember this feeling in your body. Where is it located exactly? Breathe deeply into this safe place and know that at any time you can return here.

I believe that if the necessary time is taken, individually or within a discussion group,[8] to engage fully with the questions and reflections at the end of each section (preferably using a journal), the learning will have a chance to integrate, allowing personal transformation to occur. *Mourning Has Broken*, however, is not meant to take the place of a professional therapist who is trained to hold and guide the deeper healing process. Working closely with someone you trust whose task is to totally support your healing may be essential to keep the necessary momentum toward wholeness.

Finally, I want to tell you how the name of *Mourning Has Broken* came to be, because this title was the note of resonance to which both the storytellers and readers were drawn. The last lines of the final chapter of my book, *Benjaya's Gifts*, read:

My son/sun is shining still as he did upon the earth,
                    breaking the mourning with his light.

My father, Derek, on reading this mused, "*Mourning Has Broken*, now that would be a good name for a book!" And so it is, bringing with it, for most people, a memorable tune and the lyrics, "Morning has broken like the first morning, blackbird has spoken like the first bird..."

It seems symbolic to me that the cover of this book contains my father's words coupled with my mother's image. The "dove sunrise" was captured on film by her on a trip to a sacred site in Mexico. I approached many publishers, and of all the names this work could have been associated with, the one who answered the call is named "Crucible" with its logo of the sun shining from a chalice. What is a crucible? My computer definition says it is a place or set of circumstances where people or things are subjected to forces, which test them and often make them change.

The analogy of the morning breaking after a dark night speaks volumes to me. I imagine the night's chill beginning to lift and mists clearing as the sun rises. And when I think of grief, I sense that the breaking of the mourning process and the drying of tears are as inevitable as the sun's ascent and the evaporation of the morning dew.

The experience of re-emerging into life after my own dark night of the death of my son has been very much like the first morning of the song. I have felt like a newborn with a chance to start again. My skin seems more transparent, hiding none of my deeper feelings, calling me to be totally authentic in each precious moment. I have new eyes, new vision and a passionate desire to share my insights. I want to inspire others to engage more fully with the heart of life and to connect with the vast potential we have as human beings, no matter what we've suffered on our travels.

The first story will be mine, the telling of which still breaks me open to an indescribable chasm of emotional pain. But I know that revisiting the chasm voluntarily will put me in touch again with the experience of my own depths and capacity as a human being to feel fully alive.

And so, I invite you to sit at the feet of my teacher.

The First Key

FIND
THE
BIGGER
PICTURE

*The eyes experience less stress
when they can look upon a
wider horizon.*
R.D. Chin

Find the Bigger Picture

To find the bigger picture we need to widen our perspective, notice the web of connections that surrounds us, take careful note of synchronicities and learn to speak a whole new language. Let me explain.

When the chaos of crisis hits, our first need is self-preservation. We become understandably lost for a while on the roller coaster of emotion and the effects of shock, and we need to make sure our physical and practical needs are met. It is appropriate to be "out of our minds", experiencing the impact of the events at hand. It is healthy to be howling our grief, feeling our anger and voicing our disbelief now rather than in a therapist's chair in years to come. I remember my first trip after the death of my son. I was driving to a nearby city to buy a funeral outfit, tears dripping into my lap. I drove slowly as if I traveled in a surreal bubble of total madness while the rest of the world zoomed by, oblivious. But, just as no man or woman is an island, neither is any event ever unconnected to the wider web of life. And it is in the finding of this web, this network of connections, that great comfort is experienced.

When at last we are ready and able to lift our heavy eyes to a wider horizon we may begin to see sense in our situation that we had missed in the fog of our intense emotions. However, if we are used to a scientific worldview, the wider picture may be limited. Individual events and synchronicities do seem unconnected and senseless if we are using the medical model – diagnosing only the meaning of the symptoms of the parts. When we shift our perspective to more of an overview and question how the parts might fit within the context of our whole life pattern, then our relationship with those parts, especially the painful parts, has the opportunity to transform.

Synchronicity, defined as meaningful coincidence, can be a helpful route to this shift in view. It is as if each synchronistic happening, when held with curiosity and openness, has a tale to tell that can lead us into this more expansive place where the "ah ha!" resides. Here our understanding of the nature of accidents will inevitably change and so will our language. We will become inspired to explore the dynamic interplay between our external and internal worlds and discover a whole new way of listening to and relating to life. The coming stories will reveal more.

I have chosen to place my own story with Deborah Keammerer's because they show an uncanny similarity in the way the prolific signs and synchronicities connect together to create a picture far larger than we are used to seeing. They are more dramatic and intense than most people's stories, but they do show the profound level of educational information available to all of us in the welter of life's everyday activities. Both the major events in these stories would normally be described as "accidents", but placing together the details that create the surrounding context calls to question the true nature of accidents. I will share the story of my son, Benjaya, in some detail so that the seemingly unconnected parts can be seen forming the bigger picture as the story unfolds.

My Story – From the River to the Sea

My firstborn son, Benjaya (pronounced Benj-I-a) was one of the first babies to be born in water in England, in 1986. For me it was an excruciatingly painful and yet exquisitely rich and empowering entry into motherhood. The venue was an attic room in my family home, which had been used for healing work for many years. Ten people, sitting in silence sending me love, courage and strength, plus two sensitive midwives, witnessed Benjaya's birth into the world.

I hadn't really wanted him to be born in water. It was his own doing. When I was about four months pregnant, my partner, Abel, gave me a book to read called *Ideal Birth* by Sondra Ray. It contained some educational chapters on waterbirth, which at that time was virtually unheard of in Britain. Abel was inspired by the idea – where the mother labors in a tub of warm water that eases the pain, and the baby comes from the waters of the womb into a larger body of water and then gently floats up into the arms of the mother. My initial response was "No way!" I thought it would be an added complication, given that the home birth we wanted was already being frowned upon. I had felt only the barest of movements from the baby at that stage in the pregnancy, but when I began reading about waterbirth the activity increased tremendously. When I put the book down the womb-stirrings stopped and when I picked it up later they began again. It was uncanny. I decided to do a test to see if the baby was trying to tell me something. I sat quietly, cross-legged on the bed and asked, "If you want me to attempt to create a waterbirth for your entry please give me a very definite kick." The response was immediate. The forceful kick almost shocked me off the bed! That was Benjaya's first kick, which was to change the course of our lives... radically.

Benjaya's birth experience had felt sacred to me and to all those present. In retrospect I could see that it had all the attributes of an initiation:[9]

1. May or may not be voluntary
2. Experienced in person
3. Is witnessed
4. Includes chaos
5. Requires courage
6. Requires symbolic or real blood sacrifice
7. Requires a period of isolation
8. Includes the death of an aspect of self
9. Changes the initiate's consciousness forever

No doubt these attributes were experienced by Benjaya also as he journeyed towards incarnation. He swam into life as the dawn chorus began, and continued his frog-like movements as he was lifted from the warm water into my arms. His big, magnetic, deep brown eyes connected with mine and my world stood still. This magical moment was captured in a photograph that encircled the world in newspapers and on television screens the following day. It was such a beautiful image that, despite the vehement opposition of the medical professionals to waterbirth at that time, the headlines had to match the energy of the picture with such words as, "The Joy and Miracle of Birth."

This international heralding of my son's birth seemed like a fairytale, and I have to admit that because of the impact it made on so many people I did expect his life to be unusual. He was a charismatic child, very handsome, lithe, agile, full of life and, at times, wise beyond his years. I had a sense that his bigness was trapped within his small child's body and that he was often frustrated by his desire to be free from its restrictions. Abel and I saw him as our teacher, teaching us to love unconditionally.

That first kick also created a business. Shortly after his birth we set up a company, *BirthWorks*, to cope with the prolific requests for information about waterbirth and holistic childbirth. We designed and built portable birthing tubs to make waterbirth available to large numbers of people and began lecturing on the subject all around Britain. Benjaya went with us and was always the star of the show. We also designed and made flotation tanks and spa tubs, and wrote about the healing power of water.

My mother, M'haletta, and I led workshops for midwives on Holistic Childbirth and always included a session on death. We share a passion for exploration into the mysteries of life; and death was no exception. Although I had read prolifically on the subject since my late teens, with a specific interest in life after death and its implications, I had not come very near to death in real life. The closest I had been was seeing the bodies of two of my deceased grandparents. M'haletta and I sometimes spoke about our desire to work more closely with death, and she tentatively voiced her awareness that someone within our family was preparing, on some level, to die. She was right.

The nightmare began on a train journey to London. I was off to take part in a weekend about Conscious Conception and Ideal Birth and was to be the keynote speaker. Benjaya, now age five, was staying at home with Abel. I was newly pregnant and feeling very sick, but when I reached Paddington station in London, where I needed to change trains, I felt much sicker. In-between train announcements I could distinctly hear my name being called – "Will Mrs. B'Hahn please go to the information desk." There I was told gruffly to phone my husband at work.

I tried several phones on the station concourse with no success.

Eventually, I heard Abel's voice – tight and emotionless, sending shivers up my spine. He said:

"Sorry to drag you off the platform but you must come home on the next train."

Noise...commotion...I can't hear properly

"It's Benjaya, he's fallen in the river. We don't know if he's alright, he's been taken to hospital."

... Noise... Noise

"Where shall I go?"

"If you can't find me, get the police..."

...cut off

HELP! PANIC! I could hardly stand up with the shock, and my brain was full of fog. But I *had* to move and think clearly. This was an emergency. My boy needed me more than ever and I was many hours from home. In a stupor I found a train, which seemed to take about three years to snail its way back home on its three-hour journey. When every millisecond counts, time plays tricks!

My emotions were on a roller coaster ride and normal life went on all around me. No one offered a kind word into my obvious distress. Compassion was barricaded behind newspapers that rose higher to avoid eye contact as the panic rose in me. I was angry with my faceless fellow passengers for not daring to care, and I was terrified that my sweet Benjaya, so active in his perfect body, would live with brain damage and be what we cruelly call "a vegetable." My diary was my only friend in those terrible hours of not knowing and I scribbled away in an attempt to connect with sanity:

I need to love and let go of my fear into God's hands. I mustn't blame Abel. Don't think about what might be. Come back to the now. What is, is. What will be, will be. I AM LOVE. I LOVE BENJAYA AND RELEASE HIM TO WHATEVER IS BEST FOR HIM. I LOVE ABEL. I LOVE OUR NEW GROWING BABY. Benjaya, wherever you are I am with you and am sending you love for your healing process, be that to live or die peacefully. May the will of God be done.

The loud speaker assailed me again: "If there's a Mrs. B'Hahn on the train please make yourself known." I did so and was given a message to get off at Newton Abbot station where I would be met – by a friend I thought. Eternity lived through, the train pulled in at the station. There was no friend. The platform was flanked by police, one officer at every other door, and I knew, as did everyone in my carriage, that they had come for me. It all seemed impossibly unreal. "You're Carmella aren't you," stated the policeman at my door. I nodded feebly and other police officers converged towards me to take my bags, my arms and my life force energy as they ushered me into a cold British Rail Office. A blond policewoman sat me down and spoke these indelible words into my daze:

"There's no easy way to say this Mrs. B'Hahn, but we found your son's body in the river this evening. We thought you'd want to know as soon as possible. Your husband's at home, we'll take you there."

And so my waterbaby son, born so beautifully in a pool of water had died that day by slipping into a pool in the river and being washed away. No ashes to ashes, dust to dust for him. The following day it was national news, just as his birth had been, and flowers and cards filled the house that had the same holy aura about it as the day he was born. And the heart-rending emotional pain equaled the physical pain of bringing him into the world. The song sung to Benjaya when he was six months old in a blessing ceremony had come to be true:

> *The river is flowing, flowing and growing,*
> *The river is flowing down to the sea.*
> *Mother Earth carry me a child I will always be,*
> *Mother Earth carry me back to the sea.*

The human me, the mother who had lost my son, never to see him again, was shocked to the core, incapable of making a cup of tea, dazed and physically sick. And yet, into that wretched abyss a light was shining all the time – sometimes glimmering, sometimes dazzling. It was present, by no conscious thought of my own, and seemed to emanate from me as if it was another aspect of my self. It felt as if the external me was withering and dying with the death of my most treasured role – "mother", but this light or spirit in me flatly refused to die and made its presence known like never before.

Many thoughts and memories arose in those first raw days, which had the effect of expanding the light place within and supporting my rock-solid certainty that Benjaya's death had been a perfectly orchestrated finale. Despite my anguish, from the moment I heard the word "river" I accepted my son's fate. No anger showed its face and no voice within me ever attempted to make his death wrong. It simply was what life had dealt us and it hurt like hell.

Throughout my life I have "heard" guidance in my head. In 1986, when I was eight months pregnant with Benjaya, I was sitting with a group of people when I suddenly felt choked with an emotion that was certainly not my own. I began hearing words in my head and knew, as crazy as it may seem, that if I opened my mouth my child-to-be would speak. With my heart beating fast I took the plunge and allowed the words to come spilling out. The essential message was contained within the first four sentences:

You may not think that we have fear here, but I am afraid. Birth to me and to those with me is like a death – death to who I really am. Just as there is death in birth, so there is birth in death. Please remember this and keep me conscious of who I am when I come.

Five and a half years later these words echoed into my anguish as I sat amongst a sea of flowers in my bedroom with friends and family speaking in hushed voices as if nervous of disturbing the sleeping newborn. Together with the awful agony, as if it resided in the same space, I felt an awe-filled wonder at the great mystery of death and deep gratitude for yet another life-changing shift in consciousness that was causing me to feel more fully human. In poet Christopher Fry's words this was "the longest stride of soul" I had ever taken.

The sense of living another sacred initiation equal to that of Benjaya's birth was often with me – all the attributes were there – but because I found this to be too much of a stretch for most people to comprehend, I kept it mostly to myself. Lao Tsu said, "What the caterpillar calls the end of the world, the master calls the butterfly." I craved to talk butterfly-speak but, in the face of death, few could speak the language.

The media was portraying the mass consciousness about this kind of death as – "A tragic accident and cruel loss of life." There was no room for the balance of feelings I felt; no room for a positive word about a five-year-old's fullness of life and meaningful finale. I wanted to scream from a soapbox to anyone who would listen: **Why can't you see that feeling heartache about loss doesn't make death wrong or the life lived wasted because it was short? Tell me why my boy's death was not as natural and as sacred as his birth?** Instead, I accepted all the interviews with the press and shared my unusual viewpoint in the most balanced way I could.

It soon became obvious to me, by piecing together the signs, that Benjaya had subconsciously known he was going to die, although I had refused to see it. He often initiated conversations about death just before sleep. I know that this is not uncommon for children, and rest assured it does not mean a child who speaks of death will die young, but he was particularly fascinated with the subject. He asked, "When I die will I meet your old cat?" and "Who will my new mother be when I come back again?" His favorite book was one about spiritual traditions of the world from a series called *Spiritual Teachings for Children* from the White Eagle Trust, and he would sit on my lap as we read the page about reincarnation over and over again. "Tell me again Mum," he would say. And we discussed whom he might come back to if he found himself born again. He decided he wanted to come back to me but then got his mind in a twist because he knew that if big people die first I would not be on earth when he died.

Days before he died he made me some everlasting paper flowers and said, "Don't get your hopes up Mum, I'm not going up into the next class, I've got another school I need to go to." Then he said, "I'm not going swimming on Sunday," but he didn't know why because he really wanted to go. He died on Friday. He started to give away his special crystal collection and precious toys the week before he died and wanted to stay in the house with me more, which was completely out of character. He even drew a skull and crossbones flag and played drowning his Lego pirates in a blue silk river. I took a photograph of that river with its tiny china swan swimming towards the bridge. (His body had floated downstream to a bridge where it was found in the position of the swan.)

Four other thought provoking events all involving water that occurred the week of Benjaya's death were later brought to our attention. One of Benjaya's friends, Nikhil, became obsessed with water and played a game he'd never played before of repeatedly drowning his wooden dolls and bringing them back to life. When told of Benjaya's death he said, "That's all right, it doesn't matter."

Benjaya's cousin, Sommer, who was in India with my mother, also became obsessed with water, wanting to swim every day and to play frequently a particular game of pretending to drown. "Do you think people will think I'm dead?" she asked my mother. "They might," she answered, "but I won't." "Don't let them save me will you?" pleaded Sommer. (Why did she not want to be saved?) Then she asked directly, "Who would you rather have die, Benjaya or Carmella?" "Carmella," answered my mother, "because that is what she would wish." Only a few days earlier, Sommer and my mother had been playing in the sea when a dog hurtled towards them. There was a sudden crack of a rifle and it dropped dead yards from the water. They were very shaken, and with incredulity spoke of how life could be taken so swiftly.

And yet another. The day Benjaya died, Tim Coombes, who was living a long way away from our home county of Devon, had a pain in his chest, a terrible sense of heaviness and an image of a small boy slipping into deep water whilst clambering down a bank. He sobbed and clutched his son, thinking it could be a premonition of his death. We met Tim for the first time many months later after he had moved to Devon to become a teacher at Benjaya's Steiner School. I would have met him the day of his premonition had I made it to the conference on Conscious Conception and Ideal Birth. This is where Tim discovered the reason for the key speaker's absence and knew that his own son was safe.

We had Benjaya's body cremated, as we thought that fire was a more appropriate element than earth for him. When I went to collect the ashes and held the remains of my boy's physical form in a brown plastic urn, it was torturous – the worst day of my life. His big brown eyes were in white bits in my hands. How could I integrate that reality? And yet into the anguish the light still shone in the form of a voice in my head saying, "Don't cry Mummy, it's only my body!" Wherever that voice came from, it was a healing balm. And the long-term blessing is that once you've held your son's ashes in a box, the perspective renders certain of life's lesser challenges relatively effortless.

The grieving process was far from effortless and was compounded three and a half months after Benjaya's death by the loss of the baby I was carrying, followed by a second miscarriage several months later. My study of death and my belief systems about the afterlife certainly softened the process to a degree, but as time ticked by and friends went back to their normal lives, I did not escape the inevitable nitty gritty process of grief taking its course. I realized that shock is very clever. It brings with it protective veils to shield us from the brutal truth of loss, but as time passes and shock recedes, the veils thin and blow in the wind, bringing gusts of the physical finality of death. Oh my God, I'm NEVER, EVER going to see my boy again... it began to sink in. There was an overwhelming feeling of something missing in my life, as if a limb had been severed. Lack screamed from every corner; no small shoes next to mine, no crumbs in the bed on Sundays, no place at the table, and just a space where his car seat used to be. Space... silence... gaps... holes. Easter without Easter eggs, summer without buckets and spades, Christmas with no stocking to fill, and his birthday without him. This was the daily reality of my grief.

I realized that the literature on grieving that places it on a time-line with prescribed steps that are taken before coming back to normal functioning is totally at odds with my experience. My grieving was more like a spiral on which I revisited the same anniversaries, memories, weather patterns that would cause me to physically and emotionally relive the loss. Each turn of the spiral carried a little less intensity than the tighter twist of the year before. Rehabilitation and loving support are needed for a long, long time.

When I remembered others who have lost whole families in the war and imagined the depth of their grief I wept until my heart screamed for mercy. Then compassion began pushing like a flower from the crack in my rocks, watered by my tears.

The synchronicities kept coming, bringing lots of questions and often comfort. Here are a few more I recall. My mother remembered that the name of the Indian man to whom the job fell of informing her that her grandson (whose full name was Benjamin Jaya) had died, was "Jaya." It is a name that is often used in Indian chants connected to the names of the Gods. It means "victory." The mother of Nikhil, who had been drowning his dolls, phoned to tell us that he had been singing "Spread your rainbow wings and fly into forever..." a song we had sung at the funeral/celebration that he had not attended. When asked how he knew the song he said "It just was." Another little boy, Sol, whose only contact with Benjaya had been on a walk knee-high in a local river, was asleep on his mother's lap as she was meditating and receiving unusually clear insights about her life. When he woke, Sol told her that he had been dreaming that Benjaya was alive and had come here to talk to her. He said, "It was when the morning owls came." They did not know that Benjaya had a passion for owls.

Butterflies and pennies continue to be a source of solace and joy. Since a bronze butterfly swooped down over the coffin at Benjaya's cremation I have associated this symbol with him. When facilitating a *Shedding Light on Death* workshop, I invited the presence of all our loved ones who had died. It was then that a large colored butterfly descended from goodness knows where to dance in circles around me. Everyone noticed that it was only me it wanted.

Benjaya's favorite song was called "Magic Penny" and since he died pennies have manifested on my path at uncanny moments, often seeming to be a form of confirmation. It is sometimes startling, as the only explanation for the exact timing and their sudden appearance seems to be materialization. I even found one in the middle of my bed one day after dreaming about him. This morning as I was sitting outside wrestling with how to portray the whole subject of synchronicity, my mind took to wondering if I would attract any good examples to share with you. At that precise moment the cat, which was sitting behind my seat, gave a loud screeching cough. I turned and followed the angle of her nose to... not a mouse... or a bird, but an earth-streaked penny on the ground between her paws. The intelligence at work behind synchronicity is not without a sense of humor!

There are many questions that I have been asked repeatedly since Benjaya's death and to which I have responded in *Benjaya's Gifts*. I would like to repeat and expand the answers to two of those questions here. The first is: Why do you think this happened to you? The "why?" within me has arisen from my inherent need to understand the lessons and blessings of this event rather than as the lament "why me?". I have thought on many occasions: "Thank God it was me rather than someone who has no supportive beliefs from which to draw strength."

The whole scenario of Benjaya's birth, life and death seems like a giant jigsaw puzzle, as yet unfinished. Some pieces show recognizable parts of the picture and the logical mind can say, "These are the flowers and they fit together" or "this yellow bit fits with this yellow bit." Likewise, I can say that the water birth fits with the water death. Benjaya's intense interest in death and the premonitions could fit with his early departure, and my studies of the subject and desire to work with death fit with experiencing it first hand. I could say that Benjaya came to start a trend in waterbirth, to teach us about holistic birth, love, and death. I could say that the next baby came so that I held life within me when facing death and was given the grace of holding the lifeline of motherhood for a while. Some jigsaw pieces, however, are deceptive. They seem to match perfectly at the time, but then another part of the picture just won't fit, so you have to concede that this piece doesn't fit there after all and remove it.

And what about the vast expanse of blue sky that boggles the mind with its challenging sameness? We can go only so far with our powers of understanding; to attempt to understand everything is futile. When I suffered the second miscarriage I was plunged into my blue sky – into an agony of failure because I could not understand why this was happening to me. "Three deaths is too much to bear," was my daily affirmation. It took a while of weeping and wailing before I remembered that the best way of completing a jigsaw puzzle is sometimes to leave it alone. Either someone else will put the last pieces in, or one will go back to it with a changed attitude and the pieces will miraculously fall into place.

The second question is: Why do you believe that Benjaya's death was not an accident? Firstly, let me say that my initial response on hearing of Benjaya's death was an instant and inexplicable sense of rightness – catastrophic to my senses, but right. This was not a reasoned strategy for coping but a resonance on some deep level with the drama that was playing itself out, as if I knew deep down that this was in the script. It has to be said also that my belief system about accidents – although it did not create that sense of rightness – certainly helped to underpin it. "God" describes that belief system perfectly in *Conversations with God (book 1)*:

> Nothing happens by accident in God's world, and there is no such thing as coincidence. Nor is the world buffeted by random choice, or something you call fate. If a snowflake is utterly perfect in its design, do you not think the same could be said about something as magnificent as your life?

Benjaya, of course, did not consciously jump into the river to his destined fate. Witnessed by two young friends, he fell while clambering down a riverbank as a branch snapped underfoot. This we call "an accident." My English dictionary defines an accident as "An *unforeseen* event or occurrence happening unexpectedly by chance." But it *was* foreseen, so where does that leave our language and comprehension of the nature of reality? Can any one of us explain how the stick knew to break? Premonitions and accidents don't mix do they? And if his death was not an accident, what then of the apparent accidents of others? What if they were also foreseen events but the premonitions had simply not been shared? And would we grieve differently if we knew for certain that our losses made sense in the context of an overall plan or divine design?

There are so many questions; so much blue sky in the jigsaw. Now, in an attempt to put a piece of sky in place, I will share one of my hypotheses, which may or may not fit. I think that although human beings have free will, we may well operate within the limits of a wide and beneficial life blueprint, or divine program design, which interacts and dovetails with the blueprints of others. I imagine that we have unconscious awareness of our blueprint that holds the pattern for our greatest potential, and perhaps have by some yet-to-be-discovered process given it the seal of our approval. The humble caterpillar holds the blueprint of a butterfly, so it's not too far fetched to imagine that humans have an equally miraculous potential in this world. We do, however, tend to romanticize the caterpillar's transformation into a butterfly. Scientists have recorded a screaming sound from the cocoon as the butterfly is formed and then struggles to break out of its prison. My process has been similar and I feel as if have emerged with bright wings from the darkest place I could have imagined – a statement that is echoed, in her own way, by my first interviewee, Deborah.

Deborah Keammerer's Story – A Baptism in Agony

It was a hot summer day in Boulder, Colorado when I finally met Deborah Keammerer. There was an instant rapport – two mothers of similar age, bound by the same baptism in agony. We sat in comfy chairs in the light of her sunroom, and by hearing her story my sanity was, to some degree, confirmed. Here was someone with an equal amount of blatant synchronistic events and premonitions surrounding the death of her child, a similar attitude to life and an identical conclusion: We are blessed despite the agony.

At one point Deborah described one of her experiences as "eerie", which means "frighteningly strange." Strangeness, however, disappears when you find enough others who share similar experiences. My experience has been that the more I dare to speak of the "strange" events in my life, the more others open up to their unusual occurrences, and it becomes obvious that they are universal experiences that have simply not been shared for fear of ridicule or the like. As I witnessed the unfolding of Deborah's powerful story I saw her move, like a wave, through her grief and out again into a place of gratitude.

Deborah and her husband, Warren, have a career together as plant ecologists. They bought a country house, also a healing center, in Colorado when their first daughter, Linnaea, was three months old. Three years later Holly was born. They were normal kids who played and fought together and were best buddies.

In the spring of 1992, when the girls were eight and eleven, Deborah worked away from home a lot and missed them terribly. So when she was asked to teach a class in Restoration Ecology in Idaho, she decided to take them with her for a week. She told me:

One family I worked with on this project had two children close to their ages. We'd gone for supper and the children had played happily together. The girls asked if they could stay overnight. I said 'no' and said to them later 'I can't explain this because these are wonderful people but I felt something wrong there and I couldn't let you stay in that house.'

It was Linnaea's twelfth birthday on June 10th and we went camping. Linnaea took a friend but she was out of sorts and ended up sleeping in the back seat of the car instead of in the tent with her friend saying, 'I just don't feel safe in that tent.' Her art teacher had given her materials to make a cochina doll over the summer, but, unlike her friends, she completed it overnight. Three weeks later we went to a fireworks event and I was distracted by this horrible feeling of something being wrong. I had felt death coming that spring but I thought I was going to get sick because I'd been working so hard. I recognize now that this was a premonition of the grief to come.

Later in July Deborah needed to go back to Idaho and there was no one available to care for her children at home so she took them with her again. She called the same family, thinking the girls would be safer there, supervised at a home, rather than staying alone in the room next to where she was teaching, or playing outside where there was a river. The girls were delighted to visit their friends who had also invited some neighborhood friends to come and play. On the way to Idaho Linnaea bought Christmas gifts, which seemed a little premature, and Deborah bought flowers for the family. In the florists Deborah decided to add a sincere sympathy card for the mother because she was going to deal with four children. Then she changed her mind and selected a "thank you" note instead.

The girls settled in, and Deborah, who was focused on the two-hour drive left to her destination, forgot to give them the phone number of where she could be reached. She takes up the story.

As I left, Linnaea was sitting on the front step. I kissed her and said, 'I love you honey.' She said, 'I love you too, Mom.' Then I drove for a while and stopped for supper in a little restaurant. It was eight minutes to seven and the restaurant lights went off. Pitch dark. Then they went on again. I went back to the car and there was an incredibly intense rainbow. I thought how much I'd like to share this sight with the girls. Eventually I arrived at the place I needed to be, met the people and showed them pictures of my daughters.

The next morning I got up and meditated, then started the class. About an hour later I saw a police car go by. The man who'd organized the class went out and when he came back in he said, 'There's been an accident. I need to speak with you.' He led me back to my room and said, 'One of your daughters has been killed.' I said, 'Which one?' He said, 'Linnaea.'

My whole class was stunned and one man said a blessing. I said, 'She was a wonderful child and I'm so glad I had twelve years with her.' I think everyone thought I was a saint, but in truth, if I'd had an idea of the agony that was coming I might have reacted more strongly. I just knew I believed in God's grace, had lived in it for 43 years, and nothing like this had ever happened to me.

This is what had happened. There were two boys, 18 and 13, and a 10-year-old girl in this family. The older brother had meant to go hunting with his friends but decided to go water skiing instead. He'd put his loaded 22 caliber rifle, normally locked in a case, back in his room. The kids were horsing around downstairs and the younger boy, wanting to get everyone's attention, got the gun and played "Clint Eastwood" with it, kind of pointing it at Linnaea. He pulled the trigger and it went off. She died instantly, shot through the head, at the same time as the restaurant lights went off!

Holly was in the bathroom so, miraculously, she didn't see the shot, but she came out to see the boy leaning with his head against the wall and her sister on the floor in a pool of blood. There was much panic and Holly was traumatized. When Deborah eventually arrived they hugged and wept together. Deborah was keen to see Linnaea as soon as she could and found the experience both horribly painful and immensely valuable.

> It helped to see that she was obviously not there in her body, which was lying naked on a pillow under a white blanket. I tried to stroke her face but it was stiff and cold. I didn't weep then. I just talked to her and noticed her perfection. I was afraid to hold her because I didn't know then where she'd been shot and I didn't want to find the wound.

Later the police tracked down Deborah's husband. She recalled the anguish of that meeting.

> I met Warren at the airport that night. I've never felt so much physical pain in my life. Childbirth was painful, but this was so much worse. We could hardly breathe it hurt so badly, and we just lay and held each other, weeping and feeling this terrible pain in our bodies and hearts. It was unbearable.

That first night Holly had a vivid healing dream of Linnaea who told her that she hadn't heard the gun go off and didn't feel anything at all. In the dream they were back at home and Linnaea was dressed all in white, looking angelic. She said that she was concerned about everyone, especially the boy who had fired the gun. She also said that she was fine and not to worry about her. The sisters played on the trampoline together and then went swimming. Linnaea took Holly up to her bed, tucked her in and kissed her goodnight. Then she sat by the windowsill and her body dissolved into thousands of points of turquoise light.

Deborah shared some of the ironic synchronicities that became apparent after Linnaea's death.

When I was the age she was when she was killed, I read a story written by a man who had accidentally shot his best friend. His tragedy touched me so deeply that I took it to school to share with my friends and I knew I never wanted to have guns in my life or in my house. So we didn't. It's like Sleeping Beauty where you isolate all of the spinning wheels and yet somehow that spinning wheel needs to be found.

In looking for materials for her memorial service I came across a piece Linnaea had written. It was a review of *Tuck Everlasting* – a story about a family who inadvertently drank from a spring, which made them live forever. In this paper Linnaea was asked to answer the question, 'Would you drink from that spring if you had the chance?' She said, 'No, when it comes to my time to die, that will be all right with me. We can't live forever, there would be too many people.' Also, some of her poems were eerie with how much they addressed. Here's one:

Leaving
I'm leaving so I'll say good-bye
Don't know how long I'll live
Or when I'll die.
I'm going to go across the sea
Don't know if you'll ever see me.
I'm gonna fly over unheard of lands
And walk through the jungle with helping hands.
So say farewell before I go
Into a world that you don't know.

Did she know she was going to die? My friend, who was her baby-sitter, called me one day and said, 'Debbie, you're not going to believe this. We have a video of the last time Holly and Linnaea were at our house. Linnaea, on film, is pantomiming being shot and falling to the ground.' Also, I remember Linnaea asking me what it's like to be dead and we talked about how you can move from one place to another by the concentration of your mind. A few weeks before she died we read a book together called, *Closer to the Light,* about near death experiences in children, so she knew the landscape she would be walking into.

The Keammerer family celebrated Linnaea's life at her memorial service. They had a mosaic of photographs in the church so that people would see her, not dead but alive, and they prayed for the boy and his family. The house, of course, was full of flowers and sincere sympathy cards… and the bitterness of the loss. Within a week Deborah packed up Linnaea's things but kept photographs of her around the house. As soon she recognized there was something she hadn't done since she did it with Linnaea, she did it again so that she would have new memories of the activity. This no doubt helped her avoid post traumatic stress, as the deliberate avoidance of anything that brings back the painful memory is one of the main symptoms of PTSD.

I know people usually avoid potential places of pain, but it was a healing step for me to go past the loss. I want to learn everything there is to learn about losing a child. This is graduate level parenting. God knows I would never have chosen this class consciously, but if I'm here I'm going to pay attention!

I talked about Linnaea all the time because I wanted to speak her name. I grew tired of the grief and weeping, but just had to have faith that I would find joy and sanity again one day. Someone once told me when I was learning to body surf: *You'll get tumbled by the waves, you won't know which way is up, and you'll just have to hold your breath and trust you'll float to the surface.* That's the way it was. I had to hang in there, even though I wanted to die to be with her. I was her mother and I felt I needed to care for her.

Many parents divorce after a child dies but the Keammerers set their teeth, did counseling, and vowed it would not happen to them. Holly joined an acting troupe – a safe outlet for her emotions – and developed a strong peer group who continue to support her. They recognized that in a way their family had died when Linnaea died and that they had to recreate their lives. They gave away everything that didn't have a sense of vitality. They had "travel therapy" when they went to places they hadn't been with Linnaea, and "remodel therapy" when they remodeled the house to incorporate more light. "It was an investment in our survival," said Deborah.

One family, who was Buddhist, had us over to dinner frequently and just wept with us. I can't tell you how important that was; it kept us alive. One week, two weeks – that's nothing. A year later you still need someone to hold your hand and listen to you. Another friend checked in with me once a month and we went to the movies or to supper, and she'd let me say anything I needed to while she handed me the tissues. You only need a few friends like that.

My daughter was killed on the cusp of adolescence, and a few weeks before she died I had asked her if she was excited about becoming a woman. She said, 'I don't want to grow up.' Her friends, of course, did grow up, but most of them found it too painful to interact with the reality of our lives. Linnaea's peer group no longer met together. A couple became deathly sick and her best friend had headaches so bad that she had to be in complete darkness. Finally she healed with the help of counseling. Another friend left home at 14. I think people need to pay strong attention to kids who lose close friends. Children need to be involved in whatever way possible in the healing process. One or two sessions is not going to do it! These kids had been together since pre-school. They'd slept in each other's arms. When Linnaea's friends reached their senior year in high school I invited many of them over. We sat and talked about Linnaea and how they felt about her death. It was a good thing to have a time for healing and closure.

The potential of the dream world as a teaching tool will raise its head many times in this book. Deborah's greatest healing has come from her dreams. She told me about some of them.

Almost a year after Linnaea's death I dreamed I was sitting at home with Linnaea sitting next to me. It was so natural. She went outside to roll in the grass like a pony and was ecstatic, her blonde hair shining in the sun. I held her and told her how much I loved her. Then I said, 'Why don't you call Emily and tell her you're back?' So she dialed and spoke to Emily, her best friend, for a long time. When I woke up I realized it was Emily's birthday and thought that Linnaea must have wanted to send her a message, so I took Emily a present and told her about the dream.

In the second dream I suddenly remembered that Linnaea had been imprisoned for a year and I hadn't been to visit her. I felt terrible as if I'd forgotten her. I was at this prison asking the matron to bring her out so I could speak with her. She came out and said, 'Mom, I really like it here. These people are great, I love what I'm doing and I like it better than elementary school.' She wasn't in prison. It felt like a very real communication and I woke myself laughing.

In the next dream I was on my way to a lecture hall to take classes with Holly, and Linnaea appeared next to me. She said, 'I'm going to the same class you are, I'm just going to get there a little sooner!' Then she pranced off. Her hair was longer and she had matured, as if she was aging in step with her friends. Then, in the following dream, I was sitting talking to Linnaea who was now a firm but compassionate spiritual teacher. She told me, 'It's time to move on, time to complete this phase.' She was encouraging me to step into the next stage of my life. That is what is happening now, and I feel as if the worst part of my grief is over.

To digress for a moment. Dreams can be such a rich source of wisdom, especially when the drama of waking life is in urgent need of help. I was recently told about a book by Robin Moss, called *Dreaming True*, which tells how Harriet Tubman, a freedom fighter in the Deep South, received all her information on how to organize the successful Underground Railroad from dreams. She would suddenly feel the urgent need to go to sleep and if she didn't lie down she would fall where she stood and "sleep" for an hour or two. She visited the area that was to be the escape route for the slaves in her dreams and carried a detailed aerial map in her mind.

My son, Asher, who is eight at the time of writing (born in water ten months after my second miscarriage), had a powerful dream similar to Holly's that helped to lighten his sadness about never having met his brother. He told me about it the following morning: "I was at home and there was a knock at the door. It was Benjaya but his body was blue and white like mist. His face was Benjaya's and he had a big smile. He was about seven and he said 'Do you want to come and play?' I said 'Yes, of course' and we went for a walk and then we went flying over the Atlantic Ocean. When we came back he said 'Tell Mummy and Daddy to have a good holiday,' and he sent you lots of love." Both Asher and I felt strengthened by this communication.

After the Columbine school shooting, Deborah felt moved to re-open her contact with the family of the boy who shot Linnaea. His mother told her of some amazing visitations in the night. Within a couple weeks of Linnaea's death they were visited by a spiritual presence three times. Three members of the family awoke on different occasions to see a bright orb of white light ringed with blue hovering in the family room where Linnaea died.

> My friend often hears her son speaking aloud to Linnaea before going to sleep. He discusses with her whatever is up in his life. I think there is great wisdom in this. He must feel she is alive and near him and sense her forgiveness. I think this horrible event was a unifying force in their family. They dug in and did some hard work and seem stronger and closer for the effort.
>
> To complete I want to say it is a joy to share my story and to pass the message along that it's part of life to lose someone close and to feel deeply grieved. We can't get through life without it grabbing us with all of its fullness. The loss of a child brings up some of the deepest feelings we can experience, and while it's a baptism in agony, it is part of the human experience. Those of us who have experienced it may come through it stronger. I am a new creation since this adventure with Linnaea – deeper, stronger, and wiser.

Deborah admitted to me at one point that she felt the need to make sense of Linnaea's death for people. She believed this had to have been God's will, otherwise it was an accident and that didn't make sense to her. But she struggled in the height of her anguish with justifying that God could have been behind the death of her child. I have discovered in my conversations with the bereaved that this desire and inability to justify that God could be behind the death of a loved one is common. Many bereaved people lose their faith. However, when Deborah became open to the messages and learning surrounding the trauma, she actually began to feel blessed – a far cry from being wronged by God. When we begin to notice the bigger picture, the need for justification diminishes. I venture to suggest that as long as we believe that death is unacceptable, that emotional pain is bad, and that God is the benevolent creator in charge of our lives, then it can never be justified, and God will take the blame. I feel fortunate to have retained my faith. Perhaps my God remains benevolent because I sought and found valuable gifts in Benjaya's passing, and because I totally believe what I heard him say to me not long after his death: "Death is but a dance of freedom from the body's earthly thought."

Deborah and I were both on a quest for wholeness before the deaths of our children and it was natural for us to take the time to piece together the parts of our personal stories, allowing the bigger picture to inform us. It is quite possible that many of the synchronicities and premonitions in our stories would have remained unseen, dismissed, or ignored had we not begun with this more holistic attitude to life.

To my delight I have noticed that "Nothing happens by chance" is becoming a more respectable and widespread belief. Could the happenings in these two stories possibly be due to chance? Water birth: water death. Drowning dolls and Lego pirates. A gift of everlasting flowers. The river is flowing... a child I will always be. Butterflies and pennies. Or: Lights going out in the restaurant. The rainbow. The story of the man who shot his friend. Linnaea's poems. Christmas presents in July. Pantomiming being shot. I boldly predict that the word "chance", along with "coincidence", "accident" and "luck" will fall out of common usage before too long.

In order to comprehend how to look for the bigger picture, perhaps a deeper understanding is required of the holistic attitude of which I speak, and of the language that accompanies it. Exploring the ancient wisdom, "As without: so within" is a good starting point. Perceiving the connections between the inner and outer life has become a daily practice for me. I experience myself as being in a dynamic, reciprocal relationship with my external world; an intriguing interplay which defies logic and reason. The language is one of meaningful signs, symbols, premonitions, and dreams, which inter-relate and create a profusion of what Swiss psychologist Carl Jung called "synchronicity." "Meaningful coincidences," he said, "are unthinkable as pure chance – the more they multiply and the greater and more exact the correspondence is, the more they can no longer be regarded as pure chance, but, for the lack of causal explanation, have to be thought of as meaningful arrangements."

As humanity begins, en masse, to digest the scientific information that at a quantum level our bodies and external matter are indistinguishable, that we are in a symbiotic relationship of interdependence with all life, creating a vast collective consciousness, it is inevitable that our interactions with all that enters our life path will change. And although communication is occurring on some level in every moment, it seems that the incidence of dramatic synchronistic events increases in times of important life transitions, as if some intelligence knows that there is an unmet need for a signpost to help with direction, to see a clearer picture of reality, or perhaps to show another choice. Or, could it be that we are simply more attuned to them in times of need? Many people would call this intelligence "God" and attribute the signs to God's guidance, but, call it "Godspeak" or "Signspeak", I think it is a good time to learn the language.

The universe has no doubt been presenting an unceasing stream of symbols and signs since time began, but it is only in recent years that a notable number of us in the "civilized" world have taken on the ways of certain indigenous tribes who, unlike the "civilized" world, are fluent in their ability to comprehend and respond to the messages offered. I know that the language has spread significantly because on my extensive travels I am meeting an increasing number of people with whom I can openly converse in this form. Worldwide, conferences on spirituality and all aspects of alternative/holistic lifestyles are teeming with those who are learning to speak the language, and books attempting to explain the mysteries of our relationship with the messages of life – and especially the messages from our bodies – now deck the shelves of mainstream bookstores.

Like any other language, Signspeak has a multitude of ways in which it can be spoken and comprehended. Each person relates to it a little differently and the potential usage is, I'm sure, far greater than we can presently imagine. When we become totally fluent it probably includes telepathic rapport with, and acceptance of, all that crosses our path, animate or otherwise! From my present limited awareness I can see that there is:

1. The personal message of the sign or synchronicity which affects our emotions and inner life.
2. The effect of our response on our immediate surroundings and direction in life.
3. The wider, even global, effect.

For example, I came downstairs yesterday morning feeling glum. I was craving sun and had wanted to sit outside and write, but it was raining... again. The CD player had turned itself on – how remains a mystery – and as I entered the breakfast room, Ladysmith Black Mambazo were singing in exquisite harmony "Rain, rain, beautiful rain." This was a message just for me. I laughed, all glumness disappeared and my mood change lightened my day.

If we look at the story from the introduction about the appearance of the pheasant, and the badger feather with its message that sometimes people need stories more than food to stay alive, we can see that because I was open to listening and following the pheasant, I found a treasure of wisdom that is now being shared with everyone who reads this book. And perhaps many people will now look out for animal symbology in their own lives.

Like ripples from a pebble thrown into a pool, every thought and action affects others to some degree, be that energetic, or in a more tangible way. In Jung's *Synchronicity and Human Destiny* there is a story of how such a pebble in Abraham Lincoln's life started his career in politics, which of course affected the whole global political arena. One day a stranger in urgent need of money came to him with a barrel of papers and odds and ends and asked him for a dollar for the barrel. Lincoln gave him the dollar and when he eventually bothered to clear out the barrel he found an almost complete edition of Blackstone's *Commentaries*, the acquisition of which led him to become a lawyer and later a politician. What would have happened had he said no to the barrel? My guess is that he would probably still have become President because some other happening would have occurred to help remind him of this potential track.

As I have matured in my awareness I have found myself living in what appears like a new dimension with awesome synchronicities occurring as my common reality. Some of these are hard to fathom because they are beyond my comprehension at present, but I do know that when they occur I feel a deep sense of rightness about the path that I am on, or the decisions I am making. It is as if the external world is answering my inner need to live a connected life. The downside is that the limitation of time prevents the sharing of my full complex web of reality with others. And, without the whole picture, friends and loved ones can be quick to judge and even laugh at how I use certain details of life to inform my direction. I often feel lonely in my profound and mysterious inner life and long to share it more with others. However, many marvels must remain unspoken.

Having said that, I must tell you this as a final synchronicity story before I end with the effects and benefits of opening to the bigger picture. I was working on these last few pages this morning while my son, Asher, was watching *STAR WARS Episode One*. Suddenly I felt moved to see if he needed something to eat and as I walked through the door, Qui-Gon Jinn – the Jedi Knight portrayed as the epitome of good, working with the Force – said "There are no such things as accidents"!

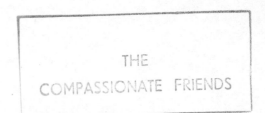

The effects and benefits of opening to a BIGGER picture

- Taking things personally and feeling hurt diminishes when we also see events as symbolic or part of a bigger pattern.

- We become more present, more conscious, as we learn to attune our antennae to the messages from both our external world and our internal, body-centered world.

- Everyday living becomes more dynamic and our relationship with the natural world intensifies.

- We notice how connected the details of life really are and our perspective widens, creating or deepening our belief and faith in a guiding intelligence and divine design.

- We are released from the uncomfortable see-saw polarity of "right" and "wrong" to rest in a place of "What is, is" where struggle becomes acceptance, and action rises from a less driven place.

- Direct or symbolic communication from those who have died may be more easily received, giving much comfort.

- Inquiry into the nature of other realms and dimensions of existence can be sparked.

- Warnings/predictions of the future can be received.

- Insight or confirmation about our next steps and direction in life can be received.

- Our dreams can become more informative.

- Clear reflection of our inner life, including what lies behind our conscious mind, can be seen in the external mirror and used as a therapeutic tool.

As I composed this list I became aware that there is so much more to be said on this topic. Then I remembered that life tends to repeat itself until it is heard, and relaxed as I realized that these themes would inevitably repeat themselves throughout the book.

First Key
FIND THE BIGGER PICTURE
Questions and Reflections

1. Sit quietly and imagine you are in a place where you feel absolutely safe. Now allow a challenging situation in your life to arise in your mind. Looking from a wider perspective than you have before, what awareness, if any, do you have about the bigger picture surrounding this situation?

2. See if you can recall a time when, despite painful emotions, you simply knew the "rightness" of a crisis or difficulty? How did this feeling affect the way you dealt with the situation?

3. Close your eyes and scan your body and inner world. Listen. Is there anything you need to take note of that's affecting your outer life in the world?

4. Have your beliefs about "accidents" changed since reading these stories? In the event of an apparent accident, how might you question its possible connection to the wider context of your life?

5. Will you continue to use the words "accident", "coincidence", "chance" and "luck" in the same way? If not, what alternatives could you use?

6. Go and find an object that represents birth and one that represents death to you. (Draw or imagine them if they are not accessible). What do these objects say to you? What, if anything, has changed about your beliefs about birth and death since reading 'Find the Bigger Picture'?

7. Write down or share with someone, "What I believe about the existence of divine design is…"

8. Sit in silence and become aware of any sense you might have of a personal blueprint that holds your greatest potential. If you do have a sense, how would you describe that blueprint? What else came up?

9. Go inside yourself and ask how you could use your dreams more as an informing source.

10. Bring to mind some of the children connected to your life. How carefully do you listen to their voices? What step could you take that might connect you further to the wisdom of a child?

The Second Key

TRUST
AND
SURRENDER
CONTROL

*Taking responsibility
and giving up control
are two sides of the healing coin.*
Elizabeth Lesser

Trust and Surrender Control

A common experience when we are in trouble is that we are losing control over life. This is usually a temporary phenomenon until we are able to resume our normal, more comfortable position at the helm. However, to believe we are ever fully in control is an illusion, and perhaps we are aiming at an inappropriate target in desiring to be so. Life, which can change in an instant, is beyond our conscious control. Even the millions of dollars per hour America spends on security cannot guarantee protection. As the intensity of initial feelings subsides after a traumatic event and the desire to re-establish a sense of security and authority returns, we should avoid retreating to the complacent illusion that we are protected from life's adversities.

Catastrophes don't just happen to others "out there." We are an interconnected web, and life is unsafe – if safety means being untouched by grief. If we are set on controlling our own sorrow-proof oasis then we are chasing the impossible. The sooner we get this message, the sooner we can grasp how precious is the life that we have and begin to live it to the full.

So, if we are not aiming for control, what is a more appropriate target? Mine is to be in balance. This means not holding the reigns too loose or too tight, not retreating in fear or reacting from anger. It means relaxing into a place that trusts wisdom to arise in the absence of a personal plan or agenda. There is only so much we can do to secure our personal safety. The rest is up to the powers that be. On my refrigerator I have a sign that says,

> *Good morning, this is God. I will be handling all your problems today.*
> *I do not need your help, so have a good day.*

To let God, or the bigger picture, unfold its assistance we need to trust, surrendering the burden of managing and tightly controlling the detailed direction of our lives. Trusting in this way is allowing ourselves to be embraced in our unknowing and vulnerability by an all-knowing source of love and compassion. It is a place where I can safely rest until spirit moves me to act.

Two weeks after the airlines were used as terrorist weapons in 2001, I was due to leave England for a working trip to Hawaii via New York City, the epicenter of danger. I had been excitedly looking forward to the trip and would be letting many people down if I pulled out. For two weeks I lived in limbo, not knowing what was truly in my best interest. People concerned for my safety were telling me I'd be irresponsible to go. But I could not allow fear to be my advisor. I waited, trusting that I would be given clear in-tuition coupled with external information. And I trusted that I would be guided to be in the right place at the right time in terms of my safety. The green light came at the eleventh hour when Linda, with whom

I was traveling, suddenly remembered what she had been told by a Hopi Elder: that she would be required to go to Hawaii with a sacred prayer bowl at a time when the world was in great turmoil. I went. Every flight was on time, every step of my journey deeply enriching, and I felt totally safe and protected. The journey ended with a powerful, moving ritual with the prayer bowl and a circle of a hundred world educators praying and singing for world peace.

Our instinctual desires for survival, safety and security propel us to find ways of meeting our needs. It is these very drives, however, that so often sabotage our true needs. Most of our strategies for directing our lives carry the seeds of two extremes. On the one hand we are attached to being always and at all costs in control. We fear letting go in case something is lost, and believe that receiving help (unless we are rendered completely helpless) is an admission of weakness. This stubborn streak is often labeled "arrogance" and has the effect of leaving others feeling disempowered. On the other hand we give away our power to a "higher" authority like our parents, the Government, God or gurus. This tack allows us to take little responsibility ourselves and then to complain about the mess others have got us into.

As within so without. Our microcosmic, personal relationship to control will be clearly reflected in the macrocosm of our nation's relationship to war. When our feelings of safety are disrupted, how do we behave? Do we want to control our world or do we want what is for the highest good of everyone? Do we want to avoid responsibility for any kind of action simply because we are afraid of conflict? Or, does our stance, whatever it may be, come from a deep, calm, inner sense of what is needed?

The following stories expand this key to handling adversity. We follow three people on their journey from a state of extreme control to a more balanced place in which both true authority and sense of deep trust are found.

Rick Curwin's Story – Some Stairs aren't for Climbing

I met Rick Curwin in the sacred Black Hills of South Dakota at a conference sponsored by Reclaiming Youth International. Here adults working in various ways with "at risk" youth gather each year to be inspired, regenerated, and to share the richness of their work. Rick, an erudite, disheveled rogue of a man with a twinkle in his eye, was a key speaker.

Adversity visited Rick early in his life. His father died when he was four, leaving his young mother to work to support three children. They had little money and couldn't buy new clothes, but Rick's mother – a Jewish mother – in her compassion and love made him feel important whatever he did. When he broke his leg in first grade it was discovered he had bone disease. Bone wouldn't form, only water. He had surgery, was given a brace and crutches, and labeled "a cripple." Rick told me, "I never thought of myself that way. I just thought I was a kid with a brace." Rick spoke of his brother who taught him that his disability need not be a handicap.

> My brother's one of the most wonderful men that ever lived. He gave me the gift of believing in myself. Our home was a third story tenement in Boston, and he would *never* carry me up the stairs. I would say, 'Elliot, my leg hurts, please carry me up the stairs.' And he'd say, 'No, you can do it.' I was so angry with him, I could have killed him, but I made it up the stairs by my willpower. Years later he told me he used to cry at how much I suffered, but he believed that the only way I could learn to take care of myself was to do it myself. He would have carried me if I really couldn't have done it, but I always did.

Now in his fifties and living in San Francisco, Rick has endured many seriously difficult times throughout his life that he's always overcome by sheer willpower and relentless perseverance. He believed until recently that there was no adversity that he could not overcome by refusing to give in. Friends called him "the ultimate survivor" because he had inner strength that most people could not comprehend. Then, a few years ago, Rick went through an overwhelming event that proved to him that some obstacles cannot be overcome by willpower, or indeed any human attribute. He told me:

> My whole world and the way I related to it changed in a heartbeat. There is a Jewish saying, 'Man plans: God laughs.' I've come to understand that every person faces unexpected trials as part of life's rich tapestry and in some ways the trials we can't conquer define us more than the ones we can.

What happened was this. Rick's new fiancée and two of her sons had moved into his home. The boys shared a bedroom on the bottom floor. One day the younger boy lost something under his bed and couldn't find a flashlight. When he took a candle to look for it the bed caught fire. Rick's fiancée went down with a fire extinguisher but by the time she got downstairs the room was already in flames.

> We managed to get her and her children out, then foolishly I went back upstairs to save her dog. I trapped myself, and the dog had already died from the smoke. I'd lived in that house for ten years and now I couldn't even find the front door! I went to the safety of my bedroom and caught my breath. My choice was to attempt to find the door through the flames and smoke or jump out the window. I did not have the luxury of time for deliberations. My fear of heights was stronger than my respect for fire, so I tried for the door. Smoke overcame me, flames were flashing

and things were crashing and breaking. Every time I heard a sound I turned to react to the noise and I got lost in my own house.

I made it back to my room, took a deep breath and looked over to the window and said, 'I have to jump.' But it was too high and it scared me too much. Then when flames burst through the door I jumped out of the window. I crashed on the ground and hurt myself pretty badly. I broke a bone in my foot, smashed all my vertebrae, and cracked my jaw so badly I had to have all my teeth surgically removed. I lost 90% of everything I've owned in my life. A few things were recovered but almost everything was gone.

This happened at the end of March and in August Rick married his fiancée. The marriage lasted three months, mostly because they weren't close enough to overcome the issues of the fire. And so, not only did he lose things that he cared about but he also lost a relationship that really mattered to him.

I'd done some work with Lakota Native Americans in South Dakota at their school, and I became friendly with the man they called 'Chief.' We joked around a lot. On my last day he had this big garbage bag for me and he said, 'I've got a present for you.' I was on a stage with a microphone in front of about two hundred teachers, half of them Native American. I said, 'you've got a garbage bag for me? I can see what you think of me!' He said, 'You have to look inside to see what I really think of you.' So he took it out. It was a star quilt that his grandmother had made for him when he was born. It came from his bed. The giving of star quilts, I discovered later, came from the tradition of giving buffalo skins to warriors in the Lakota tribe. Most Native Americans get them and birth and die in them and maybe get one or two for doing wonderful accomplishments in their life. The star is the Morning Star, the star of wisdom. They take about nine months to a year to make.

When he told me the story of what it meant and how important it was to his life, I was overwhelmed and I said, 'I can't take something like this.' He said, 'you don't understand Lakota tradition. First of all, for me to be a true warrior, when I die I can't own anything because warriors can't own things. They have to give their belongings to someone else. I'm not really giving you my quilt, I'm giving you my spirit to protect you, to help and guide you. Don't you want it?' I said, 'Of course I want it.'

I loved that star quilt and took it home and hung it on my study wall. It was true Indian art, belonging in a museum. Visitors would spend ages looking at it, seeing so much in it. In the fire the quilt burnt to a crisp. I could replace pictures because my family had pictures. I could replace just about everything, but I couldn't replace that quilt. What once inspired me, now became the symbol of the trauma of sudden overwhelming loss and the powerlessness that accompanied it. My previous life had become irreplaceable just like the quilt. It hurt and I could not recover from the trauma. I'd wake up with nightmares, and I was lonely from the loss of my relationship. I lost focus on everything I was doing.

Then one night almost a year later I woke up in a cold sweat. I'd had a vivid dream that was more like a vision. My friend, the Chief, had visited me and said in a tone that was more challenging than sarcastic, 'For a white man you're pretty stupid.' I said, 'Why am I stupid?' And he replied, 'because you keep mourning the loss of that quilt. The quilt is only cloth. It doesn't matter how old or how beautiful it is, it's just a piece of cloth. It doesn't matter on this earth. Understand this: I didn't give you a quilt; I gave you my spirit, my guidance. If you reach out for what matters most, you'll stop worrying about the cloth and you'll heal. You've been looking in the wrong place.'

Well, I don't know if his spirit reached out to me, or if there was part of me that connected to him and just awoke to his message. I only know that through some magical process, in his presence, I healed. It was the first day that I didn't cry at least once. It was the first day that I started to see that my life wasn't so terrible, that I'd gone through a terrible ordeal but that it didn't have to define my life. What defines my life is who I am and what I do, not what I have and how I suffer.

Soon after the vision Rick got a call from Larry Brendtro from the Black Hills Seminars who told him about the Spirit of Crazy Horse Award, and that he and his partner, Allen Mendler, were to be honored for the work they had done together for children. (They had created and were applying an approach to discipline based on principles of mutual respect and dignity.) Larry asked him if he would give the keynote address that year. Rick told him that he'd be delighted to because he'd got a great story to tell about his quilt, the fire, and the vision. Larry then proceeded to tell him that for the last year, without knowing this story, Lakota women had been making him a star quilt, which is the gift they give to honor the recipients of the Crazy Horse award. "Then I understood the meaning of the message that I was looking in the wrong place," said Rick. "Everything I needed was there for me and always will be. I wasn't so much stupid as ignorant in the sense of not having knowledge. I think recovery from tragedy comes from knowing how to look for what will help us and for what we need. While we're suffering we don't know how or where to look."

Rick explained his new relationship to control and surrender.

The fire was the first thing that I knew I could not overcome by willpower. No matter how strong I was, I couldn't beat this. It was stronger than me. But of course I didn't have to beat it. I made peace with it and that's a completely different feeling. The power was inside me and all around me in the spiritual realm. I feel in a more balanced place now, maybe somewhere between my brother's will and my mother's love and compassion. I want to retain the positive aspects of my will and my belief that most things are possible, but I now know there are stairs out there that I can't climb, no matter what I do. That's a place of surrender, a place of trust. So from my vision of the Chief I learned that to be fixed on climbing the stairs is not the way forward. When I can't climb them I just have to look in a different place for something else.

Where there is truth there is paradox. The paradox of control shown in Rick's story is: ultimately nothing is controllable and, as Rick points out, everything we need is here and always will be. It is, of course, easier to see the wisdom of adversity in retrospect. Many survivors of trauma say that they came out much stronger than they went in, but it is natural to be unaware of the gifts of crisis at first, because we can only see the garbage bag.

Rick's story is a wonderful example of how a crisis calls for change of unhelpful ways of being. With the help of the Chief, he was able to see and release his exaggerated pattern of using willpower to win, to beat, and to conquer – learned for his protection as a disabled child. He learned to couple his will with an openness to wisdom beyond his conscious mind. After the fire he also redefined himself in a way that gave him strength to move forward: "What defines my life now is who I am and what I do, not what I have and how I suffer."

Looking in a different place for the answer reminds me of when I used to teach holistic childbirth. The information I felt it most important to share with expectant parents was this. If you are so sure you know what the best outcome is and become fixed on a target – such as a totally natural home birth with NO medical intervention – it will seem fine if all goes according to plan. But if it doesn't then you'll probably see that you've set yourself up to feel failure at losing the game. Ideally you should stop, gather information from various sources, then be willing listen to your in-tuition before aiming at the target you sense is best, while always holding the awareness that there could be a target you haven't noticed which would yield greater results for all concerned. The continuation of my own story, which follows Karen's, will expand on this further. Karen's story offers similar wisdom in a very different way.

Karen Proctor's Story – The Control Freak's Miracle

Karen came to see me at Linda Lantieri's apartment in New York City where Linda's "Crazy Horse" quilt was laid out on the floor. From what I had heard of Karen's fairly recent ordeal I expected her to arrive in a wheelchair, or at least on crutches. She breezed in with not even a limp; a slim, well-dressed woman in her thirties – oozing confidence – with a bloom and zing of excitement on her face.

Born in Philadelphia, Karen was the third of four daughters. She had a chaotic childhood with no financial stability. Her parents fought and screamed, and her alcoholic dad drank. Her mother had a "just go for it" spirit that she instilled in her girls, telling them "You are here for a purpose. God has a plan for you." She raised them to understand that as African Americans they would face certain challenges.

> I took faith from my mother, and from my emotionally abusive father I learned to be tough. At 15 I resolved never to live like them. My house would be a peaceful house. I was very intolerant of weakness and used to say to my mother, 'Why don't you leave him? Why do you tolerate this?' I just couldn't comprehend her love for him or her willingness to forgive. I developed this hard shell and had a tough resolve to survive and to raise my status. I was going to go to the best college and to work as hard as I could to get a degree so that I wasn't dependent on anybody. I saw my mother's life and I refused to continue that circle of living. I wanted to be in control.

Karen did succeed in going to Notre Dame University in the U.S., and with no money in her pocket she had to work hard to survive the four years. She said, "I felt like a triple minority because I am African American and I'm not Catholic or male. All odds were against me, but the flip side of my hardness was my will to survive."

After graduation she went to San Francisco, got married, and started work at a radio station. At 24 she gave birth to her daughter, Chelsea, but she struggled terribly because her husband wasn't faithful.

> It was a very bad marriage. I was naive, and as hard and tough as I was, I was also vulnerable because I was desperately seeking the love I didn't get from my father. I just wanted to be loved, so I accepted infidelities and emotional manipulation. But despite our troubles, I thought 'we're going to make this work' – just like every other part of my life that I made work. He didn't share that view!

She was left as a single mother, devastated by his abandonment and now with a demanding job with a cable television network. She had lost control of her life and, because control was so important to her, she was falling apart. In the depths of her despair she cried out to Jesus to help her survive and was moved to start Bible studies.

> I learned that when you really look, you can see a plan, a divine order of

things. Day by day, as I delved into my scriptures, I realized that darkness is only a part of my life. I reminded myself of the 23rd psalm: 'Even though I walk through the dark valley of death, I will not be afraid, for you are close beside me, your rod and staff protect and comfort me.' I learned to take it step by step and stopped wishing things were another way. I accepted where I was at and dealt with it. So I started thriving, seeing the blessings that were coming throughout, especially the bond that was being created with Chelsea.

Feeling stronger, she moved to New York and started working for the National Basketball Association. "It was a tough; a sink or swim environment with no room for failure. I just dove right into that New York 'get out of my way' frame of mind and was spending less and less time with Chelsea because my job demanded a 70 hour week. I was on this treadmill just working it."

Her father became critically ill in 1994 and she made peace with him before he died. After the funeral, she went home, helped with everything and then went right back to work. "I had to keep going, got to push through and be in control of my life," she said. Two years later her mother died. She shared what happened next:

It was shocking and made me wake up and say, 'You're 33, both your parents died in their sixties, this could be your mid-life. What are you doing? How are you being of service? How are you relating to other people?'

My sisters and I were all tired and we prayed for peace and a little breathing room. I took some time to reflect on my life but I became more driven to achieve at work. It was a place to go every day, responsibilities, somewhere to channel everything. I was a control freak about my life, thinking that if I could control my situation I could control my feelings.

On June 2nd, 1997, I had a big meeting to attend. It was an inaugural year of the Women's National Basketball Association, a new sports league for women. On that day I was to give a speech to the new women players about the importance of becoming role models. I had practiced and practiced my speech and was excited. That day was Chelsea's school play so I planned to go from the play to the meeting. Chelsea's dad showed up, the play was wonderful, and I was a proud mother.

I ordered a car to take the worry out of my journey. It shows up, I jump in the back, put my seat belt on, and we start out for the hotel. The deluge that day was scary because it was the kind of relentless rain where you could barely see. I felt nervous. The guy's going kind of fast but why am I worried about that? I started drifting off to sleep when all of a sudden there is this big swoosh sound and I wake up and see all this water coming up in front of us. Everything seems to be happening in slow motion... the car is spinning on the highway... the driver is freaking out, and, shit, we're going to hit something. What? Oh my god! We hit and I black out.

The next thing I know, I am touching my face because I can hear the driver screaming, 'Are you OK? Are you OK?' Well, my face is OK, no blood, but I look down at my body and, what is this? My torso is sort of leaned over to the left and my lower body, from my hips down, is to the right. I try to sit up and I can't. I am in excruciating pain and I look down at my legs. I can see that my right leg is broken – it looks like a chicken-bone effect, and my feet are wedged under the passenger seat. I was like this wrenched thing, and I was wearing all black that day too! I am like, 'I can't breathe, I can't think, I hurt, my legs look horrible, this is really bad.' The driver is totally panicked and I ask him to calm down, get me help on the radio and to call my office.

Two young black guys lean into the car and one of them says, 'we're going to be here with you.' I tell them, 'All I can do is pray, so just let me pray and do whatever you need to do.' So I pray, 'Jesus help me get through this.' I counted on him getting me through second by second. I could feel the terrible pain and this strange, foreign heat in my body. I couldn't move and I didn't know how they were going to get me out because my feet were stuck. The only thing I knew was that I could wiggle my toes, which meant there was no paralysis.

The driver was still panicking and trying to pull me out of the car, but my two good Samaritans, soaked in the pouring rain, said, 'No, leave her alone. We have to keep her conscious and wait for the emergency crews.' They held my hand and asked me questions, and I stopped rejecting them because I knew that they were calm and would protect me.

The emergency crews came with 'jaws of life' to break things and to try and get me out of this totally smashed-up car. They broke down and the second jaws weren't coming, and I don't know how much longer I can stay with this. Those boys are like, 'You can do it, you can do it.' And I'm like, 'OK Jesus, you brought me these boys, HELP ME!' The entire car had to be pulled apart and they had to take out the seats so they could get my legs free. The roof of the car had to be pulled back and the windows broken.

Eventually, Karen was rushed off to the New Jersey hospital and taken into surgery. She woke to find herself in traction and bound up, surrounded by her sisters. She had internal injuries and both her knees were dislocated – the right knee was almost ripped off. Her pelvis was fractured in many places, a rib was broken, her badly damaged spleen had been removed, and she needed four blood transfusions. Karen continued.

> So there I was in intensive care, a rock-like woman of control, totally and utterly helpless. My sisters were panicking because the doctors were telling them, 'It's touch and go.' No one could give me a prognosis and I was faced with total uncertainty about my future. One of my doctors said after my surgery, 'I don't understand how you survived. With an impact severe enough shatter your pelvis, you should have been dead on the scene. Usually, with a knee dislocation like yours we have to amputate. And how your back did not break, we're not sure. So you survived, you are not going to be in a wheelchair forever, and you're going to have to focus on that as you go through a very difficult time of rehabilitation.'
>
> When they tried to sit me up, I was in excruciating pain and prayed, 'Lord, help me meditate through one minute at a time.' I would go into deep meditations on Jesus and knew that as he walked this earth, he suffered physical pain too. The Bible says that when we can't pray, we can groan, and that God will know what it's all about. There were many times I was just groaning, but I did keep my faith. In Romans 5 it says: 'We can rejoice too when we run into problems and trials, for we know that they are good for us – they help us learn to endure. And endurance develops strength of character in us.' That really helped.

Chelsea, who associated hospital with death, did not believe that her mother would recover and this prompted Karen's resolve to get back to normal life as soon as possible to be there for her. Karen needed an acute care rehabilitation facility and after four weeks she was flown to a New Orleans hospital, to be near her ex in-laws. These people wanted to take care of her because they had maintained a close relationship despite the troubles with their son. More good Samaritans who nurtured her, comforted her, and provided her needs. Day by day she got stronger.

She told me of her struggle with pain and the lessons the car crash has taught her.

> I pleaded to God to help me understand this pain thing because it was making me go out of my mind. It was ever present and at night it was horrible. Then one Sunday I watched a church service on television. The preacher talked about ways to cope with and understand periods of darkness. He said that there will always be periods of darkness and despair in this life – that's part of our human condition in this world – and we need to remember that even through the darkness, God will be with us providing the light to see the end of the tunnel. I realized that Chelsea's grandparents are that light for me. The preacher said that a time of darkness is also an opportunity to build intimacy with God because

you're dependent, and to learn the lessons offered by that darkness. I felt my lesson was to let go of control and soften my heart. The car accident – which wasn't my fault, it just was – told me I can't always be in control and I have to open myself up to people. I hated dependency because my mother was dependent, but I found myself in a situation where I was totally dependent on others for everything, including degrading kinds of things for someone so proud and haughty. I am so grateful that life gave me the opportunity to break down my pride and become more humble.

I had asked after mom's death to be woken up and to find out how to best help others and serve God. Then I threw myself into work and obviously needed a big shake up to stop me in my tracks and make me meditate on what needed to change. I needed to break down the idol of my job and the sense of false security that comes from the world of glamour and high money. I believe that what truly matters is God's purpose for me, and that my suffering was not in vain because it was part of the divine order.

I began to realize, as I was going to therapy and getting better, that I could help people who were just being brought in. So I offered encouragement to people who were as broken as I was. In giving to others, I started feeling like a bird – soaring through this challenge. My wings were starting to mend and I wanted to fly. I could have died at 34. Instead I had an opportunity to be very close to death, to know how instantaneous it can be, and how we are not necessarily in control of that. I've heard people who have been through near death experiences say, 'Isn't everything bluer and clearer?' Yes, it is. I see the beauty in people and my eyes are wide open now. Life is such a gift. Why we forget that is astounding to me.

Now my journey is to find out where I can shine my light. My doctors call me a 'miracle girl.' I defied all of their predictions and statistics, and four months after the crash went back to work, despite having been told that I was deluding myself to think I'd be back within a year.

Karen told me that she has some fears to work out and can't run yet, but that she can ride her bike like the wind. She continues to speak healing into her joints.

My determination was the result of my upbringing, and my power is through Jesus Christ. The Bible says: 'I can do everything with the help of Christ who gives me the strength I need.' I believe this. I spoke healing, through prayer, into my body and it healed miraculously. I may have to have a limitation because that may be the cross I have to bear, but I have learned to release to a planning greater than my own.

Karen's inner strength comes from her unshakable faith in sources beyond herself – identified in her case as Jesus and God – and her trust in the divine plan, coupled with her own determination. She gave up her tight control on life and softened into a place where she felt held by an intelligence that knows better, but at no point did she give up her will. Although she had been rendered helpless in many ways, Karen still took responsibility for responding to her condition to the best of her ability, thus retaining her self-respect. She actively flooded herself with positive messages, using her will in a positive way to direct the arduous task of becoming well and then helping others to do likewise.

Karen was called the "miracle girl" because she defied all the medical predictions and statistics. She showed her resilience by avoiding the common trap of giving her power away to the "experts" and automatically seeing herself as they did. She had called to be woken up after her mother's death, and despite the traumatic nature of the subsequent car crash she graciously accepted it as a wake up call when it came. And I wonder if the miracle pace of healing would be in the realm of possibility for us all if we stopped resisting and trying to control our pain long enough to allow the inherent messages to present themselves.

Karen admits that she needed a big shake up to stop her in her tracks, and the opportunities offered from being rendered totally helpless dovetailed perfectly with her desire to become less controlling and to break her tough shell into humility.

The most powerful truths are often the most simple. Karen's TV preacher told her that there will always be ups and downs in life – periods of darkness and light. So obvious, and yet I, for one, often feel that something is wrong if I'm not experiencing a happy life. The chase for happiness is so ingrained. Every so often I remind myself that a good fairytale is full of darkness, daring deeds, monsters, and the like. And the satisfaction gained from reading such stories comes, not from the end, but from the way in which the s/hero bravely encounters the devils of the adventure. Perhaps there is never an end to real life stories.

The story that I will tell next has no neat, happy ending but it does have inner resolution within the characters. It is a story revealing certain challenges from the opposite side of the continuum of control. Rick and Karen were both transported by their very different traumas back to times of helplessness in childhood and brought face to face with the need to alter their lifelong patterns of using will to control the world. The protective pattern I created in my childhood is one of retreating from the will.

My Story Continued – An Ocean of Trust

Another sudden shock brought into sharp focus my lifelong struggle with control. Unable to speak up for myself in childhood, I needed a non-verbal survival mechanism. My early childhood was spent in a sea of powerlessness, with tears calling attention to my needs. I cowered in the face of criticism and withdrew further into my shell, swimming in self-pity. I thought I had no power over anything, but control comes in many guises. Non-action, when action is needed, is as out of balance and ineffective as the "control freak" pattern.

As we all do, I unconsciously perfected ways of behavior to get my needs met. My vulnerability called for protection and for others to look after me. If something unpleasant occurred I retreated into books, fantasy land, or later, spiritual practice, leaving them to sort the problem out. If the problem was unavoidable and my carefully chosen, softly spoken words fell on deaf ears, my vulnerability would often induce a change of mind or heart in others. Unconsciously, I must have realized that big rolling Bambi tears are hard to resist, and for 40 years I let them roll. The emotion was real, but neither I nor the witnesses were in a place of true power. We all felt victimized.

A recent event heralded the coming of age for Bambi. To set the context: my marriage of eleven years, which by most standards was a good one, ended by my choice in 1998. It was probably the most courageous act of my life. I believed that I had to leave because I had not found a way, even with Abel's proffered help, to be fully in my power in his presence. I said "yes" when I meant "no", felt threatened and diminished by his highly developed intellect and practical genius, and then resented him because it looked like he was holding all the power. I knew full well that no one could make me feel inferior without me agreeing to it, but no amount of concerted effort yielded the inner authority for which I yearned in my marriage.

The parting was made even more painful by our shared poignant memories. In the house I was leaving we had experienced the death of our firstborn son and the birth of our second, Asher, who was four when we separated. I moved three times before finally settling happily in a terraced cottage in the same village as Abel. Asher, after two and a half years of inner turmoil and often bitter anger towards me, was ecstatic about having both parents so close. I was deeply relieved that he was healing from the trauma of our breakup, and looked forward to the childcare – which I shared equally with Abel – becoming much easier.

It was at this point that the thunderbolt struck for the first time. Abel, admitting an intense sense of guilt, told me that he was seriously considering moving to London – four hours away by car – and that he wanted to take Asher with him. He was not feeling fulfilled living in the countryside and was yearning for city life and better business opportunities. He sincerely believed that Asher would be happier with him, and if I didn't agree then we would have to bring in some outside help to mediate.

I felt as if I had been physically struck by a knife that went deep into the wound of loss created by our first son's death. I was shocked to the core.

All I could do was howl and feel pain at the possible loss of another son. The alternative – becoming a full-time single mother – would, I believed, stop in its tracks the new, exciting direction of my career, which involved a lot of travel. To me this was also unthinkable because I had been trying for years to make my work more visible in the world, and felt on the brink of success. I also projected that Asher would be devastated by either possibility and could not abide the thought of him experiencing any more pain. I felt completely controlled by Abel. The oh-so-familiar ocean of powerlessness engulfed me, and the Bambi tears fell night and day... until I began to believe, in the absence of more news, that Abel had changed his mind in response to my intense pain and inability to actively support his plan. Nevertheless, that sword of Damocles continued to swing in my subconscious and I suffered chronic insomnia and a sense of mild dread.

Then, four months later, it dropped. It was January when Abel visited again, this time visibly steeled against the intensity of my feelings. He explained in more detail why he felt he had to do this and informed me that he intended to leave by the end of the summer. Something in me knew that there was too much at stake here to remain lost in my powerlessness. I realized that if I didn't put Bambi to rest and grow up fast, I might lose my son. I was still shocked, but turned my attention to listening properly to Abel's needs. I knew that if he felt unheard, and manipulated by my feelings then he would be unable to care about my experience. Once again he would get what he wanted because I hadn't stood up for my needs in a clear adult way. He went away looking softer and feeling heard.

The timing was perfect. That same week I was going away on a short trip to the Caribbean island of Puerto Rico with my soul-friend. I decided to use the gift of these ideal surroundings to find a wise response to the challenge before me. I remembered a line which the wonderful teacher, Angeles Arrien, is fond of saying – "Solutions are not found in the extremities: elegant solutions are found between the polarities" – and I was determined to find a path to center. It was an important inner journey for me. I allowed myself to feel the rising pain without losing myself in it. I acknowledged my strong beliefs, fears and attachments around this issue without making decisions from them. And I knew that I needed to step out of my own limited perspective to allow an overview that embraced all of our needs – especially Asher's – as my input here would deeply impact the direction of his life. I knew also that as long as I was filled with my own agenda there would be no room for wisdom to enter, and so my goal was to surrender both my attachment to a specific outcome and any thought of knowing what was best.

I consulted the I Ching, a divination tool with which I have had an ongoing relationship for 20 years. This offered me sound and useful advice, but the greatest lesson was given to me unexpectedly by the Caribbean Sea. It had been very windy since we arrived at our guesthouse on the beach and despite my desire I could not get into the wild, choppy waves, which matched the waves of my inner turmoil. By the third day it was slightly less choppy – both inside and out – and I braved the surprisingly warm waters. After swimming nervously for a while through the unpredictable waves with white crests breaking over me, I lay still on my back and let the ocean hold me.

I became acutely aware of the comparative stillness of the water under me and the vastness of the deep ocean in which I was floating effortlessly. When I let go and relaxed I was carried safely up and down over the waves, comforted by the gentle rocking, with the warm sun on my face. I looked across at the surface of the sea with its wild ups and downs and realized that life is always full of peaks and troughs, and the trick for me to learn is to navigate them without using too much of my own emotional, physical and mental energy in the process. I embodied the knowledge that there is a calm core place within the roughness of life, a place of total trust. I knew that in that place I could avoid drowning and successfully ride the currents. So simple. So profound.

Over the next few days I lay in the ocean again and again, until I was also able to feel permeated by that ocean of trust on dry land. By the end of the holiday I felt rock solid in my ability to hear and trust my own wisdom and knew that answers would unfold in the right timing. I had recognized that there was sure to be a bigger picture here that I was unable to see at present, and was now almost excited about what gifts could be on the way. I had fully let in the fearsome possibility of releasing my son if guided to do so, and was equally willing to release my career in its projected form for the sake of my son's well being. I was fiercely committed to allowing the best solution to present itself, was unattached to outcome and felt truly safe. There was nothing to be lost. I felt totally alive and freed from both the need to control and the fear of being controlled.

So, I had "come to center" by moving from a place of attachment to a place of commitment; from the resistant place of struggle and "power against" to the welcoming place of "power with", and was keen to see how Abel would respond to this new embracing state. We met as soon as I returned, and during that meeting I remained anchored in that place, not even tempted to be pulled by the current of his agenda. In fact his current, which we were both used to being affected by my "weather" patterns, seemed to have been soothed into silence. What I perceived in him was a sense of awe in the face of my leap into empowerment. It was as if my willingness to embrace everyone's needs and to constructively follow the next step, created a slipstream into which he let go, because ultimately that's what he wanted too. What was in the best interest of us all had stood little chance of being discovered until Abel felt respected by me and free to explore his calling.

Abel decided to put his directive plan on hold and to attend to Asher's primary need – continuity and security for a while longer in his education at his present school, which is like a family to him. He had moved to a place of wanting to hear and embrace all our needs and to follow whatever wisdom came from the release of personal attachments. Over a year later we still live in the same village. Abel has fallen in love and so we begin the process again, this time with the needs of four people in the pot. There still is no clear plan for the coming years but we are each trusting that from this state of being the plan will reveal itself to us or through us. Lao Tzu said it perfectly:

Do you have the patience to wait until your mud settles and the water is clear? Can you remain unmoving till the right action arises by itself?

I want to affirm how vital it is to stay absolutely centered in our own knowing, once found. When mentioning this challenge about Asher to others, I was bombarded with conflicting yet well-meaning advice. Some tried to convince me that I needed my freedom and this was a way I could take it – "after all, Abel is such a good father, and boys need to be with their fathers." Others immediately expressed anger and a desire to protect my boy from Abel's selfish plan – because "boys that age need their mothers." Most of the advice was a total projection of what each person would feel and want for themselves in that situation. It was a minefield from which I learned to choose carefully those in whom I confided.

And so this major challenge helped me to deeply understand that elegant solutions are not found in the extremities but between the polarities. It also helped me to become a more grounded, responsible member of humanity.

As a tailpiece to this section I cannot resist also sharing the next piece, written by an Italian spiritual teacher known as Babaji Francisco. It appeared today as I was sorting through my old journals. Here are a few lines from one paper, the title of which is:

Stop Controlling. Lose control and you will re-find yourselves.

When you give up control then your actions, your responses, no longer belong to your mind but rather to your whole spontaneous and natural BEING – that which is not conditioned by anything. Then you will be your-Self and your response will be unpredictable. It will be a response against all logic but it will be real. You have transcended social custom, conformism, conditioning, and in your response will be a most profound authenticity... It will spring from your soul and the soul KNOWS everything. The soul acts when the mind ceases, when all control ceases.

You lose control and unbelievably it happens that you have everything under control. Then you succeed in seeing everything clearly, in understanding everything, and in loving as you had not loved before.

Second Key
TRUST AND SURRENDER CONTROL
Questions and Reflections

1. Meditate for a few moments on the stories in this section: Rick's fire and quilt, Karen's car crash and miracle recovery, Carmella's ocean of trust. What had the most heart and meaning for you? Why?

2. How could you apply the learning you consider most important from these stories to your own life? What would prevent you from doing that?

3. In your journal write the word CONTROL in the center of a page. Think about your relationship to authority and control, and using colored pens/crayons represent that relationship on the page in pictures or words. Then ask, "What does this page tell me about myself?"

4. On another clean page represent, in pictures or words, any changes you'd like to make to your relationship to control?

5. Take a moment's silence and bring to mind a time when you felt very trusting. How does this feel in your body? What was it about this situation that helped you to trust?

6. Now see if you can recall a challenging situation in which you managed to let go into a state of unknowing and a way forward presented itself. How did this feel?

7. Close your eyes and in your imagination take a trip to a place that supports you to relax deeply and let go. Make it vivid. When was the last time you were there? If you can't get there physically, know that you can get there in your mind.

8. Think of the last time you were in physical pain. How did you cope? In what way did you listen to the needs or lessons of that pain?

9. If you are totally honest, who or what do you believe is responsible for your health and your life's direction? Is that a belief you want to keep?

10. To what degree do you carry the "happy ever after" desire? What happens in you when you encounter the shadowy side of life? Is there anything you want to change about that?

The Third Key

SHARE YOUR PAIN AND CHOOSE LIFE

What is not ex-pressed is de-pressed;
the more we give voice to our pain in living
the less build-up we have between our soul
and our way in the world.
Mark Nepo

Share Your Pain and Choose Life

S haring our struggles and our pain and choosing life-affirming actions
bonds us with others, builds community and supports the healing process.
Disaster on a big scale, especially a disaster that allows useful action to be
taken by the community, breeds compassion, heroic deeds, and acts of
kindness. Kirk Humphreys, the mayor of Oklahoma City said in September
2001, "Oklahoma City developed a more powerful sense of itself after the
bombing. We feel a lot better today about ourselves than we did before. The
hardship brought about our optimism and our caring." When the story, the
grief, and the hideous details are shared with a village, a city, a nation, or the
world on television screens, a stream of compassion, loving support and
prayer is released. There is an outlet for powerful feelings, and connections
of depth are made. Both the givers and receivers are fortified to some
degree as they take the next steps in the process of integrating the difficult
reality before them.

If only this were so for all those who suffer. Except in the case of cataclysm,
there is a widespread pattern of trying to protect our soft spots by avoiding
subjects of pain at all costs. We often deny the depth of our vulnerability,
even to ourselves. Thus we block the receipt of care when we need it most
and deny others the opportunity to give and feel useful. No person or place
on earth is invulnerable and it is extremely helpful to accept that having
painful places that sometimes trigger overwhelming emotion is a part of
being human.

The infrastructure to share pain and so prevent the pressure cooker build-
up of our emotions has to a large extent broken down in the West. Separation,
fragmentation, and isolation are the sad side effects of our modern quest for
freedom and individual expression. No longer do our family and social
networks receive our daily woes, or even our pleasures. In our nuclear family
and single parent culture many of us are starved of an effective outlet, or
the time to integrate our minor daily experiences, let alone the bigger
issues of our lives. Separation from the sources of wisdom in a community
– especially the wisdom of our elders – has increased our sense of vulnerability and loneliness. If there is no one to hear our pain we can become
desperate and do anything to get attention, to be heard and noticed. There is
an increase in the ultimate acts of loneliness – suicide and explosive violence.
In the case of the terrorists who turned planes into bombs, they chose both the
extremes together to try and make their point! What were their unanswered
needs I wonder?

Certain research tells us that in order to make sense of traumatic memories
and put them in a different perspective it is beneficial to repeatedly communicate the details of the story in a therapeutic space. If a sense of safety can
be felt alongside the difficult memories then, as Daniel Goleman says in his

book *Emotional Intelligence*,[10] "the memory starts to be transformed, both in its emotional meaning and in its effects on the emotional brain." He also says, "By putting sensory details and feelings into words, presumably memories are brought more under control of the neocortex, where the reactions they kindle can be rendered more understandable and more manageable." Peter Levine, author of *Waking The Tiger, Healing Trauma*,[11] who has studied stress and trauma for 30 years, would add that a vitally important part of the healing is in the discharge of trapped and frozen energy in the body when recounting the story, followed by the realization of one's successful escape from the danger.

The following stories show various ways of sharing intense experiences with others and highlight some of the rich rewards of doing so. They also offer role models as to how, having successfully escaped from danger, we can use our experience to fuel a new, positive and useful direction in life. Mirsad's story raises questions about anger and forgiveness – a subject dealt with more fully in the sixth key. What can be done with intense anger? What does forgiveness really mean? Is it a necessary part of the healing process? And how do we reach a place of true forgiveness?

Arn Chorn-Pond's Story – Ten Thousand People Cried

It seemed incongruous to be sitting in a comfortable hotel room in Cambridge, Massachusetts, being transported by Arn's vivid memories into his war-torn homeland, Cambodia, and the shadow side of humanity. The bizarre inequality in the world seemed to hover in the room. Arn, a casually dressed, good-looking man in his thirties, had no visible scars. The scars were in his eyes and in the propulsion of his passion to save others from a similar plight.

He began by telling me about his childhood in a Cambodian city near the border of Thailand. He is unsure how old he is, but knows he was born the fourth child in a large family. He especially loved his oldest sister, who was very kind, and a younger brother with whom he recalled watching movies in the town before playing Chinese Kung Fu games. His father, uncle and grandfather were actors in the opera. All of them died young and so Arn was brought up with little money in a home of hardworking women and lots of children. His mother gave him to his aunt when he was a baby and he became very close to her. He laughed as he remembered fetching vegetables for her from the city, then gambling with the taxi driver.

His family didn't have enough money for school, so he was sent to the temple. He told me,

> I liked temples because of the many people, the ceremonies and singing and music. And there was always food there! Mom taught us how to offer food to the monks properly. It was fun. We had movies at night on a big screen in the temple. I liked monks.

Apparently the family did not know that war was coming, although they could hear artillery far away. Arn was about nine or ten in 1975 when the communists took over his country. I'll let him tell the rest of his story, as his words are so powerful.

The Khmer Rouge came into the city – thousands of them in tanks and trucks on the highway. I was cheering with everybody else because I didn't know what was going on. The soldiers were almost as young as I was, and they had guns. They had scarves, caps and frowning faces – not smiling, not happy. They said, 'Peace has come.' Some of them came down from the trucks. I began to teach them how to play ball with other kids and they put the guns down and played. They were awkward and I was scared at them because they were very angry, *never* smiling. One Khmer Rouge guy stopped a man riding a motorcycle. He wanted that motorcycle but the man said, 'I don't give you it,' and so the soldier hit him in the back of the head and he fell down. This was the first time I seen a person do this. I ran to my family and told my mom and aunt but they didn't pay attention because everybody is happy saying that peace is coming with the Khmer Rouge. My family didn't pay attention to me because I was a young person.

Two days later Khmer Rouge came to our house. My family greeted them very friendly and picked coconuts for them. I was hiding because I was scared, but I hide my fear in my heart and didn't tell because nobody would believe me; they thought I was weird. Three days later the Khmer Rouge came on a truck with a microphone and announced that in three days the Americans would come and bomb us because we won a victory. They said, 'Everybody has to leave the city to save their life.' We found out later that they lied.

Next morning, 5 o'clock, thousands of people packed the highway walking away from the city. They took what they could carry. My family was lucky that we held each other's hands. We had plastic bags and some food, some pig and chickens. It was noisy and I was scared to see people like that. The Khmer Rouge had guns, directing us saying, 'Go, move, move, move.' We walked two days, sleeping on the highway, and people were getting directed to different paths. We saw some corpses on the ground. We didn't know why. We were getting far from the city now, in the countryside. Finally they directed my family and about 500 other families into an area; others got to keep on walking. Then Khmer Rouge took our names and got a history about us. They told us we would be here for two or three months. Next day they told us to work in rice fields at 7 o'clock.

About two months later I saw some family taken away and they didn't come back. Then there was a woman we know who the Khmer Rouge killed right behind our hut. We were about to scream, then we ask each other not to scream. My mom's look said, 'You probably were right.' So now we begun to be careful. We worked every day. Later on we found mass graves in the rice field and we lived in fear.

After five months people have become sick. We had only a hut shelter we made ourselves. Then the Khmer Rouge began a campaign of hate at old people and began to kill them saying they are not useful. Children from 6 to 13 years old they took away. From 13 to about 25 they took them to live separately. The women lived with the women. Fathers went far away with fathers. They found there was no one to take care of babies so they started using old people to take care of them.

I was separated from my family and sent to a temple far away. My aunt just said, 'Be careful. We will see each other again.' They took me to a temple with 500 other kids from 6 years old to 13 and forced us to live there together. It was similar to Auschwitz but on a small scale. I lived there for two out of four years of 'the killing fields.' I was sent there to work and to die. We worked in the rice fields from 5 o'clock in the morning until 12 o'clock at night with a short time to rest in the middle of the day. Then they said we can't have food because we are not making enough food. We had a very small portion of rice put into a tank of water to feed about 150 kids. We just drank the water and that's it. Many of us were dying now.

There were many sections in the temple. Behind the big Buddha the Khmer Rouge would tie up hundreds of prisoners. They killed night and day. Over the stream that ran across my center was an orange field where they killed lots of people and they would bring us out to watch. We made a circle and sometimes they would punish them in front of us. I was asked too many times to go and watch and sometimes to help take clothing off a person before they put the bayonet into them.

In Cambodia hot season is very hot, and I hated the rains too. Kids were throwing up, dirt and smells, blood all in our center. They didn't clean. It's like hell with many kids dying every day. I spent a lot of time sitting looking outside in my dreams somewhere, hearing kids groaning in their sleep on the floor. The hardest part for me was when I was really sick. I went to the bathroom 500 times a day. My stomach hurt a lot and I had headaches. While I'm sharing this it all comes back. It's good I'm really present with that feeling now. Back then I needed to stop feeling or I'd die. The Khmer Rouge watched our faces for emotion, and if somebody showed sadness they killed them or punished them with screwdrivers. I've seen kids killed because they care about other people. Some of my close friend's family was executed. He was about to be checked out about the face and I squeezed his hand. They went past him. I saved his life I think. I was so scared. Some died in the field while they worked.

One time it was raining hard and I was looking out the window. The Khmer Rouge were having a good time punishing people in the rain. There was one muscular guy, a former soldier from the American Government, who they punished every day until he became weak, hitting him with a screwdriver in his knees. Finally they brought him close by my window. One guy was so angry, he found a stick on the ground and hit him in the neck until he was dead. They put him in a tree right outside my window, sitting there wearing an American helmet with a cigarette in his mouth. His eye was still open. These are the things I remember from childhood.

I saw the Khmer Rouge take the liver and spleen out of victims. The spleen they made medicine out of it and the liver they ate it. They wanted me to eat it too. Ten of us kids were asked to play music for the revolutionary song. An old man came and taught us flute and dulcimer and five days later they killed him. Lucky they didn't ask me to watch! Then I was asked by the Khmer Rouge leader to perform for them and I was good at it so probably I was saved. I had light skin, they thought I was from rich family and the men were after me. The leader took me to live with him, so I left the killing place to take care of the car and house, to perform and play the flute. I had more food to eat. Here I got a letter my older sister wrote me from her deathbed. I don't know what they did to her.

In 1978 when the Vietnamese invaded Cambodia, I was about twelve, and was forced into the front line and given a gun. If you refuse to carry a gun the Khmer Rouge just shoot you in the head, so I took the gun and had to figure out how to use it. Thousands of kids were forced to fight. We had a lot of spirit, but the Americans they kill us like hell. I couldn't take it watching my friends die everywhere. I felt helpless and crazy and I wanted to scream very much. If you did not make a decision quickly you died. I didn't get shot – maybe my skill or my luck, I don't know. Later I found that a quarter of my country's people died from execution, starvation and overwork in the Khmer Rouge rule.

Then I escaped to live in the tropical jungle by myself. Three months, six months... I don't know how long. In the jungle you most likely die; even the smallest snake can poison you. I saw some bones of people killed by the animals. I wanted to kill myself, but every day I went on. I walked to the South trying to get away from the sound of fighting. I had no knowledge of the world at all – I thought the world was flat. After about two or three weeks I realized I'd walked in a circle and came back to the same place, getting nowhere. I was on the edge, but I went on because I felt sure I would see my family again and tell them what I've been through. Somewhere in that jungle I would find clear sky and reach somewhere.

The monkeys also helped me survive. There were monkeys all over and they can be dangerous too. Sometimes they came with the whole pack of family and I'd get up from sleeping and see them, big guys with teeth. They'd look me in the eye; I looked them in the eye. But they helped me because I didn't know what fruit to eat – what was poison. So I followed the monkeys and ate the fruit they dropped. I also fished with my hands in the stream. I watched the mother monkeys bathing and loving their kids. I never saw that with human beings. I thought that little monkey's lucky. I was curious. They are very similar to humans and very passionate. Sometimes I killed a little monkey to eat because they're easy, but I felt bad.

Sometimes I would see a person, but no way I would talk. If you saw a human being you must shoot. You see, you couldn't trust human beings; animals are safer. I slept sometimes in a big tree by climbing up a vine. In the jungle it's wet all of the time. I hated it. My clothes were torn apart and I was practically naked. I would climb a tree to be dryer. The movie, Tarzan, is similar but I wasn't strong like that, I was a little boy shitting in my pants. There were animals sleeping up there too, especially snakes. One time a snake was across my leg and I had to be still otherwise I'm dead. If it's not a bullet it's a snake!

At last I crossed the border into Thailand. I was confused with malaria. Five Cambodian women collecting wood found me and carried me to a camp. It was like a dream when I woke up, so many people. Where am I? I was scared... blisters all over my body. The five women had medicines and tried to cure me. I felt good the first time the women touched me. They saved my life.

I went off in a car, and I've never seen a car in a long time. They put me in another camp where I lived for about two years. I was very sick and weighed about 50lbs. One night there was terrible floods, it was raining hard and I was about to drown. I couldn't move, I was too sick. Many kids drowned that night. Then someone stepped on me and realized I was a human being. I think he felt bad – he's about 200lbs! That man held me and he cried. I was lucky he stepped on me and rescued me and came back next day with food. He kept coming back, giving me food and making sure I didn't die. One day I heard the doctor tell the man, Peter, I wouldn't make it. I told them, 'I'll make it! I'll make it from somewhere!' Peter was crying. I knew he liked me this rich American. So he keeps coming, and day by day I made it.

Peter wanted to be my foster father, and in 1980 he took me to America. Lucky I didn't jump out of the window of the plane! When they said 'America' I didn't know where America is. I almost died on the plane because of the anxiousness and the nurse thought I was crazy. On the plane there were refugees from all different countries, including my three Cambodian adoptive brothers. My new dad came and picked me up. I was so happy to see him I hugged him and cried.

In New Hampshire there were hard times because I didn't know where my family was, why I was in America. I ran away from home many times. I was put in ninth grade in high school with white kids and I didn't pass any courses because that's the first grade I ever had, and the kids make fun of us because they've never seen Asians before. But, they put us Cambodians into soccer teams and we became champions three years in a row; heroes in high school!

Then I began more and more to heal myself. I met a good woman, Judith Thompson, and was encouraged by her and my dad to go out and talk. They said 'If you want more of your friends from the camp to come here, you've got to let people know about your story.' I didn't want to talk about it because I thought nobody cares a shit about my life. First I learned from my heart a few words, 'My name is Arn. I'm from Cambodia. I live in the camp. My family die.' People listened and then they made a line to hug me and cry too. For the first time I felt cared for and I felt powerful. (Underneath I think people that care for you abandon you or something.) It takes time to trust people. Peter kept coming to me every morning and saying, 'What you went through in Cambodia is not your fault.' I take it day by day. Some kids might take 10 years to change, some 20; some might not change until they die. For me I am fast and it takes me 17 years! So it helps when I go out and speak. In a way I have an urge of talking on behalf of the kids that were killed and can't speak out.

I began to work for Amnesty International and I was asked to speak at St. John the Divine Church to 10,000 people. It was about peace and disarmament in New York. I was the key speaker. I wrote it on my own mostly. There were four or five other kids from around the world. Half way through my speech I couldn't take it and I cried uncontrollably. Then there were 10,000 people crying. They asked me if I want to stop and I said, 'No, I want to finish it. This is a turning point for me.' When I finished I felt I was on the top of a mountain.

After that I started Children of War with Judith Thompson and we brought kids from 42 countries. A turning point also was meeting those other children of war, learning about their suffering. It's trouble when I think only about myself, *my* suffering and *my* world. I went through more than many other people, but if I think I'm the only person in the world that went through this I feel very bad. When a Vietnamese kid told me that he lost his family too, I choked. We're all victims of war. And who started that? Adults in their greediness, politics or whatever. In Cambodia we were taught by adults to hate the Vietnamese and the Vietnamese were taught to hate us.

I began to know we *can* do a lot together as children to stop this fighting. I believe strongly we have to start with young people if we want to teach peace or love. Those kids who risked their lives for me in Cambodia taught me about unconditional love, and continue to have their life in me. I just want to save kids. I still live in America in a town with the second largest Cambodian population and I am working with hard kids in street gangs and sharing my experience with them. It is my love for them that keeps me going. First they say, 'You college kid, what you want to help us for? You don't know anything about guns!' Then I tell my story. I relate to them on a personal level and I *know* anybody can change. So I believe in them and they believe in me. I'm facing my past every day by seeing the pain of life but I feel good about myself when I help others like me. These kids are 13 and 14 years old and shooting each other on the streets. There's a war going on in America, never mind Cambodia, and what the hell are the leaders doing?

Also I go back and work with thousands of kids in Cambodia – a dangerous situation but that doesn't matter to me. I've died a million times already. I started a project called 'Cambodian Volunteers for Community Development' a few years ago and now we have 50,000 young members. These are traumatized kids who saw family members killed by the Khmer Rouge and cleaned up bones and stuff like that. Brutalization can cause paralysis of will so it's important to get people active. We have a center and try to heal ourselves. I have 24 English classes. We made our own tables – prostitutes and monks as well. Before the war we had lots of trees, now there's nothing there so we planted new ones. I also help orphans cleaning up streets and building houses.

I was saved and others were not saved, so I'm wanting to do something good before I die. I want to grow up to be a good adult and hopefully be a role model for other kids. Also I have good reason for a lot of anger and so do these kids and it is important to make the anger produce good results.

I think I am alive today after all these years, not just because I wasn't butchered by the Khmer Rouge genocide, but because I had the courage to speak out my story and I learned how to love again and how to feel the pain of others as well as my own. Recently they found that SIDS – Sudden Infant Death Syndrome – that happens with babies, occurs in men. It's related to post traumatic stress. Men keep stress inside them more than women. Three Cambodian men I knew very close, went to sleep and died. Cambodians are like anybody else – they don't want to touch that painful spot. I think that's a weak point because if you don't you might die from holding in all the pain. I'm lucky I know that.

Since this interview was conducted I have discovered that Arn also catalyzed and co-founded several projects to assist Cambodian musicians and culture. His cultural heritage was nearly extinguished when Pol Pot's regime killed 90% of the Khmer traditional performers. In the mid-1990s, as Arn began to locate the few surviving performers, he discovered that they had not been able to teach or perform for a generation in Cambodia's crushed economy. To help these elderly "living treasures" pass on their heritage, Arn inspired the Cambodian Master Performers Program (CMPP) that enables more and more of the great masters to teach, record and perform again. Arn now lives in Cambodia where he immerses himself in cultural activities. Drawing on all the contacts he made in Cambodia and around the world during 20 years as an activist, his activities affect Cambodians from the top of society to the bottom.

Anais Nin wrote:
And then the day came
when the risk to remain tight as a bud
was more painful than the risk to bloom.

Arn's healing journey began when he reached this point and started sharing his story. Up until then it seems that his energy was utilized in simply surviving. Timing is crucial of course, and it may be too soon to expose our rawness, but the time of sharing must come if healing is to happen. It doesn't have to be a public sharing witnessed by many. It could begin by simply groaning an admission of the pain to yourself, or to God, or by simply allowing the body to tremble the pain to the surface and to complete its natural cycle of release in the presence of someone you love and trust. The question is: Are you burying your feelings? If you are then, unfortunately, you will reap the inevitable effects. What you resist will always persist. Arn ends his story by telling us that if we don't touch that painful spot we might die from holding in all the pain. Jesus said it this way:

If you bring forth what is within you, what you bring forth will save you.
If you do not bring forth what is within you, what you do not bring forth
will destroy you.

I cried when Arn said, "I'm lucky, I know that." But, having banished the luck concept, I'm left asking: if it wasn't luck, what did help him to survive against such odds and choose to live rather than giving up? He survived the brutality of the Khmer Rouge guerrillas, starvation in the Auschwitz-style camp, being shot in the front line of the war, the dangers of the jungle, the ensuing malaria, horrific culture shock, and bullying. Some would say that perhaps he was protected by the powers that be because he was meant to live to bring more love into this world. Perhaps it was his reserve of love, or his extraordinary will to survive that saved him. Love is a survival need and, according to research into resilience, to have had at least one early, trusting relationship with an adult is a key factor in thriving after trauma. Would Arn have thrived without: knowing his family loved him and holding dreams of seeing them again, observing the love of the monkeys, the

women who tended him at the Thai border, his foster father's devoted care
and Judith's mentoring? "I'll make it! I'll make it from somewhere!" said
Arn from his apparent deathbed. It sounds like there was a powerful survival
instinct in him, a choice and determination to live. I wonder if he would he
have survived if he had decided he'd had enough of suffering and wanted
to die.

After Benjaya's death, both Abel and I shared our pain freely with others,
howling our grief out loud in those first weeks whenever it arose. We threw
open our arms to the support of friends and family, who immensely appreciated being able to share in this depth with us and releasing their own grief
in our presence. Many friends expressed their gratitude for being included
in the raw reality of our grief. It was transformative for them. After an intense
week of being with us in our pain, Kitty Watkins said, "I feel indefinably
bigger, perhaps greater. My heart feels larger and holds the pain of heartache
and yet it is a growing pain. I feel dynamically rearranged – utterly changed.
I feel love and gratitude that I have been able to share something so personal,
so precious, just like a birth... I am here unclothed in my newness." In those
early days we never once entertained the thought that our pain could be a
burden for others, because it was so obviously having the opposite effect.

On a precautionary note, as time went by I learned a salutary lesson in
relation to sharing pain. I realized that showing it too often with too many
people can become damaging to self and others. How so? Caroline Myss
Ph.D. has invented the word "woundology", which means becoming
addicted to using our wounds to attract certain kinds of attention. Many of
us learned at an early age that when we are hurt, others will take notice of
us and we may get more love. Staying in a place of pain and letting others
know how difficult life is becomes a misguided way of enticing the love we
crave. When this occurs others may be fooled for a while but will soon become
uncomfortable with the "stuck record effect" and avoid our company unless
they have a neurotic need to be a helper and giver. It is important to become
attuned to whether this is the right place, the right time, and the right person
for such a sharing.

It is also important to avoid trying to make someone else talk about a
traumatic experience in order to get the feelings out. This could cause
retraumatization. Simply being fully present and creating a container of
safety will enable feelings to flow through the body when the person is
ready. Don't resist and don't push – just allow.

Almost every year, on the anniversary of Benjaya's death, I have felt
moved to facilitate a workshop on death and dying. It is as if the flow is
stronger at that time and I seem more able to catch the essence of my learning
and use it constructively to help others. I have also discovered that daring
to stand authentically naked before others in my vulnerability, which
includes being open to my joyful, playful self, is the quickest, most effective

way to help others step into intimacy and to create the safety for them to share what is ready to see the light of day.

Over the years I have observed a changing perception of the quality of vulnerability. It is increasingly recognized as a strength that can heal rather than a sign of weakness. More of us – especially men – are discovering the richness of our emotional selves, and a move towards greater intimacy is in process. It may be worth asking ourselves if we avoid weepy movies because we are embarrassed to be seen expressing sadness. Or, do we weep freely and allow ourselves to feel connected to another's pain, not caring what others might think? Do we think less of men who cry? Or, do we welcome their depth and vulnerability? Arn has spent many years learning how to cry because his healing process depended upon it.

Judith's story expands this theme of sharing pain and graphically describes some of the immense benefits of being present in our vulnerability with others.

Judith Thompson's Story – Suffering as a Sacred Doorway

Judith, the "good woman" mentioned by Arn, is slim and elegant, with a sharp, clear mind and a history of actively engaging with the world to create positive change. Her story is less personal than others in the sense that she speaks of her invaluable work with children in grief from all over the world. However, we are given enough of her own story for us to see exactly why choosing this particular work was part of her personal quest for wholeness.

Judith had an intimate connection with death before she was even born. Her twin, who she always felt was boy, died in utero. She was delivered by cesarean section because his body was blocking the birth passage. Judith was a sensitive child who felt very spiritually connected. But she was ridiculed for that, and the message from her family was about the need to conform and to play the game by the rules. She saw facade and superficiality, and often questioned her parents about the suffering of the world. They had no answers. She told me "I adored my parents, but this is how they were and I'm sure I chose them for a very good reason!"

For most of her life Judith didn't think much about her birth and her twin. But eventually it began to surface in her deep memory and she realized that this early loss has played significantly in her life. She reconnected to the deep love she had for her sibling and how much of a loss it was when he died. And then, like many others who have lost siblings in the womb, she set upon a path of searching for the deep connection she had lost, a search for close intimacy – "like looking for myself!"

When Judith met 14-year-old Arn in 1980 she was able to become intimate with the suffering and pain in the world – precisely what her parents had tried to protect her from. She told me, "What is beautiful about working with pain is that you can't be false about it." At that time, Judith was in a national program that required students to go overseas to do internships. Her friend, Jack Kornfield, had just come back from the Thai border and she called him to ask what was going on there. He led her to Arn's foster father, Peter, whom she called. He said, "I'm just going to New York to pick up three orphan boys and a monk, do you want to come?" She couldn't go but invited them to brunch on the way back. Arn sat on the floor and told his story in broken English and Judith was captivated by his charisma.

Judith worked as a community organizer with Cambodian refugees for two years with Peter, Arn, the boys and the monk. Arn had become fluent in English and, said Judith,

> He was knocking them over everywhere he went, not just because of his powerful story, but because he is totally present with his feelings, sharing them in complete vulnerability all the time and weeping freely. There is no falsity, no facade. He is totally unfiltered.
>
> Arn doesn't always share this, but he watched one of his sisters, whom he loved very much, die of starvation, and at one point he had to just leave her. He has had a sense of her spirit coming back to him, easing him and telling him not to worry. So because of my brother dying and me leaving him to continue my life, there is an understanding between us that feels as if it is the recovery of a lost relationship.

As Arn mentioned in his story, he and Judith co-created Children of War, which began with the seed idea of bringing children from war-torn countries to the United Nations to speak to the leaders of the world. Initially it was seen as a way to help motivate U.S. teenagers to get involved in issues that mattered in their communities and overseas by working with role models of courage. The young people would go into schools, tell their stories, and motivate the children to respond empathically and compassionately. However, it was healing that became the signature of the work.

Judith spoke at length of that healing work:

> Children of War built a container that brought people together from all over the world, of every different color, language, and belief system who had a common story, or common bond of suffering. Through their sharing they transcended culture, class, and race, and became a unit. They had the experience of being 'one with' and it was their pain that opened the door to that. When people who have had that kind of pain share it, there is what I call a covenant. I always felt graced to be engaged in that covenant by midwifing the process. When I went with a Children of War theater group to Bosnia, a director said to me that he was scared of going because he felt he would rip people off. He didn't want to listen

to their stories and then go away and feel he couldn't do anything about it. I said to him, 'You can't solve the big problem, but just being willing to be truly present with the pain and to hear and hold each story in that moment is the greatest gift you can give. And it holds within it the power of great transformation.' I think this listening work is what more people need to do.

People often ask if it depresses me to listen to these stories. It doesn't. It's a blessing and a joy. It's connectedness. It's reality. It's stripped away of anything superficial and it is a great gift to be in the most vulnerable places with another human being. I don't mean that I don't grieve and weep with people. I'm saying that the opportunity of going through that doorway is rare and we don't offer that to ourselves in the world very much.

I have a beautiful example of this arc of movement from suffering to joy, using suffering as a doorway. We would bring these young people together, share movies and information about the more socio-political part of the story like: What happened in Cambodia? What is apartheid really about? What goes on in Central America? Then the young people from that region would get up and share their story. One evening we showed a tough movie about the Cambodian story. It was three days into the process and people were already very close. It was a safe environment. The Cambodian young people got up to tell their story and they just couldn't. They started weeping and saying, 'No more war!' Everybody in the room started to weep; a truly sacred moment because you had the sense that this was the collective, the world grieving for itself. All parts of the world were represented there. It was everybody's pain and everybody grieved. I remember there were one or two people who were kind of outside us and said, 'Can't you make this go away?' But I said, 'No, let the process run out.'

Very organically one or two people stood up and then other people joined them and formed a circle. We were swaying, and the South Africans began to sing their freedom songs as a way to bring courage. There was a sort of snake dance all around the building, then everyone was dancing. Within half an hour they had moved from being in complete pain to being in ecstasy. You could look anyone in the face and they were completely unveiled of whatever it was they had brought into the room earlier. We danced all night.

There was that release which is so crucial; a cathartic birth passage through pain. In a sense it was keying into the grief of the world that released the incredible energy of compassion. And the joy was the joy of connectedness, because grieving together allowed them to touch each other on the deepest levels. To share and relieve that burden in a group was the ultimate act of trust. You couldn't separate them from each other for the rest of the three weeks! We were all in love – a phenomenal experience. Pain is a very sacred thing.

What happens so often is that people share and there is no container, no one there who is willing to hold it. Relationship is part of the healing process. Crying alone has some value to it because you can get it out, but when you have someone who is willing to be there in the process, that is what creates the loving part of the healing. This is classic in Post Traumatic Stress Disorder literature:

1. Share the story
2. Find a constant ally
3. Survivor Mission (meaning taking the pain and using
   it to help others).

So most of the people we worked with became engaged in activities to transform the situations that gave rise to their pain, which helped them feel as if they had recovered some meaning in life. We created about 42 new multi-cultural youth groups in 16 cities and they all utilized the same story telling process in their groups to share with each other. What we called 'Support Group Peace' was central to all the children.

The young people, feeling empowered by this healing and the connect-edness they had made with their peers, went out to do public speaking and to motivate others. This was Survivor Mission – a way to find meaning. The fact that someone's mother got tortured and killed motivated them to find some way that the world would not have to go through that again.

How well they can maintain it when they go back into difficult experiences will vary depending on how much support they have. A young man wrote to me from a bomb shelter in Beirut. He said, 'Here's what life is like in this bomb shelter, but the fact that I know that there are other people around the world who are connected to my story keeps me going.' It's like the mountain top experience. When you've reached the mountaintop and seen what life is like from up there, you may not always be there, but you can always reference that memory. Positive experience and the memory of it are transformative.

Judith then went on to describe how she was affected by the death of Princess Diana. Her words about the global nature of the impact of her death could easily be applied to the effect of the terrorist attacks on the Twin Towers and the Pentagon.

The death of Princess Diana was a global phenomenon that said to me that the world is hungry for the kind of transparent compassion that she, like Arn, was able to show, and thus we mourned the loss. I was completely glued to that phenomenon because I wanted to be in the global mind. This grief was in the nervous system of the planet. It is phenomenal to know that you are in a moment that other people are sharing so powerfully. That globalness of the collective grief was happening spontaneously – as with the children of war – and large groups of people were grieving together openly. What might have healed globally? We certainly tapped into and released immense grief – personal and planetary.

Judith concluded by saying,

I now understand how my whole life was a set up for me to come in with the particular issues that I came in with, and that my story of loss is what motivated me to found Children of War. A lot of my issues that I have worked through are not only about loss, but also the survivor guilt. Why did I live and the other die? When that happens you can say, 'I don't have a right to live.' This is what survivors go through. In a sense we are all survivors faced with the question, Do I really want to live?

Judith introduced the possibility that we have chosen our parents for a very good reason. This may well be so. There is a fast growing body of belief that a conscious matching process does take place in the spirit realm before conception. Many people under hypnotic regression or similar therapeutic journeys have reported being part of such a decision making process. However, whether we choose them or not, as our listening skills and compassion increase and our impulse to blame decreases, we will perhaps stop pushing our parents away. We will begin to appreciate their more difficult characteristics as an opportunity to find our own inner strength, and will come to accept responsibility for our part in our personal family drama.

Judith's talk of global grief tapped me into a vivid memory of the exact moment I stepped out of "my" pain and into "the" pain of the world. I was visiting friends in a wooden house in a tiny hamlet in England. It was a few months after Benjaya's death, and I was triggered into grief by seeing his five-year-old playmate, Fin, playing happily with his toys by the wood burner. I remember being in this triangle formation – a friend at each elbow supporting me as my feelings became more and more intense. As the pain grew I sensed that my consciousness was expanding in some way. Visions of people all over the world who were torn with grief at that very moment flashed into my mind. Scenes of war, of whole families being killed, cyclones, rapes, starving children and much more, showed themselves. It was a timeless moment. The room was filled with the energy of world grief.

The surprising thing about this experience for me was that it felt like a holy awakening. Just like Judith's children of war, although the others in my case were not physically present, I connected with a communal sea of grief, realized that I was not alone and opened up to an immense sense of compassion. Compassion seemed to flow from every pore for a while. I even sensed the pain of people in the street and my heart went out to them. It hit me that *everybody* has pain. My pain is the same as anyone else's, just as my joy is the same (and it resides in the same place). About a quarter of a million people die every day, which shows how many are in mourning in each moment, but it became totally irrelevant to me that my pain was triggered by a death. Pain is pain is pain, be it from your beloved daughter leaving home, sickness of a pet, loss of a favorite possession, or whatever. All pain deserves recognition and respect, not sweeping under the carpet because it is less than another's. My spiritual teacher once said, "Comparison is one of the worst sicknesses on this planet. It either falsely lifts you up or plummets you down."

And so, in my experience, there certainly is a global mind where our consciousness merges with others – what Carl Jung describes as "collective consciousness." In his book *The Conscious Universe*,[12] researcher, Dean Radin, describes experiments that suggest that people's consciousness affects matter at a distance. By using an electronic random-number generator (RNG) – a machine that generates chance events like an "electronic coin-flipper" – the team at Princeton University showed that the stronger, the more coherent a field of consciousness, the more order would be evident in the "random" system. Readings taken from five different RNGs at times where millions were focused on the same thing – such as the televised verdict on O. J. Simpson in 1995 and the Opening Ceremony of the Centennial Olympic Games – showed a startling change in the chance order. In graph form it can be seen where the graph peaks at high interest points in the programs and plummets at the commercial breaks down to the level of the control. This leaves me questioning the effect of mass emotion on other people – especially those who are particularly sensitive.

The giant step I took as I opened to the sea of global grief is, I believe, a microcosmic example of the inevitable leap humanity will take. It is the leap from three dimensional, localized thinking into a realm of greater awareness of the rich non-physical realms where our connection with all living things is apparent. I see the World Wide Web and email facilities as an obvious symbol of the movement toward this recognition, offering a practice ground for more conscious global connections.

Following on from there, when individuals make the leap of recognition of the sameness that lies beyond our superficial differences, then surely nations will do likewise? Perhaps then we will release both our individual and national territorial consciousness and will find a way to combine taking responsibility for ourselves with reaching out to others in need, thus healing the global wounds.

One of the basic tools that we need to heal our wounds is, as Judith points out, the simple skill of listening to the pain of others. When Thich Nhat Hanh, the Vietnamese monk nominated for the Nobel Peace Prize by Martin Luther King Jr., was asked what he would say to Osama Bin Laden he said this, "The first thing I would do is listen. I would try to understand why he had acted in that cruel way. I would try to understand all of the suffering that had led him to violence." Then when asked if listening can be used at a national level he spoke of his work with Palestinians and Israelis at a retreat. He said, "They appreciated the practice of deep listening and made arrangements to share what they had learned with others upon returning to their home countries. We recommended that the Palestinians and Israelis talk about their suffering, fears, and despair in a public forum that all the world could hear. We could all listen without judging, without condemning in order to understand the experience of both sides. This would prepare the ground for peace talks to occur. The same situation now exists with the American people and people of Islamic and Arabic nations."

As Judith emphasized, no one can successfully share their pain without a good listener as a supportive ally, and so it would benefit us all to practice both the giving and receiving in communication. Perhaps then we could speak out if we believe these skills should be included in the school curriculum so that the next generation might choose dialogue instead of war.

Mirsad Jacevic's Story – Peace Now

Someone wise once said: "Live the experience 100 percent because wisdom is nothing more than the sum of the experiences you have lived with your eyes wide open." Mirsad role models living at 100 percent. I met Mirsad, otherwise known as Miki, for the first time at the Fetzer Institute in Kalamazoo, Michigan, on an exceptional retreat. (He is a Fetzer Fellow). His whole charismatic way of being suggests spirit in action. He is physically demonstrative and refreshingly free with the whole gamut of his emotions, crying at the drop of a hat with both joy and sorrow. In my room overlooking the lake, Mirsad divulged his story in his singsong Bosnian voice.

He was born in October of 1972 in Sarajevo, Bosnia, which, he told me, "more than anything else has shaped my history and my future." His family is multi-ethnic and multi-religious – Christian, Jewish and Muslim, so it was hard for his parents to agree on his name. He was nameless for three days until his dad's best friend came in to yet another quarrel and just said "Mir sad!" There and then he was named Mirsad – Mir meaning "peace" in any Slavic language, and sad meaning "now." His last name, Jacevic, apparently translates as "the little one who yells the loudest"! "It is important," said Mirsad, "to pay attention to our names and to ask when naming children, 'What do we want this child to be?'"

Mirsad's grandmother took care of him until he was seven. She was his guide and teacher. He would ask her, "How come I'm not going to church when all my friends are not here to play with me on Sunday morning?" And she would say, "Because your God is too big to fit into one little religion and he can't really decide which one to put you in." "In her whole life," said Mirsad, "grandmother knew nothing but war, violence and losing people but she was a source of wisdom and knowledge. I experienced from her simple and natural ways of bringing spirit alive. She did God's work in the community by example and lived her life to the fullest. She prepared me to eventually deal with everything in my life, be it the extreme joys or the extreme pains." Mirsad's mother, father and sister were "always a love nest of joy" despite their many struggles.

Mirsad, at 18, was a typical European teenager for whom the reality of war and suffering was far away on the television screen or in history books. He told me,

I was living a wonderful life of a crazy teenager, partying 'til 5am, going to school, speaking French, traveling around the world. Suddenly I was reduced from that worldly person into a young person in Sarajevo who had lost everything. I lost not only material stuff. I had little food and water, and was delighted to have had one apple in a month. I lost 40 pounds in three months and grew to cherish a glass of water a day as the biggest treat I could dream of. But also I began to lose belief in human power and my belief in God because I started asking: What did I do to deserve this? How did this happen to me?

What did actually happen is that in the early nineties the society of the former Yugoslavia broke down. Groups who lived there were divided to such a point that the only step they knew to take was one of brutal violence. Ethnic cleansing – meaning whole groups or populations being erased by concentration camps, mass rape, genocide or expulsion in horrifying numbers – was happening in Mirsad's country. His city, Sarajevo, the capital, was targeted heavily. In 1984, ten years before the massacre, the mountains surrounding the city had brought Sarajevo to the international scene during the Winter Olympics. But then the Olympic spirit of peace was transformed into the weapon of war. Forces surrounding the city were placed in those mountains creating one of the largest city concentration camps.

Mirsad's personal nightmare began on April 6, 1992. Violence was already going on but he believed there was enough power in people to prevent war from fully erupting. He led a group of students through the Parliament building in downtown Sarajevo where there were at least 10,000 people protesting and singing songs. Mirsad takes up the story.

There was beauty and connection in the belief that by us being there and by the world watching, hearing our voices demanding peace and the resignation of gunmen, that peace might prevail. Then, out of nowhere, three sniper shots were fired that killed the first student of the Sarajevo war. She was killed on a bridge, ironically called the Bridge of Brotherhood and Unity. She fell and I saw her. I saw the transformation from this powerful force through this single shot that cut life off for a

21-year-old human being who demanded peace. That's when my paradigm broke down. Until then I knew the war was going on but I had never seen anyone die in front of my eyes. I also hadn't seen a death violently and in public, and that pretty much is what war is about – seeing people die, en masse and in public, where the human spirit gets destroyed. So that single act of atrocious violence caused all 10,000 of us to panic. One shot had killed one person but also killed the peace and power of thousands.

A rapid transformation followed. You could hear the shelling constantly. Those who had no basements to hide in would risk either running into a basement of another house and being shot by a sniper or staying home and being hit by shells. A lot of people died from the shells that came through the window and exploded in the air. My sister experienced a shell explode not too far from her head and she was totally untouched. Another time you could be 20 meters from where the shell would fall and a metal piece could kill you.

Being forced into hiding denied our humanity. Many people did not see a light for months, a lot of people didn't have a proper meal for most of the war, but mostly it deprived us of our daily routine of being human. The war brings a meaningless existence that I don't want to call life. The maximum you can push for is survival. I was reduced to running back and forth between basements being like a civic guard. I was forced to carry a little gun that I was supposed to use to shoot at the shells. I didn't know how to use it and it was useless as protection. That role caused my real trauma. I was put in a cage of a city that was shelled and bombed, in a cage of a building that was shelled and bombed, no electricity and no food. The only reason for me sitting there for 24 hours was for me not to be killed. I was dying inside, the worst Chinese tap water death. More than 10,000 of our population of 500,000 were killed, approximately 200,000 fled, and 50,000 civilians were wounded.

My beloved grandmother starved to death because she lived in an area where there was no food. That was so hard, but everybody who was there has died one way or another. Some of us survived because of our spirits and some of us have survived in a physical presence but are not alive. These are people who might be outwardly successful now but they are dead people walking because they have no mechanism to cope with what has happened.

In the summer of 1992, dying that slow death, I reached a point that I was thinking a lot about life and human nature and those things that people don't usually ask themselves at 21. It cracked open the beauty of inquiry for me to see the bigger picture. I went inside because that was the only way to go. Outwardly there was nothing that would have protected me. I asked myself 'Do I choose life-affirming, respecting ways of existence, or do I just choose to die inside?' It was a fantastic inquiry. And I wish

I had the vision now that I had then. I went into a space of deep inward searching for what I could scratch and cling to that could make me open my heart to this experience. How could I learn from it to become a better human being who will then go to my neighbors, friends and family of the world and say 'What has happened to me should not happen to anybody else. Let me tell you why and what we can do to prevent it happening.' It was as if I'd been given a test to find the answer to the question: Why should I live? I was searching for something that was worth living for – meaning and purpose. And I think I did find the right one to have stayed alive to the extent that I have today.

At first it was hard because I could not deny the outward reality: the shells, the snipers, and people being killed, my sister almost losing her leg, my best friend dying, and other friends being committed to institutions, going nuts because of what they were seeing. For a couple of months I went into a period of denial. I couldn't deny the shells, but I could deny my role in it. My skin and my senses knew I was cold and hungry but I was just observing those experiences because I was not agreeing with what was happening. Once I began this inquiry things started opening up for me to see the light. I began to see rays of sun that showed me where to go in order to stay alive. I started taking more life-affirming action to support my family, waiting in food lines and becoming more engaged in the neighborhood. I recognized my reality and asked, 'How do I start making sense of this?' and 'What can I do here?' I found a way to position myself so that I could avoid participating in the war in any other sense but being helpful.

I realized that my generation were targets of this war experience. None of us had ever done anything to contribute to the creation of war but we were the ones being sent to the front lines – snatching water for our families, being shot down by the snipers, sneaking about. I decided then to pursue life-affirming actions and began to fulfill the prophecy of my name, to create peace now and to yell about it. I started an organization called Academic Life-line for Bosnia that was able to support 15,000 students. It was called 'Life-line' because it sustained life, and 'Academic' because to prevent my generation from dying we reopened the schools and started education in any form so that young people could say 'I'm going to school, not to war.' According to international law regulating warfare, young people who are in school have a legal right not to be killed. I am not a coward and a pacifist. I am just a common-sense person who was trying to figure out a way to save my friends from getting killed.

I feel anger on a daily basis and I have learned that the only way to deal with it is to recognize it, shed a light to it and find ways daily of transforming it into creative action. Anger is a real part of our human picture and I see a danger in people denying it. Ecstasy really means the state in which you are fully endorsing suffering and joy, in which you are seeing all faces of God. I believe we become so much more what we are meant to be by our Creator if we can freely express our suffering. I believe that the pace of your healing will be in direct proportion to the depth of your endorsement of your suffering and pain as something that can affirm life and bring you joy. Encountering evil has been the greatest learning experience for me. Who I am now came from seeing the full-blown face of suffering.

Once we started to enroll the young people in the program, people flocked to it and the spirit spread. They saw life-affirming action in the midst of war, which got them out of their suffering. Those people are not healed but they chose life and that made a difference. What happened in my city was different to other parts of Bosnia and the Middle East. If you had a thermometer to measure hatred in people and took it to Israel, South Africa, and Bosnia, I believe that Bosnians would show the least, comparatively. But you must not compare in terms of hierarchical suffering. I'm saying that our communal approach to endorsing suffering, spreading the joy of life, and making a conscious decision to try, worked.

Also, we saw community. I believe that a 'common unity' can only come when people are ready to sit in a circle and share our deepest sorrows and our deepest joys. When you become a member of a community it's like a clan of love that you now belong to. You have a reason to fully live – although outwardly the trauma is still there – and it's far easier to heal.

I spoke last year at the conference of the International Trauma Society and these professional trauma psychiatrists saw a person who should have been a nut-case being joyful. I was singing, enjoying life and telling them they need to go to Bosnia and shift their paradigm because what they and their colleagues are doing from a medical per-spective is not helping us. We are not objects against which they can project their scientific methods. I had a standing ovation. This new para-digm of dealing with trauma is such common sense: accept the pain, move forward and claim life. I believe that the spiritual task of our times is simply to find ways of enhancing life and to live a life consistent with the message you choose to deliver.

What has happened to me was a horrible experience. It still is. I'm dealing with grief on a daily, hourly, basis because of my friends and family who were either killed or who have been changed. So in that regard I do not wish war upon anybody, however, it has also taken me into spaces of professional, personal and spiritual ecstasy. I have felt compassion at such a deep level, and this created a passion for life and a joy of being fully human that I had never experienced before. I'm not saying that to be fully human means you have to experience both suffering and joy. I suggest people don't go experimenting with suffering, however if you are experiencing it, face it, embrace it, and make it your own because you can grow. I would not at the age of 28 be considered one of the peace leaders in the youth movement and be recognized in these ways that are humbly honorable if I hadn't done this. I would not have been my name, who I was meant to be, unless I had gone through this. My transformation was due to the trauma; therefore I think the earth-shaking human volcano we went through was meant to be. It's so hard to say but I am glad it happened.

When you have accepted the gift in the difficulties, you already are in a state of forgiveness because there is no blame. The word forgiveness I break into 'for' and 'giveness' that means it was meant as a gift for me. This was meant in order for me to be able to give full giveness to the world. I cannot be fully me unless I accept the experiences that are given for me. Unless you forgive yourself and start answering the questions in your heart, you will not even be able to begin this healing process. Healing happens only in a container of forgiveness.

The wisdom, positive action, and stamina of both Mirsad and Arn in the face of adversity are awesome. However, there can be a temptation to put such people in the category of "special" and to conclude that we could in no way measure up. But how do we know how we would cope with the horrors of war? When I was a young mother I was told about a woman whose son had fallen in a canal and drowned. I remember clearly trying to imagine what that could be like and how I would feel. It was unthinkable! My mind wouldn't go there without visions of madness. Then it happened to me. Not only did I have no signs of madness, I was astounded by the amount of inner strength that surfaced in the place of crisis. The times I have felt the most powerful sense of my true self and the most aliveness were scattered among the nightmare days when my heart was breaking. Facing my worst fears with a willingness to be open has moved me a step closer to feeling invincible! It makes sense that we cannot possibly know the capacity of our dormant strengths without them being well tested... unless of course you trust from stories such as those in this book that the human spirit in each of us is formidably resilient.

Mirsad was conscious of being faced with the question that all of us inevitably wrestle with to a greater or lesser degree with all of our challenges: Do I choose life-affirming ways of existence or do I just die inside? He chose to actively seek meaning and purpose in his situation – something worth living for, and in so doing he saw a bigger picture and stepped into a future in which he feels ecstasy alongside the inevitable pain. There is no chance whatsoever of meeting our potential on this earth as long as we are attempting an escape from the pain of life. Unless we step in totally to the present, with all that it contains, and make a stand for what we believe in we cannot be fully alive.

Like Mirsad, I discovered my main survival tool to be my willingness to feel and share the pain coupled with my ability to seek the life-affirming balance. I was blessed to have found a way of switching my focus at will from the loss to that which would nourish me. I had learned this lesson well three months after Benjaya's death when I was in hospital miscarrying the precious baby who was my last vestige of connection to motherhood. My light was going out, a black pit was beckoning, and part of me wanted it to swallow me up. The part of me that didn't like the dark sat on my hospital bed and prayed for help to save me from insanity. A familiar voice responded bringing with it that healing balm:

> *Mum, it's simple. You have a choice. If you focus on things that make you sad, like losing me and the baby, you will get small and turned in on yourself, but if you think about things that make you happy, like God and all the things you love, you will get bigger and shining like a sun.*

I walked out of the hospital humming "My Favorite Things" from The Sound of Music and mystifying the staff with my sudden brightness. Then, when Benjaya's sixth birthday approached and I ached with his glaring absence, I tried to switch my focus. I realized that because I believe he's still alive in spirit, I could choose to celebrate with him and send him gifts of joy and gratitude for his life. Thankfully Abel agreed, so we threw a party, invited all his friends, played party games, ate birthday cake and sang Happy Birthday to him at the tops of our voices. We connected to the life of Benjaya; we felt his essence and added sweetness to the bitter sting of lack. This is not suppression or denial. Notice I said the sweetness was *added to* the bitter sting of lack.

It is natural to find it difficult to choose a life-affirming action when heavy emotions are pulling us down, depressing us, but I have discovered that almost always I can exercise a choice of focus. Only today, out on a walk, I found myself drawn to visit the spot at the river where Benjaya took his last breath. I observed my mind and the accompanying emotions as I allowed myself to recreate his last minutes of life. As I let myself imagine his help-lessness, his thoughts, his small body flailing in the ice-cold water, I knew I was causing myself the instant nausea and indescribable stabs of pain in my heart. Quickly, I changed my thought track and was able to allow my sense of gratitude for having been given him as my son to join the pain. That gratitude seemed to open my eyes to the exquisite beauty of this river that was his exit place, and I again felt awed by the mystery of death. As Benjaya had said I would, I felt bigger and shining like a sun.

It is a question of diet. What are we putting into ourselves as nourishment? What images and thoughts do we choose to feed ourselves? If we are on automatic pilot, perhaps feeding ourselves repeatedly with graphic images of either our own traumatic life scenarios or television images of violence and destruction, we cannot expect to be moving forward with our healing process. According to James S. Gordon M.D., who uses biofeedback in his cutting edge work with trauma, when "negative" images are replayed in the mind and when difficult scenarios are imagined, the impact on the body can be equal to that of the original trauma. And when we feel shocked and threatened we will automatically affect all those around us. Conversely, when we feel love, even in the presence of the pain, we will create more of a desired effect on others. It may take an enormous act of will to take a life-affirming stance, but one step could turn our world around.

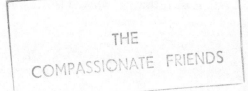

Third Key
SHARE YOUR PAIN AND CHOOSE LIFE
Questions and Reflections

1. Go inside yourself and recall a time when you had a "receiver", an ally to hear your deepest pains and joys. If you needed someone today who might that be?

2. Take a moment to identify a vulnerable place in yourself. To what extent have you shared this vulnerability with others? How would things differ if you shared more?

3. Do you tend to minimize or hide your pain, open and allow it, or perhaps exaggerate it? What is your pattern? What changes would you like to make, if any, in terms of this pattern? What would help you do that?

4. Draw a tear in the center of a clean page in your journal. Brainstorm and depict the messages you have received about crying. Become aware of what your body does when you feel intensely sad, and write down how you feel about crying, especially in the presence of others?

5. On another clean page, depict how you would like to be in relation to crying. What is stopping you from being this way, if anything?

6. When you feel lonely in your pain, what is one way that you could reach out and help someone else in pain? What is preventing you from doing that?

7. What life-affirming activity could you involve yourself in that would put the energy of your pain, grief, or anger to good use?

8. In what situation in your life right now would you like to follow Mirsad's suggestion: Accept your situation, move forwards and claim life?

9. Telling and listening to life stories can be profoundly healing. What part of your life story do you feel it would be healing to tell? To whom would you tell it if it could be anyone?

10. Is there anyone whose life story you'd love to know and never dared ask... until now?

The Fourth Key

REASSESS RELATIONSHIPS

Intimacy is the key to happiness and healing.
Without intimacy there is no joy,
no love, no healing,
no medicine,
no remission,
nothing.
Patch Adams

Reassess Relationships

Severe life challenges will always affect the way we relate to ourselves, to others and to inanimate objects. Change is to be expected, and we must give both ourselves and others the space to be different. Sometimes we are affected slowly over time and sometimes we are flung overnight into new ways of relating. Abuse in childhood, for example, will undoubtedly affect our trust in others and may take decades even to be acknowledged, which must happen before the wounds can be tended. Whereas a sudden traumatic event can catapult us into an instant change in relational behavior followed by an opportunity to consciously reassess our relationships to ourselves, to others, to love, to gratitude, and to life itself.

Many of us have a habit of putting ourselves down when things go "wrong", saying things like "I'm hopeless, I can't get anything right," or "I'm just so weak, look at the state of me!" In times of trouble we need more than ever to speak to ourselves kindly, because anything less could lead to depression. We need to imagine that we have an inner parent who is capable of loving us unconditionally – that means whatever we have done, whatever state we are in. Catching that critical inner parent in action and choosing encouraging words and a supportive tone is a way of creating resilience that is within the grasp of us all.

Rudy Giuliani, who was Mayor of New York City in 2001, is a prime example of how the experience of trauma can change a person and their attitudes to others forever. Having been battered by cancer and by a bitter divorce, then the terrorist attacks on his city, this man with many critics emerged as a hero. Grief such as this can crack us open so that we drop the defenses that keep us from being truly authentic with others.

This sudden experience of depth and connection can be invaluable. However, it will not automatically remain and is not always appropriate. The long-term challenge is to be in charge of our level of openness and choose how much of ourselves it is appropriate and useful to share in each relationship. If our aim is to be governed from within – like those with single vision – rather than controlled from without, we need to continually fine-tune our intuitive antennae to strengthen that place of inner knowing. Then it can inform us when and with whom to give and receive energy.

"It is in the shelter of each other that people live," says an Irish proverb. But there are some people in whose shelter we would not thrive. Some relationships nourish and support us; others deplete us. In times of difficulty, when our defenses are low, we need more than ever to identify areas in our relationships that drain our energy, and we need to make effective changes. Sometimes the change will be within ourselves and other times it will be about clearly defining our boundaries with others. A good question to ask ourselves is: Do I feel nourished by the presence of this person? (This question equally applies to an event, television program, or environment of any kind).

There are some people who actually feed on the passionate energy present in grief. They are usually people who have little emotional expression in their own lives and crave to be part of the action. Then there are the "helpers" who need to be doing something so that *they* feel better. People with patterns such as these will only add stress and complication to the situation and would be best served by either a clear "I appreciate your offer, but no thank you," or by being given a useful task on the periphery.

The shelter of a strong support system is essential for maximum healing; and the greater the network we have to choose from the better. And so, although it is important to identify any drain on our energy, it is unwise to act too hastily. It is easy to make quick judgments about people when feeling vulnerable, so beware: if friends are not there for you in the way you expect, it is worth remembering that some people may be great with one kind of trauma and hopeless with another, or might be struggling with their own difficulties when you need them.

Friends and colleagues often need to know for sure that help is wanted from them. They might assume that if you don't ask then you don't need help and that they might be an intrusion into an already charged situation. Times of crisis are when most of us are least likely to reach out, and yet these are the times when we most need to ask for help. Delegating someone to be in charge of informing people of what help is required can work well, or simply taking a deep breath and picking up the phone and saying "please help." Then of course there's email.

Not only can friends be invaluable, our relationship to physical objects can also be far more powerful and potentially transformative than we imagine. When adversity hits us we can see how symbols representing our pain or our lost love become charged with meaning. I'll just mention this subject here and expand on it later. Rubble from the fallen twin towers became precious overnight. Mahogany containers of consecrated, powdered debris were given out to relatives of those who died at that site in answer to the craving for something solid and symbolic of their loved ones to hold onto. Such transference of focus to a transitional object can be extremely helpful in the mourning process, especially in the absence of a physical body.

Another area we will be exploring in the second two stories is our relationship to sexuality. Most of us tend to keep our sexuality under wraps, although the media bombards us with the message of its power. It is a central, animating force in our bodies, and its misuse continues through the ages to be the cause of untold traumas. Sexual abuse happens to children of all classes, races, religions and cultures. In the U.S., studies show that approximately one in three girls and one in seven boys are sexually abused by the time they are 18.[13] As we saw in the last section: what is hidden cannot heal. I firmly believe that it is time to bring sexuality out of the closet; time to speak out about it and free it from the veils of embarrassment and shame. I suspect that there is a strong connection between the way cultures relate to sexual passion and their level of desire for war. If this is so, then addressing any imbalance in our sexuality will ultimately contribute to much more than our own sense of internal peace.

We know a lot about human relationships and how to transform them and yet they are an area that is still filled with mystery and unanswered questions. I sometimes wonder if the main purpose of being on this planet is to explore these questions. What magnetic chemistry draws us repeatedly to the same types of people, offering us the same lessons in different guises? I had a friend who had been attacked and stabbed with a knife three times by different people over a five-year period, not a common occurrence in London. Do we all play out a subtle version of this, seeking the type of conflict that we need to address? And would a simple change in us break the pattern? How come some of the greatest spiritual teachers seem to be more out of balance sexually than the rest of us? And is it good to be in intense relationships, using them for our growth? Or better to protect ourselves and live a more peaceful life? How do we discern what is harming us and what is grist for the mill?

And then of course there is the bigger picture. We can see that our nation's relationships with other countries are paramount, and that if one country is out of sync in some way then none of us can truly live in peace. Nations, like parts of ourselves, also carry wounds: think of the German national shame, the Americans' treatment of the Native Americans or the white South Africans' apartheid system. When all countries are capable and willing to relate both to their own issues and to those of other countries honestly and with integrity, then perhaps peace has a chance. As nations consist of individuals, this work must begin at home, by admitting our personal weaknesses and putting our own houses in order to the best of our ability.

Janet Patti's bolt from the blue gave her the opportunity to do just that.

Janet Patti's Story – No one Else Can Fill My Empty Places

Janet has become a close friend. She is co-author with Linda Lantieri of *Waging Peace in our Schools*[14] and, as a university professor, is committed to helping change the face of education. She is an attractive, fiery woman of Italian descent, and even in times of depression she still manages to burst into an infectious, raucous, laugh and see the lighter side of life. The greatest trauma of her life – the loss of her marriage – offered her the opportunity to reassess all her relationships.

The end began in 1994. She had been married to a handsome, charming Frenchman, Jean-Paul, for ten years, and although some things were not right in the marriage, she loved him deeply and took it for granted through all their arguments that they would be together forever. There were lots of differences but they kept getting through them and had just begun counseling.

> Jean-Paul had become angry, yelling at me in ways he never had. We were building a Japanese garden as a metaphor for our marriage, trying to do something to keep us together because we knew we were drifting, but I had no idea how much.
>
> One night he came home late when I was sleeping. He woke me up, sat on the side of the bed and said, 'I am very unhappy and I don't think anything's going to change it.' I hadn't even the foggiest what it could be. He started to cry and said, 'I have to leave you.' Half asleep, I asked him why. 'I don't know myself, I need time, I'm suffocating and I have to go,' was all he could say. I remember thinking he wasn't really going to do this, but I was also petrified. My world was about to cave in.

Next morning Janet got up to go to work in a total daze. Her husband was still sleeping so she wrote him a note that said, "If you really have to go, then you must go. I can't hold you."

> It was really hard to write but I went inside myself and knew that you can't hold anybody. When I came home that night he was gone and at this point I plummeted into an abyss. I was functioning but numb, not sure of what I was feeling, not wanting to wake up to the knowing that my relationship was over. I didn't realize the emotional connection I had to that man until then. The hardest part was that he disappeared and left me no number. There was no helping me through it.

Three days later, looking an unshaven mess, he visited home to get some things. He couldn't handle talking, and told Janet that he just needed time. He said that he was staying with a friend but refused to give her the phone number. He assured her that there was no one else, said he would be in touch to sort out the details, and left.

Janet found it very hard to be in their house alone, but she didn't want to be anywhere else. She had insomnia, was depressed and riddled with anxiety. She found herself constantly on guard... waiting, ready to do anything to have him come back. At night she imagined hearing the key turn in the door and that he was coming home.

> The process of letting go was so difficult. He kept saying he was in love with me but couldn't come back, and repeating that he needed time. The most difficult parting is this kind of 'limbo' separating because, unlike with death, the person is still there and you think you can do something to get them back.

Janet's is a classic story. Soon after her husband left, a friend, Gary, went to visit her to try to cheer her up. Jean-Paul had a motorcycle, which she loved so they took it out for a spin. It was fun until they stopped for gas. Gary opened up a compartment and discovered a love book that said, "Kisses" on the front and "Remembering the moment of our kisses, love Ruth," inside. Then Janet understood what was going on with Jean-Paul, but felt terribly betrayed by his lack of honesty.

> I was so torn with ambivalence. Should I put on a suit of armour, be the champion and fight this woman, the foe, for him? Or, should I let him go to do whatever he wants to do? What are my rights and responsibilities in this? What do I want to have happen here? At one level I wanted him back at all costs and her gone. At another level I didn't want him if he didn't want to be with me. In my heart I didn't want to do anything to manipulate him, but in my physical and emotional self I wanted him to want me so badly that I was desperate for him to come back. I was tempted to use all my tools as a woman to do whatever it would take.
>
> Then there was another level. I knew there were difficulties in our relationship that I'd never had the wherewithal to deal with. I knew he couldn't meet many of my needs, but nevertheless, I put myself in the horrible place of the victim. During that next year everything in life that had hurt me surfaced and deepened the pain; it wasn't just about the abandonment of the marriage.

Janet was a mess, retching and rolling on the kitchen floor and screaming like a child in the fetal position, "How could he do this to me?" She wanted to be able to accept this new path, but couldn't escape the victim role. However, it was from being there that she learned that you can't hold anything.

> I think that whoever or whatever you love the most desperately can best teach you how to let go. I wish there was another way to learn it. I have moved to a place of acceptance and really letting go now, but I am not yet able to open my heart completely. I have work to do. I've always been a survivor, but I haven't yet learned that fine line of loving enough to trust, knowing that this could be gone at any moment. It's a process that takes time. This separation was not about me and my inadequacies or him and his. It was about each of us needing to be on our own individual path. I've seen Jean-Paul a few times since the break up and it's been clear how much we love each other, but we can't be together for whatever reason. And I've learned that I can love without having to be together forever.

Janet had been sexually abused as a child and had been working for many years, especially within her marriage, to release her belief that all men should be castrated. She had succeeded in coming to trust men again during this relationship, and so when he left this increased her sense of devastation.

I had to get to a place where I trusted myself and I eventually found my own safety rather than deriving it from external sources. Now I can see that if Jean-Paul hadn't left, I would have thought I'd found safety when actually I hadn't.

If he had been able to say, 'I've met a woman, this is what's happening,' before he disappeared, it would have empowered me to some extent to deal with it, to have choices. I might have been able to say, 'I don't want to be with you, you need to go and do what you have to do.' Dishonesty leaves no personal empowerment, it gets ripped out, and being left in this kind of way, creates trauma. I've talked to people who have both agreed to end marriages. It's still hard and there are things to work out, but there isn't this sense of horrible loss, betrayal, abandonment and victimization. I think my soul had to go there to grow, so there's that element. At another level I think it could have been done differently with more consciousness and care, and less hurt.

What helped my grieving process? Catching myself as I speak about my marriage break-up voicing old victim beliefs that are ingrained in our culture and to which I no longer subscribe. I mean that when I take time to listen to my inner knowing, I see and hear the situation from a very different perspective where only I am responsible for the pain I felt. I really believe that no one ever has the power to hurt me unless on some level I allow it. My husband behaved in the only way he knew how and I judged that behavior to mean that I was unloved and less of a person. Also, I had an attachment to staying with him and saving our marriage, which caused me pain and a sense of failure. It really helps to dare to look at what each of our souls truly needs.

Physical exercise helped tremendously and jogging provided a safe place for me to actively release my emotional energy. Initially, I took medication for the anxiety, but not for long because I wanted to get through it. I needed an aid then and I think it was okay. I also reached out and asked friends for help. I needed non-judgmental people who could just listen, just be there, knowing that I was a mess. I left my job because I was not able to go on as life was; life had to change drastically. Pain is too easy to mask; then it just comes back. I'd rather go through it. Talking to other people who have been through it was really wonderful (there's comfort in having the same pain) and so was being by the ocean.

I went through bouts of anger about the lack of preparation for pain in life. There was nothing in my Christian background, nothing in my family, and nothing in school that prepared me for pain. How to move through challenges and trauma should be part of the school curriculum. We have to know life isn't a storybook. There are going to be hard times and we need to know that we have the wherewithal to get through them. Divorce is really a commodity right now – almost a way of life in the U.S. I want people to realize the trauma of it.

What has this experience taught me? If I'm honest, I think it was necessary for me to go through that pain to become a whole person. Can change occur on such a deep level without pain? I believe that to change such set behaviors needs a great awakening. You have to be invested in wanting to change, and if you hurt that badly you damn well better go there! If you're not hurting much you might think, 'Oh well I'll get there.' But you don't. You're not propelled. The pain propelled me into a deep search of who I am, who I want to be, and what I want to do in life. I'm in the process of becoming very much myself with both my strengths and weaknesses, embracing all those parts of me. I've also learned how important it is to be gentle with the side of myself that is still growing.

I'm now loving consciously and cautiously and am determined not to lose myself in a relationship again. Loss of identity is one of the main causes of bitterness for which we tend to blame our partner, even though it is us who have let it slip away. Many people, after separation, go right into other relationships without realizing the extraordinary level of personal work that has to happen before you can get into another relationship that will not repeat the same dysfunctional patterns. We have a habit of putting Band-Aids over the wounds.

It is such a temptation to go unconscious and 'fall' in love, wanting to believe the romantic fairytale image of meeting my other half, my perfect prince, who will make me feel complete. Only disappointment will follow this way of being, because that dream is about what *he* will give, what *he* will be and do to fill my needs. Sooner or later he will fail to live up to my projections and will resent me trying to make him change to fit my image of what he should be. I am seeking to become interdependent now instead of co-dependent so that, whatever occurs in my outer life, I will have the inner resilience to avoid a repeat performance of the collapse of my world. I am focusing on who *I* am, what *I* have to give and what *I* need to create for myself to feel more whole. I have learned, above all, that no one else can fill my empty places.

Also, choosing a partner in the past was never based on what could best complement my soul. Soul didn't come into it. It was based on a wonderful passionate feeling, which perhaps I'll have again in life, or perhaps not. Now it has to be more than that, and I am looking to always be moved by inner knowing rather than the impulse of chemical attraction. The passionate impetus feels wonderful but the other pieces have to fit as well. I need to know where someone is spiritually, emotionally, intellectually and financially, and to look at the whole person and the relationship with a different set of eyes.

I felt in my heart that Jean-Paul was the man that I loved and would always love, but that does not mean that I still want him back. I don't. Divorce does not mean to me that I have to stop loving him and love another partner instead. Love isn't rationed. I'll love him till I die, and maybe beyond. I believe that love can traverse distance and will be felt by him in some way. I'm thankful I've had the blessing of loving this man and being loved by him.

Janet's story is packed full of nuggets of wisdom about healing after a broken relationship, and about love. I have taken some of that wisdom and woven it with understandings of my own to create the model below. It is a simple model trying to encapsulate a complex subject, but it can help explain why so many relationships break down – especially at this time when more and more of us are on a quest for wholeness.

It is clear to me that there are two kinds of love. 1. Conditional love that is limited and allows manipulation, blame, and secrecy. A love based on the belief in separation that is experienced by those with a two-eyed viewpoint. 2. Unconditional love that takes personal responsibility, is aware of the bigger picture, surrenders control, and communicates honestly. It is based on the belief in unity and is practiced by those with single vision.

Conditional Love

- I love you because you fulfil my needs.
- I'll love you more if you change.

- I am right, you are wrong, and I can judge you because I love you.

- I'm afraid to show you who I really am so I'll keep part of me hidden and protected.
- Not telling you about my transgressions will spare you pain.
- What you don't know can't hurt you.

- If you love him/her you can't love me as well/as much.
- I love you because you're the right shape/ size/color.
- Don't leave me!

Unconditional Love

- I love you because you are you.
- I accept you as you are and practice being the change I wish to see.
- I seek to understand you and will lovingly challenge you to reach your highest potential.
- I dare to stand before you in my vulnerability and strength, my ugliness and beauty.
- Honesty and trust are the foundations of my intimacy with you.
- All of our thoughts live in the non-physical space between us. We are energetically connected.
- My love is unlimited.

- I love you whatever "package" you come in.
- We must each follow our own soul's path, be that together or apart.

If one partner or friend expresses mainly conditional love and the other expresses mainly unconditional love, which has totally different ground rules, then a committed relationship has little chance of working. Either you have truth, trust, and self-responsibility or you do not. To relate on the middle ground would necessitate one partner seriously compromising their values and having to live with the consequences.

These two "takes" on love often battle within us as we are seeking to become more conscious human beings. Janet's struggle is an excellent example of the process to be expected when daring to take that stride into a deeper way of loving. She speaks of wanting Jean-Paul back at all costs, and yet still she listened to her inner knowing and knew that manipulation would not work to get their real needs met. She spoke of catching herself voicing old victim beliefs, to which she no longer subscribed, that are ingrained in our culture. This is the kind of work necessary if you want true intimacy, which the famous doctor, Patch Adams, claims to be the key to happiness and healing.

And so, going back to the kind of people we would most benefit from having around us after any major life challenge, the answer could lie in that second column: people who love and accept us for who we are, who seek to understand rather than judge our state of being and are comfortable in the presence of vulnerability. The Dalai Lama says "Remember that the best relationship is one in which your love for one another exceeds your need for one another."

I also want to expand on the issue of betrayal because this is a word that is rife in the scene of break-ups. It is a very loaded word, which usually heaps on blame. My understanding is that there are two levels to betrayal and that it helps to be aware of them both. On one level Jean-Paul did deceive Janet. He did cause unnecessary hurt by not speaking the truth, and was disloyal. Judas did likewise to Jesus. It is for the perpetrator to take responsibility for those actions. And yet, when Janet changed her perspective to take in the bigger picture, she could learn from Jean-Paul's actions how to find safety and trust in herself rather than in external sources. Her conclusion is that she needed that pain to become more of a whole person. And by Judas playing his particular role in the Christian drama, Jesus was able to model to the world the potential resilience of spirit in the face of cruelty and death.

Yes, it would be deeply gratifying to hear our betrayer say "I am sorry, I caused you suffering," but we cannot make that happen, especially if we insist on venting our anger and convincing them how wrong they were. We can only speak our truth, without malice, and let them sort out changing if they choose. Then we can get on with maybe even feeling grateful for the catalytic role they have played in our drama.

As Janet pointed out, pain seems to propel us into necessary change, but

I do believe that it doesn't have to be that way. Those of us who are on an active quest to become more conscious of our ineffective behavior patterns, which are most obviously visible in our close relationships, are less likely to need the pot to boil over before we notice that we need to pay attention to what is brewing.

The next story moves us into the arena of sexuality, taking us on a dramatic journey from the extremes of imbalance to a place of integration. It emphasizes the truism I mentioned earlier – Solutions are not found in the extremities: elegant solutions are found between the polarities.

Mark Josephs-Serra's Story – Mending the Sex/Spirit Split

Joseph, as he likes to be called, his wife Elisabeth and her children, have become my family. I love them dearly. It was to my local town that Joseph was guided in the depths of his despair, for which I will be forever grateful. His commitment to creating holistic, intimate community has deeply enriched this community and my personal relationships within it. He walks his talk with absolute conviction and inspires others to do likewise – especially in terms of relationship, both human and divine.

Joseph has always had an inner drive to expand his life and to find truth. He described himself at 17 as "a podgy Jewish clever-dick from a soul-dead London suburb, suffocating from central heating and monotonous comfort." He took off and became a barefoot hippy overnight, sleeping on beaches in Morocco and Greece. He traveled through Turkey, sold his clothes to make money on the streets of Afghanistan, and hitchhiked to India with a young woman. "It was spiritual, romantic, and we were out of our heads," Joseph told me.

Later he realized that he had been running away from truth, from his fear of sex, conflict, challenge, and success. He returned to Europe urgent to discover true community, and praying for a spiritual teacher. A guru dutifully appeared and for ten years he unintentionally continued hiding inside the Hindu religion as a shaven, robed, vegetarian, celibate, monk.

Joseph relates the rest of his story.

I became a part of the fundamentalist backlash to the artificiality and emptiness of modern techno-culture. In a way I was living a caricature of the mindset that we have all inherited in this modern culture: the split between denial and purity on the one hand, and pleasure and indulgence on the other. We tend to see spirituality as disembodied and good, and sexuality as materialistic, selfish and ultimately bad. These extremes I call the worlds of sexless spirit and spiritless sex. I was living a life of total identification with the non-physical, with spirit and all that is beyond this world, and totally repressing all that was physical and worldly.

Hand in hand with the sexless spirituality that I was living was a belief in obedience and collectivity, and the oppression of individuality. We were expected to obey the scriptures and the guru, who would obey his guru. To think for oneself was the height of arrogance because how could we, as insignificant beings, have any perspective on the absolute truth that has been revealed through the scriptures to humanity?

In the modern age we have rebelled against this way. Many of us have rejected spirit in favor of the world, and we have rejected collectivity in favor of individuality. Spirit has become irrelevant and all there is left is the absorption in our physicality. The ethos used to be about traveling together in community, obeying, and sharing a journey, which had its beauty but was a kind of mindless togetherness and a repression of individuality. In the modern age most of us have swung to the other end of the pendulum and are completely identified with the individual as the ultimate unit and reference point. We see nation states, organized religion, community, extended and nuclear families all collapsing. We see ourselves as individuals on an individual journey more and more.

So there I was in my monk's robes, having entered very deeply the whole world of Hinduism. I had visited India on pilgrimages, lived there, and taught the scriptures. I was extremely absorbed in this world of sexless spirit and for a while was in bliss, reveling in the community I had found. There was a kind of ecstasy in the mindless togetherness. However, having worked my way up the hierarchy, I began to reclaim my individuality. I'd seen great gurus disappearing with attractive young women, highly placed monks becoming addicted to drugs, and all sorts of bizarre happenings. I'd even heard reports of sexual abuse of children. All of this made me question, and I was no longer so obedient or faithful. To then maintain the strict repression of my sexuality became an issue. After all, I was a child of the 20th century west.

Everything that is repressed will rebound. The harder we push it down the harder it will push back and will eventually explode. In the temple there was a fraternal love between fellow monks, but should a monk deviate, that love would fall away into a patronizing need to save their soul. There was awful repression at the emotional level, and natural open relationships were impossible. The teachings say that woman is mother, and a monk should bow in humility and only look at her feet. Woman is mother, and as lovely as women's feet are, woman is also lover! I was going out teaching, addressing hundreds of people and there were half-dressed hippy girls. Much as I tried to keep my eyes on the ground, I would see the beauty of woman. Then I would chant harder, pray harder. It was total torture.

In this tradition a monk can relate to a woman by marrying a nun and my superiors suggested this. But, sexuality is confined to reproduction, and even then it can only take place once a month after about ten hours of purification ritual! I did marry, but it became even more torturous because the fire of the attraction was too hot. Inevitably, we began to break the rules and this made us feel worse. The chasm of torture opened up. We would live apart and try to obey the teachings, then come together and break the rules. Gradually I became quite mad. I was trying to eliminate all sexual thought, and the more I did that the more obsessed I became. I felt completely torn apart.

Then one day I just walked out. I had to. I couldn't have gone with their blessing. Arriving in the west and being in the outside world was awful. I'd so long looked upon it from the side of the split I'd been on – it was the world of spiritless sex. I didn't belong here, but I didn't belong there either. I was like a ghost. I visited friends who I'd known before I was a monk who said, 'What's happened to you? We expected you to be pure and elevated but you look a wreck.' I was. I was transiting from 15th century Calcutta to 21st century London overnight, and that is culture shock! A few days later after my 'escape' I was arrested – found frozen solid in a shop entrance at 5am. My wife, who had also walked out, rescued me and we lived together for a year in my sister's flat before splitting.

I ended up in an abandoned property in London with bohemian artists – drumming, smoking drugs and partying in a world of avoidance. I was a fallen monk, cracking up. Everything seemed stuck and ugly and loud, and I was desperate. I had left a world of certainty – where everything was referred back to the scriptures and had an answer, to a world of uncertainty where everyone had a different opinion that was equally valid. There was no reason to hang on to purity and abstinence, and I reached out for what my starved senses wanted. I wanted sex with as many women as possible and at one point was juggling five girlfriends at once.

I had certain spiritual credentials after all those years as a monk and I used them to seduce women. I objectified women – measuring them by the curve of their bodies – and the irony was that the objectification of them objectified me. So, just as I'd experienced the torture of sexless spirit as a monk, now I was tortured at the other extreme of spiritless sex. Everything became meaningless and empty and I felt alienated. Sexuality for its own sake has no real emotional or spiritual content and is about using others for one's own pleasure. The other becomes like a substance. I was in an addictive cycle, trying to relieve my pain with more sex, which left me feeling drained and filled with guilt and shame.

One night, on a mushroom trip, I felt dragged into purgatory. I heard a voice in my head telling me that the most noble path I could take would be to kill myself. But then, another voice came in saying 'you are very confused, this isn't the right moment, you need to get out of the city and go to the countryside where you'll be able to heal.'

A month later I moved to a town in the rolling hills of South West England where I began the healing process of integrating my sexuality and my spirituality. I was still on the sexual rampage and I knew that just as I tore myself away from the other world with an act of will, similarly I had to stop this with an act of will – there has to be a renunciation of the object of addiction. I joined a support group, learned about owning my emotions and speaking from the heart and began to tend my wounds with compassion and forgiveness. I took workshops, began men's groups and became integrated into the holistic healing and alternative spirituality movement.

Then I met and married Elisabeth, which above all has been the ground for the integration of my physicality and spirituality. She had been deeply involved in a renunciate-focused Buddhism for many years and we saw that our coming together was to both become spiritual, earthy, human beings. We committed to bringing forward all the levels of ourselves and each week we put a morning aside to see how the journey was progressing. At last I felt enough unconditional acceptance to confess, both to her and to myself, the extent to which I had become split. I broke down sometimes and, with a fear that I might be rejected, I'd confess something like obsessively looking at women on the streets. I felt terrible shame in front of her, but feeling it and being accepted in it was an essential part of the healing process. It was often very painful but our openness, our ability to listen, our love and dedication to each other and to truth was the context that held us.

Healing takes place where there is love and trust, and this developed in our men's, women's, and couples' groups. I believe that in order to be in a relationship with a woman I need to be rooted in my masculinity. Our models of masculinity are the macho man, who is too hard, and the new man, who is too soft. I don't want to be a dominant, ruthless, hard man or a wimp at the beck and call of the feminine. A satisfactory definition of masculinity is still emergent and for me the only way to directly experience a new kind of masculinity is to be with other men who have the same goal. I was able to stand in my sexuality within the sacred space that we created in the men's group in ways that I haven't with Elisabeth.

Elisabeth also entered an exploration into true femininity with other women. Femininity, of course, is not about crippling her feet in high heels and wobbling around like a chick or putting on business suits and trying to be a man. So in order to come together sexually, we both rooted ourselves in our own gender.

There needs to be a breaking away from stereotypical behavior, from the attitude that the male is voracious and active and the woman the one who is chased and passive. Sometimes I could be feeling broken or exposed and might want to be held tenderly. We need to be present to what's real, and if we want to mend the sex/spirit split we need to be totally honest. It has also been useful to admit that sometimes we hate each other and that we are sometimes so cut off from ourselves that we don't even have feelings for each other.

I've been doing movement work, which is about being totally tuned in to one's body and allowing spirit to move the body in complete spontaneity. In moving this way with others, fine-tuned to ourselves and not pushing our bodies in any way, we can feel the natural exquisite nature of our sexuality. This has been tremendously healing. More and more I stand before my God as a physical creature, and although I may not have the body of a male model, I feel beautiful in my body.

It is so easy for us to generalize about all the things that sit in the same category of our minds. So, firstly, I want to offer a reminder that Joseph's experience of the struggles of being a monk are highly individual and influenced by one particular order that may or may not bear any resemblance to other spiritual orders.

Joseph used the experiences that led to his breakdown as compost to create especially fertile ground in his new neighborhood. Concluding that the pre-modern, sexless spirit culture and the modern spiritless sex culture are severely damaging, he set about exploring how we could build a new kind of culture that places holistic relationships at the heart of the community. In his book – *Sex, Spirit and Community*,[15] Joseph explains his ideas in detail.

Living in this same area, and having seen the fruits of Joseph's labors – combined with the labors of the many others here with similar goals – I can vouch for the vital importance of creating solid, connected communities. Joseph and Elisabeth were instrumental in seeding several of the men's, women's and couples' groups that create intimate bonds in this community. We also have grandmothers' circles, creativity groups, authentic movement groups, fathers' groups – you name it, we have it. How this relates to trauma and loss is simple. Large numbers of people know each other's stories and weaknesses and therefore have an idea of where support may be required. This definitely prevents, minimizes, or helps deal with the effects of personal crises and life transitions that can be notably painful.

To offer some examples: the men's groups (which together run a yearly camp called "Manifest" for men and boys) not only explore their role as men in the world but also create rites of passage for the youths who are urgent to be recognized as important members of society. And my women's group creates celebrations for girls as they reach the often unmarked but deeply symbolic passage into fertility and womanhood. We honor and support pregnant women and the incoming newborns. Also we celebrate and honor the transition of menopause as women move into their elder years.

Recently one of our women, whose mother had died when she was nine, decided she wanted to create a funeral to let her go. She had not been allowed to attend the funeral and had been holding on to her mother ever since. For the ceremony she made and decorated a cardboard coffin in which she placed mementos of her mother that represented what she wanted to release. Together, out in nature, our group witnessed the burning of the coffin and the immense release of decades of grief. One of the grandmothers, Detta, on her 80th birthday invited large numbers of the community to come and paint inspiring messages on her cardboard coffin. Her invitation said, "It is time to honor together the wonder of my future transformation, which we could not share together once I had already left." These non-hierarchical ways of relating in groups create an ongoing sense of value and belonging – a container in which transformational healing can occur.

Now back to Joseph's story.

As with most of the stories, many of the eight keys I have used as section themes are to be seen in operation in Joseph's story. I will explore briefly how he moved into balance with his sexuality and will look for signs of the keys so far explored in this book.

Firstly, after realizing that he had swung out of control to the two extremes and was in crisis, Joseph listened to his inner voice that guided him to a place of safety – the countryside. He was at that point close to suicide and made the conscious decision to choose life. Then, he recognized that he needed to assert his will appropriately to move back to center. He had experienced how dangerous unfulfilled desires can become if swept underground, and found a supportive network to stand by his healing process. Most importantly, Joseph had the ongoing support of Elisabeth – his "constant ally" – who listened with unconditional acceptance as he shared and released his pain. He also states that involving his physical body through movement work has been tremendously helpful.

Joseph and Elisabeth's conscious work with their masculinity and femininity is reflective of the work of great numbers of us across the globe. There is a global shift toward balanced expression of our male and female qualities and it is not necessarily happening consciously. It seems to be part of our evolutionary process as a species. In her wonderful book *The New American Spirituality*,[16] Elisabeth Lesser says:

> We are going to have to add enough of the feminine into the patriarchy so that what emerges is neither a patriarchy nor a matriarchy, but a human-archy. And not even that. What we need is a being-archy, where all beings are granted mutual respect and where decisions are made with the whole circle of life in mind.

This circle of life, in my mind, includes the inanimate world. I believe that it would be incredibly useful for us to reassess our relationship with all that is inanimate, because physical objects can be a godsend in assisting and enriching our lives in many ways – especially the mourning process. In my years of working as a workshop leader with my mother, M'haletta, we have frequently used objects as a valuable tool for personal growth work, and looking back at how my mourning broke I can see that creating simple rituals using meaningful objects played a big part in my healing.

The body is the most obvious material symbol of death and to relate to it directly can be an important part of the grieving process. My heart aches for those who have had to face funerals without the body of their loved one. When I reached home that devastating first night I had an overwhelming urge to go and be with Benjaya's body; a desire echoed by his father. Now, as I think about it, that urgency seemed to be propelled by a need to connect with the physical and to capture some of it before it disappeared forever. I remember being deeply concerned that my mother would not be able to see his body before the cremation as she was in India and proving difficult to contact, so I took photos. It seemed important to capture one last image of our boy, albeit in the mortuary. Abel cut a lock of his hair to keep. We were desperate for something of him to hold onto.

Abel spent those first few days and sleepless nights clutching Benjaya's jacket, breaking periodically into howls of grief. God forbid that anyone should have taken it away from him. It was a conduit for his raging emotions and allowed him to be in touch with the vibrations of his boy. I kept his favorite teddy, Albie, close by and put him to bed every night telling myself that Benjaya would feel terrible about leaving him, and that it was my responsibility to look after him. Actually I was drinking in one of the most tangible memories of him – his relationship with his bear. (As I write Albie is in bed with Benjaya's brother, Asher.)

The morning of the ceremony/funeral, surrounded by children, I prepared two tables that I felt intuitively were required. The first consisted of a spiral display of pictures of him from his birth to the last weeks of his short life. The second table contained a collection of all the things that meant the most to Benjaya in his life. The many children present were transfixed by this table and memorized the objects, as if by doing so they were embodying part of him. I felt as if by using things to which Benjaya had been closely connected, I'd built a bridge to him over which people could travel in their minds and be with him in thought more clearly.

The clothes I wore for the ceremony were very important to me. Black would have depressed me, and so I chose my Indian-style, ivory white silk wedding trousers and a new simple silk top to match. Around my head I tied a thin band of black velvet in an attempt to balance my desire to be uplifted with recognition of the stinging reality of my loss. It worked for me, and it affected me positively when I looked out into a sea of brightly colored clothes that the guests had intuitively chosen, as we sang Benjaya's favorite song "Magic Penny." And, of course, the pennies that then began appearing were a tangible form of connection to one who is no longer physically with us.

From the first night of his death to the day after the cremation we kept a candle burning in the home for him. We asked friends and neighbors who so much wanted to be of help to give us candles and to burn candles for him so that we could all remember him in the light. At Abel's instigation it became a ritual in our family that we burned a candle at every mealtime in memory of him. I still do it today.

The job of sorting out Benjaya's room was one I had been dreading. What should I do with these precious remnants of my dead boy's life? I'd had no practice at this. All I knew is that I wanted to recreate the room as a writing room where I could have some quiet space to work, and hopefully feel a strong presence of Benjaya in his present form. With the support of my mother, I took my courage in both hands and we began. I asked myself, "Will keeping this give or take from my energy?" If the answer was "take" I gave it away.

In his last week of life Benjaya had painted three most extraordinary bright, swirling pictures, which totally belied his age. When I saw them I thought, "That must be his idea of Heaven." I framed them for the walls, and along with the everlasting flowers he had made me two weeks previously, they served to raise and lighten the energy. I felt that in using his belongings in this way, Benjaya had been "lifted up" rather than "cleared out."

To touch upon his ashes was initially harrowing and yet important for me. I took them to the river to the exact spot where Benjaya had fallen, and played out a simple spontaneous ritual. While my mother stood downstream throwing flowers into the mill pool where his body had been found, I tossed Benjaya's home-made wooden airplane with BENAIR written on it into the water and watched it circle round and catch the current before taking the same journey his body had done. I then took a handful of his ashes and scattered them over the same spot, mentally committing his body back to God, back to the waters through which he had come. I was both grateful for having been given the gift of mothering this boy and sad to be performing the last act in his earthly play. Then, I stood in awe as I heard the words: "This is my beloved son in whom I am well pleased." Afterwards we agreed that these simple acts had served to deeply nourish us.

The rest of his ashes went home with my mother to the place where he was born. There are several memorials which keep his memory alive: a "Benjaya's Bank" in the garden of my parents home – now matured and blooming beautifully in summer, several trees planted in his name, and a stained glass memorial which captures his essence, and lives in my front room.

Many people speak of wanting to make their mark in life. After Benjaya's death I was seeking to gather up, make visible, honor and celebrate the marks he had made in his five years of living so that people could relate more clearly to them. For certain I wanted to make it known that he had lived, and I used physical objects to draw the attention in a positive way to his existence. Like many thousands of others suffering the loss of a loved one, I wanted his name to be sung loudly from the hilltops, lest he be forgotten. Someone wise once said something along the lines of, "There is one thing worse than speaking ill of the dead, and that is not speaking of the dead at all!"

If each of us approached every day as an opportunity to relate appropriately to all that crossed our path, we would not need to reassess our relationships should a major life challenge occur. Whether grieving or not, today is surely a good day to create more nourishing relationships with ourselves, with others, and with our environment. In this way we will naturally make positive imprints that will be remembered when we are gone.

Fourth Key
REASSESS RELATIONSHIPS
Questions and Reflections

1. Thinking back through this section – Janet and Joseph's stories, the love model, and the ways in which we can use the inanimate world – what particularly struck you as being relevant and useful to your life?

2. Write down the names of those with whom you relate on a regular basis and circle the name of anyone in whose presence you often feel depleted. What action plan will you make to stop this occurring?

3. Identify a relationship in your life to which you may be holding on for inappropriate reasons. Consider asking, "What do we need in relation to each other to reach our highest potential?"

4. Turn to the model of conditional and unconditional love. What insights do you have about your present way of loving? What would be in your best interest to change?

5. Identify a "betrayal" in your life. Name any opportunity this presented to you? How could you release any remnants of bitterness about this betrayal that continue to affect your life today?

6. Who or what do you hold responsible for your state of fulfillment? In what ways does that work for you... or not? What two steps are you willing to take to fulfill yourself more?

7. Imagine a line about 4ft long on the floor. Find an object to symbolically represent spirituality and one for total embodiment (full connection to your body and the earth). Place one object at each end of the line and then stand on the line to reflect where you stand on this continuum. What do you need to move toward a place of greater balance? Invite that into your life now and change your position if you feel moved.

8. What prevents you from being fully present and authentic in your close relationships? How would it be if you were even more honest than you are now?

9. How does your local community support your needs? What constructive action might you take to make a difference, however small, to your relationships within the community?

10. Think of a simple act or ritual you could create, alone or with others, using physical objects as symbols to help your healing process. When will you make it happen?

The Fifth Key

IDENTIFY
AND RELEASE
LIFE-LONG
PATTERNS

Thank God our time is now,
when wrong comes up to meet us everywhere,
never to leave us till we take
the longest stride of soul men ever took.
Christopher Fry

Identify and Release Life-Long Patterns

Adversity attracts our unfinished business. Wrong comes up to meet us everywhere and results in the magnification of our ineffective life-long patterns. Crisis flings open the floodgates, bringing apparently unrelated wounds to the surface and leaving us with a sense of being overwhelmed and a fear of opening up to such a powerful tidal wave. Our unresolved issues, usually begun in childhood, arise like never before, confronting us with both past and present difficulties to deal with at once. This can make our emotional responses seem exaggerated. The key is to be prepared to take the longest stride of soul we've ever taken – to reframe our thinking so that we welcome the intensity as an opportunity to release and heal these long held blockages and hurts that could, in some cases, even be the root cause of the present circumstances.

Not only our personal past, but also our national and global history – if not dealt with in an appropriate manner – will come back to haunt us. Any areas of numbness – places we have frozen over in our attempt to hide from the difficult reality of what we have done or experienced individually or collectively – will begin to thaw if the fire is hot enough.

To continue the water analogy, feelings of grief often begin like drips from a leaking pipe (maybe one that has been frozen). We rest in the safety of knowing the drips will be caught in our bucket, then suddenly the bucket is overflowing and our emotions are spilling out of control. And when the flood happens we kick ourselves for not fixing that leak when it started dripping. However, once the shock of the damage has abated, there can be something very satisfying about clearing up a big mess!

The body has an intricate flooding system that works overtime when we meet with challenges. On each side of the brain at the side of the head lie the amygdala.[17] These almond-shaped clusters of interconnected structures gauge the emotional significance of events. They act as a storehouse of emotional memory and personal meanings, and scan for trouble, asking: is this something awful, hateful or fearful? A retrieval process is triggered to discover relevant past experiences, and if the answer is "yes", a message of crisis is sent to all parts of the brain. Fight or flight hormones and raw emotion then flood the body and override the slightly slower rational mind.

The implication of the amygdala response is that time will not heal trauma on its own. The impact of the event remains embedded, ready to send its powerful protective reaction in similar situations. If a more normal response is not actively learned to a frightening trigger, then Post Traumatic Stress Disorder (PTSD) is the result. Daniel Goleman, in his groundbreaking book *Emotional Intelligence*, supports what I have personally discovered – that it is possible to dramatically reduce the impact of even the most shocking memories and fears. Referring to specific research on holocaust survivors he states: "This finding, and others like it, hold out the promise that the brain changes in PTSD are not indelible, and that people can recover from even the most dire emotional imprinting – in short, that the emotional circuitry can be re-educated."

My simplistic understanding, reached by having experienced such change, is that if we successfully create a positive imprint connected with and equal in power to the disturbing one, then the amygdala fight or flight response will somehow be neutralized. This might seem a very tall order, but each tiny proactive step we take toward healing begins to lessen the threat of a flood. This section will give ideas of how to take those first steps. And, of course this whole book is about creating new imprints in various ways.

Before we move on, I want share some of the useful information I learned from the approach adopted by James S. Gordon, M.D., Director of the Center of Mind-Body Medicine in Washington DC. He warns against using the medical model to attempt to correct the symptoms of trauma. It is a model of pathology, meaning that you have to be sick in order to be treated, and states Gordon, "PTSD is a perfectly reasonable and comprehensible response to trauma, not a sickness." He says that becoming self-aware is the most important way to heal: seeing the symptoms as something out of balance and asking "What can I discover about myself through these symptoms?" This more holistic approach is the only way in which past patterns and feelings, tapped into as a result of the present crisis, will have the chance of seeing the light of day. Drugs will mask the body's messages, and although a case could be made for their use in the short term for serious situations, they are unlikely to be a satisfactory solution for coping in the long-term.

Certain holistic remedies can be an effective alternative to drugs. Rescue Remedy (available in most health food stores) was composed specifically for shock, and homeopathic remedies are frequently used to great effect. A homeopath will give individualized help.

The following stories clearly show the necessity of this fifth key – identifying and releasing life-long patterns – in the healing process. I hope they will open up the question, "Where are the roots of my present emotions and how can I release them?"

James Owen's Story – The Big Secret

I heard about James – artist, actor, and caregiver – long before I met him. This English/Welsh man with his home in New York City is a close friend of a dear friend of my mother, M'haletta. My mother had spoken of him to me because she had been so touched by his kindness. Never having met her, he had sent her an extraordinary hand-painted cloak across the Atlantic Ocean – an amazing gift. After a lively greeting, he sat on the sacred star quilt and began his story with the passion of an orator.

When Gregory, James's partner, was 34, he was rushed into the hospital with meningitis. The following day he discovered he had AIDS. Within a week the meningitis had gone to his brain, and within six months he became like a child. He asked James, "I have AIDS, does that mean I'm going to die?", to which he could only reply "We're all going to die, Gregory." At this point James didn't know if he was HIV positive. He told me, "Intern doctors would tell me to get tests done but it frightened the life out of me, so I focused on Gregory's comfort and didn't concern myself about me."

This was 1994, when there were no protease inhibitors to fight the virus, and unfortunately Gregory died in horrific circumstances in the emergency room of a hospital. By the time they had contacted James, Gregory was in the morgue, so he didn't get to see him, which made him very angry.

> I was also angry with his family because they absolutely abandoned him, even though they lived nearby. Gregory's mother kicked him out years before because he was gay... nobody had anything to do with him. I was at the hospital every day for six hours to take care of him, because if the patient isn't compos mentis they get treated like a lump. His step-mother and two sisters came once. He was sitting in bed talking because his brain was still okay then, but they never came again. I have felt so much anger for six months – anger at the family, the inadequacies of the hospital, the filthiness of the floor. I was fighting for him because he was helpless and brain damaged. Deep down I knew he was going to leave us so I grieved for six months before he died.

James told me that there was no funeral because there was no family, although he managed to find a brother who signed for Gregory to be cremated. James was left with the ashes.

> They came in a box – not an urn, and I put them in a bag. On the way home I went into a thrift shop for homeless people with AIDS and I had to have the bag checked. It was very heavy. The little lady said, 'Well, if what you've got in here is gold, you are a wealthy man!' I thought, 'How can I tell her that the remains of my loved one, is in that bag!' So I came out of the store, half laughing and half tearing, with Gregory in the bag, and it was like I had this big secret.

James went to England shortly after this to visit his parents, which was extremely difficult because he felt unable to share his pain. They knew Gregory was a close friend who shared his apartment, but he'd kept being gay a secret because that was something that his generation didn't talk about. He used to date girls and was even married so they had no reason to think he was gay. He told me that he was afraid that if he "came out" he would be abandoned again. His mother had put him and his brother in an orphanage at a very early age, where he'd spent most of his childhood. When they came out of the orphanage they were told never to tell anyone that they had lived there for so long. So James had carried that as a shameful secret most of his life.

James revealed that he had once had a very good relationship with a woman, during which he realized he was gay. He told me that in an understanding way he had formed his first relationship with a man, who then abandoned him to have a relationship with his girlfriend. He admitted to having been abandoned in many situations since then and that this was a familiar theme to him.

Back to James's more recent pain. He was in deep grief when he returned from England but managed, together with friends, to bury Gregory's ashes.

We put him in the sand of a rather deserted beach when it was getting dark, and let the tide take his ashes out with it. We didn't say anything out loud; we just played his favorite music.

Christmas was coming up and I felt lonely. Gregory had bought a beautiful white azalea the year before which had become like a bush. I had looked after it well but the most extraordinary thing happened. This Christmas only one bloom came out. One! And it bloomed; I kid you not, for four weeks, all by itself. 'That's Gregory,' I said. I didn't know what the sign meant, but it was uplifting for that time.

I carried on until April getting very depressed and sleeping a lot. I hated that Gregory's life was cut so short, and I kept thinking about how he was abandoned by his family. I guess I also felt abandoned again. Eventually, I plucked up the courage to take the test at an anonymous testing place. I was HIV positive but it didn't hit me and I carried on for months just mourning Gregory. Eventually the various negatives surrounding being HIV positive started creeping to the fore. Who should I tell? How can I tell people? This is going to mean further abandonment!

When I was walking every day to see Gregory in hospital I met people who said, 'How's Gregory?' and I would say 'Fine.' They didn't even know he was in the hospital because I couldn't open up and tell them. Then I would stand there crying and it would open up the wound of holding a secret that I had covered for all that time. There was no way I could keep exposing myself to being hurt. I wasn't in denial. I was protecting myself from, 'Oh, this is terrible,' 'Oh, I'm sorry.'

From this point on in the interview a dialogue emerged, which I believe is of value to share here verbatim.

Carmella: Do you think the need for protection is different with AIDS than with other kinds of illness such as cancer?

James: Yes I do, because with AIDS you don't know if you're going to get compassion, whereas if you have cancer, you know you are going to get a bit of sympathy. I worked for the British Leprosy Relief Association in a leper colony in Africa for almost a year. I saw what went on there and I've seen it go on here with people with AIDS – "Look at him! Look at her! She's got AIDS!" If you got it because you were a hemophiliac or that sort of thing, then I think there is great pity for you, but not if you're gay. It's God's way isn't it? That'll teach you for fucking around.

Carmella: I'm hearing you say that you believe it's vital for gays with HIV to protect themselves because of the mass consciousness around AIDS. I totally understand that. *And*, that protection would not allow anyone without that prejudice to get close to you. Do you attempt to discern how people might respond to you, or is it a blanket automatic defense?

James: I think it's a blanket automatic defense. I don't personally know anybody who is completely open about having HIV. Generally it's very private, but once you've stepped over into the full-blown AIDS category, inevitably it is written on your body and you can't deny it. It forces you to come out. In New York you will see young, drawn-looking men walking around with walking sticks and you know people are whispering "He's got AIDS" – that whole finger-pointing thing.

Let me digress to explain the difference between HIV positive and AIDS. HIV positive means that you are infected with the virus but you could remain healthy for many years. It's when you come down with what they call an "opportunistic infection" like pneumonia or meningitis that it swings over to full blown AIDS. However, this isn't happening to a group of people who are now on protease inhibitors.

There are millions of us looking as healthy as I look who are HIV positive, which is very strange, because when you are infected it rarely leaves your mind. You meet and greet people in your everyday life, you are smiling, but of course you have this little secret. You're acting as if things are normal because you want people to treat you normally. If they were to find out you had HIV they would treat you very differently – even if they are not bigoted, racist, or homophobic. If you told me that you have cancer and that you've got to have your breasts removed, I would think to myself, "God, what she must be going through!"

Carmella: I can really relate to what you are saying because of having lost a child in a shocking way. I suddenly became the mother who had suffered the unspeakable. I was acutely self-consciousness of my radically changed identity from "normal person" to "bereaved mother." So there is a similarity, except that I didn't have to carry any judgment. I didn't want the "Oh, isn't that dreadful... what a terrible waste... you must be feeling..." comments. However, I did want true compassion and openness, which I experienced as forging a useful and deep connection with others.

James: Yes, it's like all the other facets of you have become unimportant. It becomes what they think is you. At the time I was diagnosed, whether it was going to be this month or in ten years time, HIV was a death sentence. Doctors, with the knowledge they had then, would say, "Why don't you take yourself on a world cruise? You might as well have a ball and go out with a bang." A lot of affluent, HIV infected gays sold their life insurance, went on tours around the world, and came back only to find they might not die. They're now on protease inhibitors, their T-cells have gone up, but they have no money left.

Carmella: So how did thinking you had a death sentence affect the way you lived life?

James: After I was diagnosed I found that I am still me and I'm still in the life that I'm in. It made me re-evaluate my sense of priorities. I have difficulty when people complain about little things that I consider now to be absolutely minor. I have learned to value what I do have, especially my friends, and I don't "kiss ass." It also makes me want to accomplish as much as I can while I'm here. I want to be remembered for something – my work, my talents, my creativity. I would love to leave something behind.

I'm a caregiver to one of my neighbors in the next building who has full blown AIDS and is terribly depressed. He lives alone because he lost his partner, and suffers terrible isolation. So, I go around there and I cheer him up almost every day, which cheers me up.

Carmella: Do you feel there is more heart within the gay community now because of having to face death?

James: Oh, yes. In the same way that the British people during World War II got together when they were under a threat of death, it awakened a deeper sense of compassion for other people.

Carmella: My sense from what you have said is that the gay community may have hostility towards the straight community, or those who have not had experience with AIDS. I wonder if the gay community would be willing or ready to consider sharing their newfound heart? I know you feel you need to protect yourselves and yet a part of me still says, "Let me in! I want to share your heart."

James: This is true; maybe it is an opportunity.

Carmella: With each person I've interviewed so far I've noticed that patterns, usually begun in childhood, have repeated themselves, so that whatever trauma they have been through seems to be very much related to those early imprints. And I can't help noticing the obvious abandonment theme with you.

James: Yeah, yeah.

Carmella: I'd like to put it to you that perhaps the anger you feel about the way people treat the gay community and those with AIDS has much more punch in it because of having felt abandoned as a child. Is there an opportunity here to break through that automatic protection barrier that says, "I refuse to be abandoned again"? Your mother told you not to tell about the orphanage; she didn't say you must keep HIV a secret.

James: Yeah, I agree. There has to be a big change in my life. This abandonment theme keeps coming up. I'm a good cook but I have not cooked in my kitchen since Gregory died. I'm not nourishing myself. In fact, I can see now that I have been abandoning *myself*. I've been living in the fear that I'm alone in a fourth-floor walk up, where I don't have friends in the building. Should I get sick, well Lord I'm going to feel abandoned, aren't I? How can I change that? Well, I'm starting to reach out now.

I have a friend, a 79 year-old singer, an African-American, who's like an adopted grandmother to me. Because I have nursing experience they want me to move in with her. I would be company for her, and she for me, and if she should die, the apartment would become mine. Also I have agreed to be the creative director for a museum/multi-cultural center. I will be running a workshop there for kids, which I'll love doing. I'm going to teach the talented kids in the neighborhood who don't have opportunities.

Carmella: Would you say that you are actively taking steps to avoid being a victim to that wound of abandonment by creating a secure set-up for yourself?

James: Yes. I guess I am. The way I saw it is that I can't live in this state of mourning forever, re-enacting situations that disturb me, and fueling my anger. Gregory is somewhere else, and my life has got to go on. My involvement in the museum is wonderful because people are going to be learning, and it's for the good of the community. I really like that you can trust children to tell you the truth.

Carmella: Do you see a time when you will be able to reveal your truth?

James: Oh yes. Yes, I'm going to do it. I'm a good speaker. I'm doing it now with you. It's not difficult, but it's something I cannot do in one quick change of thinking. Rest assured, I've seen what the disease has done to so many people – not just physically attacking their brain – I mean killing their spirit. I've seen other people with great strength dealing with it and turning something positive from it. That's the way I am going. I am not going to allow my spirit to be killed.

Carmella: I was surprised, given that you are such an orator, that you had not yet made that step to sharing with other people. And I can see why now – all the fear, all you've had to go through, and the deep abandonment issue. Now I am excited with the idea of you finding enough safety within to not give a damn about the disapproval of other people. You can at least give them the opportunity to be real with who you are, including the HIV positive, as it is very much a part of your life. I can see you have needed the level of protection that you have put around yourself, and now you are feeling stronger and ready to open the doors a little wider.

James: Yes, yes, that's right! Incidentally, this is off the subject, but when I sent your mother the hand painted robe, I had not met her, but I had heard all about her and her healing and ritual work through Linda Loffredo. I said, "M'haletta is going to freak. She's going to trip over this!" To me that was the most joyful thing to do. This was a special robe. I loved creating it. It had hung in my apartment for so long but nobody had come along who was worthy of it.

Carmella: It's amazing you brought this up because it connects to what we are saying. I was there when the cloak was last used at a workshop M'haletta and I were co-leading. We'd all decided to change our names for the time of the workshop, and one man, a social worker, chose to change his name to Merlin because he wanted to invoke the ability to stand in his power and to speak his truth. Merlin wore the robe in order to feel that power. He became an awesome presence, expressing his joy at reconnecting with his whole self and feeling totally witnessed in his power.

The reason I'm telling you this is because I see *you* symbolically wearing that robe! When you mentioned the robe "off the subject" I realized that you needed to receive that image of a man standing in his power, being seen in his wholeness, and speaking his truth. When you said that no one was as deserving as M'haletta, I wondered why you don't think you are. You made it! I'd like to see you powerfully speaking your truth – talking to kids about homophobia, racism, and AIDS, and how it feels to be in a body that has an illness. And then, perhaps, the little boy with the secret will be relieved of his heavy burden.

James: Yes. Thank you for that. It is an important image for me.

Carmella: Come and get a card off the table. I suggest you ask to be shown a card to represent the next step along your path.

James: It says "FREEDOM!" Yeah, because my current state is not that of freedom.

Carmella: I think freedom is a great place to complete.

Freedom from the burden of the onslaught of emotion that his life-script has brought him would indeed be an excellent completion. In *Emotional Intelligence* Daniel Goleman writes of the work of Dr. Judith Lewis Herman on the recovery from trauma.[18] He describes the three stages she outlines in the process of recovery:

- Attaining a sense of safety
- Remembering the details of the trauma and mourning the loss it brought
- Establishing a normal life

James seems to be juggling all three stages at once. His sense of safety had been seriously undermined by the threat of early death, coupled with his deep-seated belief that he would be alone and abandoned again. We can see that he is beginning to allay these fears by securing a safe place to live where he will give of his strengths to his older friend. As the interview progressed he was bringing to consciousness the level of trauma that has been affecting his everyday life, allowing himself to remember the details and to feel the pain and anger. There seemed to be a growing willingness in him to share the story more with others, and this retelling will in time hopefully re-educate his emotional circuitry.

Whether a "normal" life can be achieved with HIV as a companion is questionable, but James is now constructing a realistic future for himself – a very good sign – and, most importantly, is refusing to let his spirit die.

Remember that to avoid re-traumatizing, it is important to ask whether it is the appropriate time and place to share the details of a particularly horrible experience. James had not felt ready until this point to divulge his story and, given his heightened fear of releasing the secret, he would have probably made things worse by doing so.

James's interview also reminded me of the importance of acknowledging the hidden needs that bubble up from our past patterning. I've learned to be aware of the places in me that are off-center and have discovered that when I feel driven to reach a certain outcome, or when I feel most uncomfortable, these are usually signposts to some important truth. This awareness has attuned my antennae to sensing when others are doing likewise. To be specific here: James was making a very good argument about the appropriateness of not telling others about his HIV status. But what I wanted to know was what energy fueled his argument. Behind the rational words I could feel an edge, a trapped wound that was crying out not to tell the secret. It is the same lesson as in my story about Abel wanting Asher to live with him in London: no decision can be made wisely unless we are unattached to outcome. As James brought into consciousness what he already knew about his abandonment, I could feel the angry edge softening into a place where he felt the freedom to contemplate sharing his secret.

Seemingly unconnected pieces of information often turn out to be highly relevant to the specific moment at which they are yielded up. When James suddenly changed the subject to the cloak I thought he was going way off track. But this surprising direction revealed the image of a man standing in his power speaking his truth – a new and constructive imprint to help release the emotionally charged image of himself as a guilty secret holder.

Joan Alden's Story – Coming Out from my Mother's Shadow

Joan, a striking, confident woman with short brown hair and a sense of no nonsense about her, strode into the apartment where we were to meet. She had heard of this book project through a friend of a friend, and wanted to be a part of it. I could well imagine Joan at work in her chosen profession – writing novels. In fact, I could imagine her being the lead character! She made herself instantly at home on the star quilt and candidly revealed her story.

She told me she was "the perfect baby" who could be put in anyone's arms – easy to take care of. She often felt ignored when the troublesome brother and sister got attention, and she craved her mother's love. Not only was she the good girl but also the pretty, talented one. Her mother, according to Joan, had a narcissistic need to make her the jewel in her crown, to use her beauty to raise her own status in the world. Joan's mother had come from an impoverished, lonely childhood that she was embarrassed about.

> My mother's greatest ambition was to create the perfect family and be seen as the perfect mother. I was analyzed, criticized, and judged on the most unimportant details as well as the large ones. My mother wanted me to succeed but she put me in a terrible bind. I did succeed: in high school I was lead in my senior class play; I was cheerleader; had dates every weekend; was the star athlete. But I didn't see myself as a winner because when I came home I was told my pants were too long, my socks the wrong color, my hair all wrong. My mother would often shake me or scowl and tell me not to be conceited.
>
> When I was four years old and still sucking my thumb at night, she told me, 'We're going to get some beautiful material and I'm going to make you a special little jacket to wear in bed.' I was so thrilled that I was getting something special... until I saw that the sleeves were sewn shut. It was a straight jacket.
>
> The Sunday before my high school graduation (at which I was to

give the commencement address) we had a Baccalaureate Service in our gowns and marched into the auditorium for the service. Afterwards, my mother came to my room to tell me that I looked like a jerk when I walked down the aisle. I was mortified, and the next day at graduation I was so self-conscious I totally blanked when I got up to give the address. I didn't have notes because my mother felt they would spoil the effect.

Joan's athleticism and tomboy behavior embarrassed her mother, who mocked and ridiculed her for being too masculine. Soon Joan confirmed these fears when she fell in love with a woman. She finally felt loved in a real way, but her mother could only tolerate her if she stayed completely in the closet. Joan refused to be a closeted homosexual and her mother did not speak to her for five years because she would not go to her grandmother's funeral alone and pretend she was straight.

When Joan was diagnosed with multiple sclerosis her mother called a temporary truce. By this time Joan was deeply involved with Catherine, who said to her, "You cannot let your mother do this to you any more, Joan. Tell her it's over." So Joan wrote to her mother and told her, "Because you clearly will not let me be myself we cannot have a relationship." That was twelve years ago and they haven't spoken since, despite Joan having reached out to her by letter.

> Catherine experienced her own mother as suffocating and so she was uncomfortable with too much intimacy and was not interested in mothering me. However, we were so in love that we kept breaking through our defenses. Over the years I taught Catherine how to nurture me, and I learned from her to be independent and less needy. We both grew, but I was a long way from being as strong as I would need to be. Clearly I hadn't finished that lesson.

In 1993 Catherine was diagnosed with advanced ovarian cancer. It soon became obvious that Catherine was going to die, and Joan knew she would lose not only her lover and best friend but also her only family, repeating the pattern of losing her family and intensifying her levels of grief. Joan felt overwhelmed. She was afraid that she would crack up. She had the challenge of giving total support to another, something she had never received herself. If she could do this then maybe she would find inner strength and love for herself that her family patterns had made so difficult. Supporting Catherine was something Joan felt compelled to succeed at, and for three years she dedicated her life to the task. She stopped writing and they decided that however long Catherine had left, they were going to spend together.

> It was like a three-year honeymoon. We had our disagreements but they always led to greater understanding and deeper love. We were present

with our love and our fears. Catherine talked about what might happen to her when she died and I spoke about my fears of surviving without her; we wrote her obituary and planned my future. Many of Catherine's friends didn't know how to react to her openness and honesty. I would tell them, 'talk to her about what is in your heart. You may not get another chance so seize the opportunity.' And so they did and it really helped Catherine. She said good-bye to her friends and gave each a gift.

In Catherine's last months she couldn't eat and had a stomach tube, which emptied into a glass jug beside her bed. It was hands on work from morning till night. I had to empty the jug and clean and dress her wound several times a day. As her organs failed she retained so much water that her limbs had to be massaged to move the fluid along. She needed to be lifted out of bed and to the toilet, assisted in bathing, and rolled over in bed to prevent bedsores. During this period, I was given more patience, love, and physical strength than I normally would have had. I felt good about myself, knowing that I was giving Catherine what she needed – what I had not had. Each gift to her was a gift to myself because I loved her so much.

The week before she died I was sitting on the bed weeping and saying, 'I don't think I can live without you.' She looked at me compassionately and said, 'There are some people up there above us in the corner of the ceiling and they are here for you. You're going to be sad but it's not going to be forever. They will look after you as they have done all your life.'

The next day Catherine crossed her fingers and repeated, 'Four by four by four.' I asked her if she was making a crucifix and she said, 'Tell me what that means to you.' I told her that whenever I was suffering and thought I couldn't take any more I remembered Jesus on the cross and knew I was in good company. Pain is a part of our experience, and it's all right. If Jesus had to live on Earth and suffer rejection and pain, why not me? And as he suffered he cried out with doubt, asking God why He had forsaken him. When I get mad at God, I know that He understands and forgives me. 'That's it,' Catherine said, and she repeated, 'Four by four by four.' I didn't understand that, I thought the morphine was talking. I would discover later that this was an important part of her reassurance.

Catherine had a difficult death. For several days she woke choking and struggling for breath. She was also nearly blind. She'd wake and ask me if she'd died. When I said no, she would frown sorrowfully and say, 'Oh, I wish I would.' Then, one morning, Catherine complained of increased pain. She began to choke again and reach for help but I stood back. The hospice nurse assured me that drowning on her own saliva would not be painful because her brain would be dulled and she would sink easily into unconsciousness. Standing back, I remember thinking, 'this is the hardest thing I will ever have to do.' I couldn't rescue her any more; it was time for me to let her go.

She gave up on me and lay back. For the next three hours while she took raspy breaths, I petted her head. Then suddenly, she began to make a loud racket. Her niece, who was in the house, came to be with me in the bedroom because I was frightened and feeling helpless. It would have been so easy to put my hand over Catherine's mouth and stop her breathing, but I had promised her I would be her witness. I would have been interfering for my sake, not hers. An hour later, Catherine went silent and her head fell. She was gone from her body, but I felt her presence in the room in a remarkable way. I wasn't alone, as I'd thought I would be.

Waiting for the hospice nurse to come I sat beside Catherine's body in the dark room, my hand on her head, which was still warm. The first thing I noticed about the nurse when she arrived was that the crucifix around her neck was the exact cross I had imagined when Catherine crossed her fingers. I suddenly understood what 'four by four by four' meant. I had made note of the time Catherine died. It was 4:44, and the day was January 4th.

When the nurse left, I bathed Catherine as we had planned. I had trouble moving her limbs because her body was growing stiff. As I turned her head, I noticed one eye was closed and one open. I jumped with a start at this freakish expression and spilled the basin of water. In spite of my nerves, I was aware that I loved the body I was washing and it did not seem strange. How wonderful it had been to be so in love.

Later that day, as Catherine's body was wheeled into the chapel of the crematorium, a stream of extraordinarily brilliant light from a stained glass window above shone down on her body and on me. Catherine was there in the light.

Her ashes were hand delivered the following morning and I leaped for joy and raced to the door. Everyone looked at me as if I were mad, and I told them, 'The hardest thing has been the separation.' We joined hands and said a prayer. A week later, when the house was empty, I put a pillowcase on Catherine's place on the bed, then tipped her ashes onto the pillowcase and went through them with my hands. It was a lot like touching her. I could feel the same electricity I felt when holding her hand or rubbing her back.

I asked Joan about the keys to her healing and she told me that writing nightly letters to Catherine, pouring out her despair, had been vital. Six months later she began to feel Catherine wanted to write, so she turned the writing over to her. Once Catherine advised Joan – much like Benjaya had advised me – "Whenever you are in the shadow remember it is the sun which has created this; you can always turn from the shadow and put your face towards the sun." When Joan's grief was such that she couldn't catch her breath, she turned to the Buddhist practice of living in the moment.

> I would pour myself a cup of coffee, very slowly, stir in the milk and watch it change color, then lift it to my lips and taste it. I'd look down at what I was wearing and examine the details. Then, perhaps, I would go to a window and watch what the birds were up to.

She also found it useful to allow herself to cry and not stop until she began to yawn, then she would take a nap, always feeling restored when she woke.

Six months after Catherine died, when she hadn't heard from her parents, she reached out, asking how they might heal their relationship. They told her that she had been a disappointment and that they wanted nothing to do with her. And so members of her church had functioned like her family; called her, took food, and sat with her.

Joan told me how her desire for life returned.

> At one point I realized that I was focusing on darkness. It was as if I went out each day to my garden to pick the dead flowers, not the vibrant blossoms. It was a matter of choice. With Catherine's help I began to see that the world was still beautiful, full of live flowers and things that could feed me and make me joyful. I began to actively look for those things. I realized that when I'm despairing and wish I weren't alive it is because I've lost touch with the notion that 'this too shall pass.' Survival takes desire, something to strive for, something to look forward to, a desire to be loved, to learn something, to see spring, to have a tuna fish sandwich for lunch.

While Catherine was sick Joan didn't do anything about her own health because it would have been good news to be told she was dying. However, a year later she was dating again and wanted to live. Ironically, she was then diagnosed with breast cancer. Both breasts had malignant tumors and would have to be removed. Joan said, "It was not the illness but the mutilation that frightened me. It was a familiar feeling connected to my mother."

Joan and her new girlfriend said goodbye to her breasts and filmed her for the last time with breasts the night before her surgery. She woke with bandages where her breasts had been and was very sick. The anesthesia had aggravated her MS, but by the end of the week she was home dealing with the wounds.

Joan wrote a poem about her breasts saying that, as she looked down at her girlish chest and the two red raw cuts on it, she felt like the ten-year-old she had been, cut down and through by her mother.

> On some level I also believed that this was punishment for having all the wonderful things, for being beautiful and talented. It evened the score.

Not allowed to enjoy my successes, I had developed my esteem by being a good failure. To be a success and be on top of the world was forbidden but I could celebrate, privately, how well I handled tragedy.

I'm working in therapy with this. My therapist wanted me to write on a piece of paper, I AM A STAR, put it in a prominent place, and then tell her how that made me feel. I was so embarrassed; it was such a conceited statement. What if someone saw it? I wrote the words then I camouflaged them so well you couldn't make them out. My therapist said I was cheating so now a new sign is hanging in my closet where only I can see it.

The other thing I am working on in therapy is my sadness. I am told I don't have a good interject of Catherine. As a therapeutic term, an interject means an inner voice which speaks up, or interjects, when there is doubt or worry. A constructive interject would speak supportively and would realize that Catherine, who was very special, loved me. This would make me feel strong, glad and blessed. A destructive interject would be false, judgemental, non-supportive. My negative interject, which comes from the repetitive criticism of my mother, is still at work in me, although I am attempting to release its hold.

Joan's consistent problem in life has been not believing in the constancy of love – afraid she will lose love if she does one little thing wrong, like wear the wrong socks. She believes that if she doesn't behave perfectly she'll be alone, abandoned like James.

Even with Catherine loving me I was afraid to be me, afraid to test her love. I'm working on creating new imprints to replace the old ones that don't work for me, and I've begun to feel Catherine's gentler voice in me. I'm starting to allow her love to take the place of my mother's fear. I think Catherine was given to me as an opportunity to neutralize my mother's negative imprinting.

Six years after Catherine's death, I wrote to my parents, not to make amends but to tell them that they were not the only ones who had been disappointed and hurt, and I described the effect the straightjacket had had on me. I have given up wanting something from them. I have let go of them, finally, and I am better off. I am becoming the authentic woman I was meant to be. In particular, I no longer want or need to be a tragic inspiration; I am compassionate, bright, and growing.

Both James and Joan's stories show how grief is cumulative. We can see the drips that went into their buckets from an early age. It feels sad that it took such big traumas to hit before they were able to make the necessary moves to begin to release those life-long patterns, but thank goodness the build-up was brought to their attention at last. The opportunity to clear up so much more than the obvious mess by constructively repatterning ineffective ways of being is generally present in crisis.

Remember how Karen Proctor's car crash brought to the surface her control-freak patterns set in childhood as a reaction to her parents' way of life, and Janet Patti saying, "Everything in life that had hurt me surfaced and deepened the pain; it wasn't just about the abandonment of the marriage." We saw that James, in the intensity of his anger and despair at the abandonment of Gregory and those with AIDS, finally realized that he needed freedom from the far-reaching effects of the shameful secret he'd carried since childhood and took active steps toward taking care of himself. And Joan, in the face of crisis, was shown how deeply she was still being affected by her mother's critical voice, and saw the need to create a new, positive inner voice.

Joan may have been enhancing her self-esteem by proving to her mother that she was good at dealing with failure – a useful revelation – but her positive attitude to her troubles is inspirational, and probably pulled her through as much as anything. She models the important truth that it is not the experience itself that traumatizes us, but the way in which we interpret and respond to the event. Our mindset and belief systems will cause the degree to which we break through or break down. In an excellent book called *The Phoenix Factor*,[19] the authors describe this very well:

> *Using growth words means adopting growth-oriented concepts to help you describe the present and carry you into the future. ... Early in the crisis your thoughts (and speech) probably contained many sentences like: "I can't go on!" "I've had it!" "I'm terribly afraid!" "I'll never make it!" Describing the crisis in this way – which is certainly appropriate early in the crisis – will ultimately lead to a dead end unless you take steps to change it. As you move through the crisis, allow your language to reflect the opportunity aspect of the crisis: the opportunity to learn new skills, to broaden your perspective on life, to deepen your appreciation of others around you, to discover hidden strengths.*

Joan's attitude was a "growth" one. In many ways she was creating positive imprints that sat alongside the horrible pain of her experiences. This will no doubt reduce the level of discomfort she will feel in the future through the amygdala channel. She was totally open and truthful about her feelings, always seeking the most nourishing solution and actively engaging in the most appropriate next steps. How many of us would wash the dead body of our loved one, even if we wanted to? Go through their ashes with loving hands? Or film our breasts before having them removed? She wanted to. She did it, and consequently felt no regrets about the way she'd handled the situation.

I imagine that the Buddhist practice of slowing things down and living in the moment is an excellent antidote to the amygdala response. Joan said,

"That was the way I got out of terror." The neocortex area of the brain informs us of the facts of what we see. It unfolds its appropriate and refined plan for action at a slower pace than the amygdala, and although it is short-circuited by the amygdala's danger signals, it surely must have more chance of kicking in when we consciously calm our rhythm.

Joan mentions crying as a kind of therapy. Here's a word or two about tears, also taken from *The Phoenix Factor*:

> *Tears play a direct role in alleviating stress by releasing two important chemicals – leucine-enkephalin and prolactin – which are thought to be part of the body's natural pain relieving substances called endorphins... Tears resulting from some other cause, such as smoke or onions, do not contain the important pain-relievers.*

Joan and James both felt their partner's presence in the room after death. Joan says, "I suddenly felt Catherine's presence in the room in a remarkable way." Also, later when the brilliant light shone into the chapel, she thought, "Catherine's here." On seeing the single bloom on the azalea, James said "That's Gregory!" There was no question in their minds, as there is none in mine when I sense my son's presence in a multitude of ways. It is a knowing that has no argument and a balm to the sense of loss.

Back to the theme of identifying and releasing life-long patterns: I'd like to share an experience I had recently of discovering and releasing a life-long thread that led from a current minor crisis to a distant past root. All of my life I have had trouble sleeping. I have been a very light sleeper, aware of almost every noise or movement in the night, and prone to bouts of serious insomnia. After spending quite a stressful Christmas in New York City with my son, and hearing personal stories from several people who were closely involved in the Sept 11 events, I returned home feeling not only jetlagged, but also deeply anxious about the future of life on this planet. Night after night at about 3am I resorted to sleeping tablets after failing to sleep naturally. I knew that my mind was working overtime at night, and that looked like the cause, but during those many hours of tossing and turning I became aware of a level of fear that seemed unconnected to my thoughts. My sense was that it was old fear. By the tenth day I was getting desperate and put out a strong prayer for help.

A friend, Christoffer, visited that evening and began talking of an exercise to help people free themselves from fear. I said, "I need that exercise and I need it now to help me sleep tonight." And so he led me through it. He asked me to go back to a time when I first experienced the fear. I was totally ready for this. It was as if the memories had been bubbling under for days and on the edge of erupting. I went straight into a vivid scene of me as a nine-year-old girl in a bedroom in a house in France. It was not from this life because I knew I was French. I was lying in my bed, desperately tired but awake, with this immense sense of fear, knowing that my father was going to come at some time in the night and sexually abuse me. I was debating whether to put a chair under the door handle or not, and was petrified about the outcome of doing so.

My vulnerable nine-year-old needed help. I felt overwhelmed by the power of my fear and helpless in the face of this brutal man. So, Christoffer led me back to my present self, and the adult me asked for higher guidance as to what this child-self needed. I heard the word "invincibility" in my head and was told to bring that quality fully into my body. I was then guided to return to the young girl in the bedroom to surround and infuse her with my sense of invincibility. I found myself also presenting her with a golden key. This, I said to her, would give her the power to lock the door if she chose to keep out the perpetrator, or to unlock it and use her invincibility to deal with him. I then visualized the nine-year-old coming back with me into my adult body where she would remain protected by a responsible adult. I felt her enter into me and stand in my protection. She was holding the key. It was like bringing part of myself back home; the part of me that has felt so alone and vulnerable in the night.

That night I took a small gold-colored key to bed with me along with my now protected nine-year-old and the feeling of invincibility. I held the key all night and slept blissfully, waking periodically to revel in my newfound sense of safety. I have not taken a sleeping tablet since. This is an example of how it is possible to create a new imprint strong enough to neutralize the ongoing effect of the original trauma. My amygdala no longer send me fight or flight messages in the night.

Jack Kornfield has this to say about these parts of us:[20]

That which is unattended will come to find us; the lost parts of ourselves will present themselves, knocking even louder if we don't listen to their cries. We end up hearing their voices in divorce or depression, in illness or some strange failure. If we do listen and welcome all the parts of the self, we will find they enrich our garden as compost, as nourishment for life itself.

To digress slightly, I recently read about a book called *A Change of Heart*, written by a woman who had had a heart and lung transplant. Shortly after the operation she had a vivid dream of the man who had been the donor, was given his name, and felt herself inhaling him into herself. Then she started to acquire different tastes for things such as beer, green peppers, peanut butter cups and Kentucky fried chicken. A second dream was of flying through the air on a motorbike. She eventually found and met the family of the donor who confirmed his name, that he did have all the tastes she's acquired, and yes, he died in a motorbike accident. Doctor Pearsall of Wayne State University, in the U.S. has recorded 70 such cases.

I have no idea how these impressions could be explained by the amgydala circuit, but what struck me is that if this woman could pick up a taste for beer from someone else's organs, surely, in comparison, there must be a body-memory screaming from our own organs and cells that hold an energy imprint of the traumatic incidents in our lives. And, given this body-memory, I am intrigued to know how any therapy aimed at dealing with the impact of trauma can completely succeed without including some form of work with this stored energy in the body. And I am left wondering about the stored energy memories from previous lives. If indeed past lives exist, where exactly are those memories stored? And how come some people seem to have ease of access to such memory and others do not?

Psychotherapists working at the Hakomi Somatics Institute,[21] specializing in trauma recovery, believe that "the behavior of traumatized individuals is often governed by disrupted, incomplete, or ineffective physical processes, which tend to persist in altered or exaggerated forms such as hyperactivity, hyper-arousal, and numbing... Trauma therapists are in need of a practical method that works through the body to resolve trauma." In his book *Waking the Tiger, Healing Trauma*,[22] Peter Levine espouses the same message,

> ...*leading edge research echoes what ancient wisdom has always known: that each organ of the body, including the brain, speaks its own "thoughts", "feelings" and "promptings" and listens to those of all the others. Most trauma therapists address the mind through talk and the molecules of the mind with drugs. Both of these approaches can be of use. However, trauma is not, will not and can never be fully healed until we also address the essential role played by the body... The living body, a condition we share with all sentient beings, informs us of our innate capacity to heal from the effects of trauma.*

To end, I want to go back to the Benjaya story to share how an interesting therapy naturally emerged to free me from a flood of memories that had plagued me on and off from the moment Asher was born. It took one session! Firstly, I'll set the stage to explain the extraordinary time warp I was in then. I am aware that parts of this particular experience may clash with some people's belief systems, but please bear with me because this is a crucial piece of my unusual life story.

Asher Sai B'Hahn, my second son, was born at home in water on December 1st, 1993, almost two years after Benjaya's death. The Press, shocked that I had dared to give birth in water again, had a field day, and again the news went national. Handsome with big brown eyes, charismatic and full of life and action is Asher – startlingly like his brother.

When he was nearly two we were walking by the river, and there, lying right near the place where Benjaya made his exit, was a dead cormorant – a big black bird. Asher became very excited and kept pulling me closer. I was nervous. This spot and death were already too connected for my liking. Struggling with his limited vocabulary, he proceeded to show me that he inherently understood the concept of death: "Bir dead... bir gone body," he said with his face beaming, pointing from the bird to the sky. Why this spot? How did he know that death means leaving the body? And why was he excited?

A couple of months later Abel and I were in the bathroom when Asher burst in and exclaimed, "Asher... Benjaya. Benjaya... Asher. Benjaya died water: Asher born water." Then he toddled out. Later, when I was trying to teach him to answer my question "What is your name?" the only response I could get, accompanied by howls of laughter, was, "I Benjaya... I Benjaya!"

Age three, when walking by a river with friends, he informed them, "Don't worry I won't fall in the river again." Then, age four, an experience happened which topped them all. For a week or more Asher had been in a strange kind of space, wistfully repeating, "I want to go home, I want to go home," even though he was at home. When questioned what he meant, he replied, "I want to go to my light house." It was during this "light house" phase that he said to me, "Please pass my books," pointing to the bookshelf, which to my knowledge held no children's books. I told him that there were none of his books up there, but he was so adamant that I eventually lifted him up and asked him to show me.

He reached up and pulled out three of the set of *Spiritual Teachings for Children* books that I had put there after Benjaya died. They had no spines and so I couldn't see them. I was astounded. "Do you know that these were your brother's favorite books?" I asked. "Of course!" he said, with incredulity that I should need to ask. "Well," I said, "there was one page in one of these books that I had to read over and over again to him." "I know," said he. "Do you think you can find it then?" I asked. "Yes," he said and proceeded to flick through the first book. "No... no... no... that's not it." Then the second book, "No... no... no." Then the third book, "No... no... YES, THERE IT IS MUMMY!"

He was pointing to the page entitled "Reincarnation" and pushing to get on my lap. "Read it to me Mum." And so we read it time and time again – "the person is in the light and then comes into a baby's body and grows up and up until the body is old, and then goes back into the light." "Yes," said Asher, "but sometimes people die young like Benjaya." As I read, time warped, as it has done so often in my mothering of Asher, but never to this degree.

Every year for six years after Benjaya's death my body seemed to express a cellular memory, as if the wound of the trauma went deep into the invisible parts of me and automatically connected itself to the seasons. A sense of anxiety, which was unconnected to conscious thoughts or memories, would begin to rise some time in October, the month of Benjaya's birth. The feeling gradually increased so that by February it had brewed into a sense of mild dread – an expectation that something terribly shocking was about to happen. I didn't know about the amygdala circuit then, but this to me seemed like a natural occurrence. I remember telling myself that if seeing a boiled egg and white crusty bread can plunge my sensory self back into my child body, sitting in grandmother's big feather bed, with the smell and surroundings still vivid after more than three decades, how then could I expect the sudden death of my son to have less of an impact? Perhaps for some trauma victims this does not occur, due to an internal blocking mechanism aimed to keep them safe from the pain. But I never have been good at blocking, which may or may not be to my detriment.

In December 1998 Asher was to become five years old. I was sick with fear, which seemed to rise from depths I never knew I had. My experience, my programming, told me that no child of mine lives past five years and four months. I had lost two "babies" after Benjaya died when friends were saying, "You'll see, you couldn't lose another." And here was Asher telling me in many ways that he is his brother, with every phase of his life so far mimicking Benjaya's. He even told the same jokes and missed out number 15 when counting, just as Benjaya did. My logical self fought for recognition saying, "Of course he won't die," but my body's deeply embedded patterning was unimpressed by logic.

I recently discovered a research study by Patricia Hentz[23] that clearly shows that it is normal to have a body experience around the time of the anniversary of a loved one's death that relives the original experience. She says,

> *As women in the study listened to their bodies, there was an understanding of a process of mourning that included a cyclical pattern. 'Knowing the time' was not just measured in calendar days or months. Knowing the time was as the body perceived the time, like knowing the time to get up without an alarm clock. The body just knew. It was not a conscious, rational process.*

And so, as I approached Asher's fifth birthday, which was only four weeks later than Benjaya's birthday, a large part of me, which I felt incapable of controlling, was experiencing this time as my second son's last days on earth. Abel and I had separated that year, adding to my intense pain levels, and he took Asher to America for Christmas – a trip of a lifetime, which I knew I didn't want to veto. I waved them good-bye, and the scene of waving good-bye to Benjaya for the last time as I sped off on a train was superimposed on my present reality. Benjaya had died in Abel's care. I have no blame about that, but letting Asher go away with him stirred that imprint along with a tidal wave of grief. I went home and howled and shook for a long time. But nothing could shake the fear of the imminent death of my son. I understood that to break this pattern I needed to create an experience equally as strong, but positive. HOW? was the question.

When I had purged the grief to a state of emptiness I sat and asked for help, repeating my simple prayer – "Please do this through me because I cannot do it alone." I picked up my pen and my journal and caught down the thoughts that streamed into my head in response.

December 16th, 1998

It is indeed a point of release and new beginnings. In a sense it is important to relive the death of Benjaya's body, catalyzed by Asher's departure and age, so that a full and true release can occur, taking with it the roots of the pain.

*The challenge for you is: **Can you totally release to the will of God?** Your trust and faith have shone through, but they are not total. Could your faith stand strong in the face of a repeat of the death of your first son? Can you look your God/Goddess in the face and say with all your being: **Take him if it be the divine will?** Or do you in part cling onto "No, it cannot be!"?*

Think on it. Severe test it may seem to those in a non-warring Western culture, and indeed it is, but there are those who love their God in total when whole families have been murdered, whole communities slaughtered. The human soul is capable of carrying the unthinkable when the sight penetrates the illusion of flesh and separation.

If you can give your second son fully to his destiny and can sacrifice the security of human attachment, then, and only then will your inner security blossom. "Don't leave me, don't die" is the cry of the mother of flesh for her beloved child. It is understandable, it is instinctual, and is fully supported by humanity as the only expected response to your particular challenge. And yet we, in the world of spirit, knowing no separation, would say to you as a reminder of that which is so near already:

Raise yourself when the tears subside
into the truth which wraps like a comforting cloak around you.
*Let the words **I and my sons are one in spirit***
wave in soothing sound through the cells of your being
and know that the great mother's ocean of love
is endless and can hold the flowing tears from every mother's
wounded heart.

And so remember this: Mother, father, daughter, son is but a playing out of the one spirit dressed in the garb of flesh. With love bursting forth into your domain I leave your mind that you may continue the play. A breakthrough is at hand.

I was moved to tears, although I was by no means a stranger to words and love coming through me from a source beyond my mind. I have been receiving help in this way since I was 21. And so a shift began to take place in me that day as I realized that, beyond the fear, I did trust in the divine design in everything and could let go of Asher to the safety of his destiny.

That evening was my weekly women's group, a circle of women supporting each other to become more whole. Through gasping sobs I shared with them my morning's crescendo of grief and read my writing out loud, asking for their help in completing the process of letting go. As I sat taking big shivering breaths of release they began to sing, to chant, "I and my sons are one in spirit," the harmonies bathing me like a cloak of mother's love, and the message that there is no separation penetrating every cell of my being. I literally felt a new positive imprint enter my body and my consciousness.

Then, as is our pattern, our healing stone was passed around the circle for each woman to imbue with specific prayers for the one in need. I asked for prayers to help retain this sense of peace in relation to fear for Asher's life. I carried that stone around throughout a highly enjoyable childless Christmas, and since that evening I have not experienced a mere inkling of that fear, even as we approached the five years and four month date that had held a menacing grip on me for so long. This was a transformational healing ceremony of such simplicity, borne of me asking for the help I needed. Fortunately, I had a support system in place to answer the call in a way that worked for me.

Asher has made no mention of being his brother since that time. What he has said is "Now that I am older than he was, I can live for him the life he didn't have." I have a sense that when he passed the age Benjaya died he no longer felt that he was walking in his footsteps and now feels free to be entirely himself – whatever that means!

It is my wish that the telling of the stories in this section will give hope that, however long the painful patterns have been there, and however deep-seated they may be, there is a way of releasing them – a way that may be totally unique to you. I am convinced from my own experience that if you ask sincerely for help to be given, trusting that this will be so, then the answer will not be long in presenting itself.

Fifth Key
IDENTIFY AND RELEASE LIFE-LONG PATTERNS
Questions and Reflections

(Questions 1 – 6 are part of a continuous exercise)

1. Bring to mind a time in your life when you felt especially safe and strong. Intensify the image and feelings. How does it feel in your body? Know that you can always bring this memory into the present if you are feeling unsafe.

2. Now think of your most difficult recent challenge. Identify the powerful feelings connected to this challenge. Go inside yourself and ask: When have these feeling responses occurred in my life before? Is there a theme arising?

3. Allow memories of the first time you had these feelings to arise. (If intense put them on a screen in your mind to watch). How did your responses help or hinder you in that situation?

4. Ask yourself: What quality (patience, invincibility, courage to ask for help, etc.) did I need then that I couldn't access?

5. You are now older and wiser. See if you can access that quality now and bring it vitally alive in your body, maybe by recalling a time that you did experience it.

6. You may want to take that quality back as a gift into those past situations when you think you needed it, before returning to ask: How would this quality help my present situation? Exactly when and how will I use it?

7. Is there someone whose negative influence lives in you (like Joan's mother's critical voice continued to affect Joan)? What first step could you take toward releasing this and replacing the imprinting with a more positive inner voice?

8. Identify any dead end language you are using such as, "I'll never make it." How could you turn this around to growth language? (eg. "I'll make it a step at a time. This too shall pass.") Write out new statements in color and stick them somewhere that will remind you to use them.

9. Take a moment to ask: What parts of myself have I hidden or ostracized? How would you go about welcoming them back home?

10. What specifically would you most like to remember and use from this section about identifying and releasing life-long patterns?

The Sixth Key

CULTIVATE COMPASSION: SILENCE THE JUDGE

Whoever opts for revenge should dig two graves.
Ancient Chinese Proverb

Cultivate Compassion: Silence the Judge

Jalaluddin Rumi said:

Out beyond ideas of wrongdoing and rightdoing, there is a field.
I'll meet you there.
When the soul lies down in that grass, the world is too full to talk about.
Ideas, language, even the phrase each other doesn't make sense any more.

The sixth key to handling adversity is to learn how to meet each other in that field that lies beyond right and wrong. It is about learning to empathize; about imagining how the situation looks from another's point of view.

Our pervading paradigm, nourished unashamedly by the media, is divisive, creating "us" and "them" consciousness. Vast numbers of us are insidiously judgmental and frighteningly devoid of compassion; consequently we have become experts in creating enemies. I say insidiously judgmental because of the clever cover-ups that we manufacture to make our position appear whiter than white. The accepted norm is to sit in moral judgment on others. Anyone who commits a "wrong doing" is on the other side; there is zero tolerance, and the enemy deserves punishment. Revenge, subtle or blatant, is sought and justified as "righting the balance."

The question asked is: who is to blame? Scapegoats are then needed to carry that blame. More often than not we don a self-righteous cloak and project a demonic mask over the humanity of the "culprit", creating an enemy that we can justifiably attack in some way. This, in the long run, escalates our pain and our wars.

Not only do we judge the external enemy, but also, if we allow our defense systems to drop and glimpse our own part in the conflict, we often then judge ourselves as being to blame and beat ourselves up with guilt, or worse. We put the demonic mask on ourselves. Many of us, mimicking our societal role models, have sent our own shadows underground, down the well-worn escape route from the world's eagle eye; hoping that our sunny sides alone will draw the love we crave. But the guard of our shadow-dungeon will make sure that anything that reminds us of those hidden realms is in some way annihilated. Far from bringing love and acceptance, this brings us a world with prisons full of those who have "acted out" rather than suppressed their darker sides.

We tend to judge the polarities of good (love) and evil (the absence of love) as forces of opposition – duality that cannot be bridged. But the paradox is that we cannot know one without the other. Without evil we would not know love, just as without sweet we would not know sour, and without hot we would not know cold. What would the world be like, I wonder, if it had nothing to kick against, nothing to say "no" to, nothing to compare with, and was filled only with sweet and lovely experiences?

I believe that when we come to accept that we are *all* capable of the highest and the lowest actions in life and begin to comprehend all expressions of violence as a calling to meet unmet needs, we will come to know compassion. Only hurt people hurt people; and no one does anything wrong, given their model of the world. Even the suicide bombers, whose actions catalyzed such horror that fateful September day, truly believed, however misguidedly, in the rightness of their cause. Mohamed Atta Jr., one of the bombers, in a document called "The Last Night" wrote – "Be happy, optimistic, calm, because you are heading for a deed God loves and will accept." He was instructed to pray continuously on his mission, and to end his life with the word of God on his lips.

The following stories offer examples of how, even in the face of atrocity, we can make those seemingly impossible, much needed steps towards silencing our judgmental selves and cultivating compassion.

Arun Gandhi's Story – *Grandfather Would Have Forgiven His Assassin*

Arun Gandhi and his wife, Sunanda, who work together with total dedication helping youth to deal with conflict nonviolently, graciously welcomed me and my ever-supportive friend, Linda Lantieri, into the Gandhi Institute for Nonviolence in Memphis, Tennessee. Around the walls hung a series of enormous photographs of Mohandas K. Gandhi, Arun's grandfather, on loan from an exhibition. They depicted scenes from his life, into which we felt as if we had walked. There was a still, peaceful presence in the room, which remained as Arun began, in his soft, lilting voice, to tell his story. At one point he admitted to feeling that his parents and grandparents were guiding him, and we felt profoundly connected to history and the wisdom of his ancestors.

Arun was born in 1934, in Durban, South Africa. His father, Manilal, was the second son of Mohandas K. Gandhi's four children. His mother, Sushila, and father adopted voluntary poverty and devoted their lives to nonviolent and political change in South Africa – a movement started by his grandfather in 1893. He became aware of suffering in the world at a very early age, as he lived daily with the prejudice of apartheid.

> In South Africa we were made aware of skin color from an early age and it was apparent that we were second-class citizens of the wrong color. There were no public toilets for us. We had to find the house of a nearest friend. The best part of the beach was reserved for the whites, and the amusement parks were always in white areas. I was beaten by white South Africans for being too black and by black South Africans for being too white, and it affected me very deeply. I felt terribly inferior and my self-esteem was very low. Of course I was lucky my father campaigned

against all of this but he spent about 14 years of his life imprisoned.

In his early teens, during the most tumultuous period in India's struggle to free herself from British rule, Arun was taken by his parents to live with and be tutored by his grandfather in India. "His love was overpowering" said Arun, "and he lived out in front of me the values he wanted me to learn. 'Be the change you wish to see,' he used to say."

It was heartbreaking when the family returned to South Africa 18 months later. Arun's beloved grandfather was old and they were deeply concerned for his safety. India was torn with violence between Hindus and Muslims, and Mohandas Gandhi was in the thick of the fighting having made it his mission to bring about peace there. He accepted no security, even when his life was in danger. He said, "If I am destined to live I will be protected by God; however, if God does not wish me to live, no human can protect me."

Arun and his family lived in the Phoenix Center for Nonviolent Living – the Ashram that his grandfather had started in South Africa in 1903. The normal routine was that on Thursday night the weekly *Indian Opinion* would be printed, and on Friday morning it was taken to the post office 18 miles away in the city and mailed. However, on Friday January 30th 1948, two months after they returned, the routine was changed and instead of the normal group of people going to town, only Arun's father went.

This day will be etched in my mind forever. My little sister, Ela, who was eight, and I were on our two mile trek back from school through muddy roads across sugar cane plantations. It was about two o'clock in the afternoon. My sister was creating a big fuss to make me carry her home. During this argument I saw an old gentleman who used to live in the Phoenix Ashram walking hurriedly towards us with an agitated look on his face. He told me, 'Run home as quickly as you can, your mother wants you. I'll bring your sister.' I realized there was something very urgent, so I ran home... fast.

My mom was on the phone, tears streaming down her face, sobbing. I stood there silently, not knowing what all the commotion was about until she put the phone down and told me, between sobs, that grandfather had been assassinated. He had been shot at point blank range and fell to the ground with his hands together in prayer saying, 'Ram, Ram,' – the Hindu name for God.

I was absolutely stunned. In that moment I could see the time I had spent with him flash across my mind – the love he showered on me, the lessons he taught me. And I couldn't understand how anybody would want to kill somebody who had so much love and affection for human beings. My immediate reaction, after I got over the shock, was one of tremendous anger. I wanted to throttle the person who committed this heinous crime. When my father returned home I expressed my anger saying, 'I wish I could strangulate that person.' That's when both my parents reminded me of the lesson I was taught by grandfather about using anger positively. They told me that grandfather would have wanted me to forgive his assassin. I said, 'Yes, I must find a more positive way of dealing with my anger, but I don't know how to forgive him.'

Arun's father and brothers in India were able to forgive him and wrote a letter to the Government requesting them not to punish the assassin but to forgive him because that is what their father would have wanted. Gandhi apparently had looked at his assassin with love and forgiveness in his eyes as he fell to the ground speaking the name of God. Not surprisingly, the Government upheld the law and tried and hanged the assassin for his murder.

Much later, in the seventies, I went with my wife, Sunanda, to visit Gopal Godse, brother of the assassin, who served a life sentence as an accomplice. Although I found him ignorant and unrepentant, I saw the wisdom in forgiving. I could have carried hate in my heart forever and ruined my life, but instead we left him to deal with his life and his conscience.

I think what really helped all of us get over the sense of loss was becoming immersed in creating a special memorial edition of the *Indian Opinion* to commemorate grandfather's life. It was a labor of love that diverted our attention from the tragedy toward something constructive.

My father continued to defy apartheid and suffered the consequences by going to prison, while the majority of the non-white South Africans accepted the prejudice and tried to keep away from it. Father used to tell us to stand up to injustice but often he was the only person who was defying injustice and being taken away by the police. At times it seemed ridiculous. He would defy the injustice and court arrest but the police didn't want to arrest him. Even the non-whites ridiculed the idea. 'What do you gain? Follow the mainstream,' they seemed to be saying. These two extremes tore me up during my teens, but in my twenties, after reading grandfather's writings, I realized my father had done a tremendous thing. Even without support, he had refused to bow down to injustice. I realized the power and the potential of nonviolence and it began to strengthen me.

The reaction of the masses to grandfather's death was divided. During his last days grandfather made a sad prediction – 'They will follow me in life, worship me in death, but not make my cause their cause.' That is exactly what happened. A small group dedicated their lives to continuing his work, but a very large number worshipped him saying, 'We are ordinary people and we can't achieve this.'

The death of grandfather, and subsequently my parents, became turning points for the better in my life. Of course death is sad in the fact that you are never going to see the person again, but philosophically grandfather used to say, 'The physical body is like clothes. We change our clothes every day and wear fresh clothes. The soul continues to be, just goes into another body.' I understand that the souls of our ancestors continue to live and in some ways influence us. Life and death is transition, one to the other, and it's not something one has to regret, but just take in one's stride. Each of these tragedies consolidated that belief. Mysteriously, sometimes things that I say are the exact words my grandparents or parents would have said. I feel that from somewhere they are guiding me and helping me in the work that I am doing.

After his mother's death in 1988, he saw the total destruction of the Phoenix Ashram, where he was born.

I had a tremendous attachment to that place, such strong memories of my life there. The buildings had been raised to the ground by arsonists instigated by the apartheid government, the land occupied by 30,000 squatters. Gangs, murders, rapes, are happening there where peace and nonviolence was being taught and practiced. That was a major shock and another source of anger, but I was mature enough now to understand what grandfather meant by using anger positively. One could so easily scream and shout, be violent and make enemies of people who have perpetrated that kind of crime, but the positive use of the anger is to turn things around and see that you can make some change.

Arun and his wife, Sunanda, used the energy of that anger to start the Gandhi Institute for Nonviolence in the U.S. as a replacement for the work that his grandfather started in South Africa.

We began by using nonviolence to resolve conflict and developed programs helping children to do so creatively. One day, coming from within the spirit, I knew that this is not enough. We have to discover where these conflicts start, get to the root of them and show how to avoid them. Many of our conflicts come from two main sources: our inability to deal with anger positively, and our inability to build meaningful relationships.

Relationships are so fragile because they are often built on selfishness: I want something from this relationship and if I don't get it then I don't want the relationship. Or we base it on tolerance. I found that ideal relationships must be built on the four principles of respect, understanding, acceptance, and appreciation. We have to respect ourselves, each other, and our connection with all of creation. We have to purge our minds of the thought that we are independent individuals and can do whatever we like.

We are all interdependent. Whatever happens to one person eventually happens to others also. If we respect that, we reach an understanding of who we are and what our role is in life. When we stop judging each other and reach an acceptance of our differences, then we begin to see others first as human beings and not by their gender, skin color, race or religion. We have created so many labels we cannot see through them to the soul of the human being. It's a tough sell, but I think we have planted a seed in thousands of young people, which will eventually germinate and make a difference.

If we learn to be both verbally and physically nonviolent towards self and others then we will understand more about suffering. And one of the cardinal principles of the philosophy of nonviolence is developing compassion. There is a thin line that divides pity and compassion. We generally act out of pity but think we are acting out of compassion. We are often willing to give to somebody who is distressed or hungry saying inwardly, 'Take this money and get something to eat but don't bother me, I don't have time.' That is acting out of pity. When acting out of compassion you would wonder why that person is suffering and question what problems they and others are facing in your neighborhood. You would share some of your time, talent and resources to enable them to rebuild their self-respect and to stand on their own feet. Showering charity on people cripples them and makes them dependent on us, but by making them worthy citizens who can fend for themselves we are lifting them up. I learned this while working with Sunanda in India with the poor and low caste people, including the "untouchables", in economic programs to rehabilitate them – an area that had so pained grandfather. We were able to change the lives of over half a million people in 300 villages and the people we helped are now empowered to help other people.

One of the ways we can develop compassion is by developing humility. If we are arrogant we will pity people. When we are well fed and cared for we don't really understand the suffering of the hungry or homeless because we've never really been hungry and haven't had to sleep out in the open. So compassion requires a lot of humility and that's what grandfather was trying to do when he chose to go third class on the trains at great personal discomfort. He was coming down to the poorest of the poor and reaching out to them. That's one of the reasons why he alone could touch the hearts of the poorest and most distressed people in the world.

The example of nonviolence, modeled by Arun's father and grandfather, shows us the immense potential and influence we, as role models, have on others. By defying injustice in a nonviolent way, the Gandhis have beautifully modeled the middle way – that place of center between the polarities, which in this case are revengeful attack and turning a blind eye. It is the place where compassion resides and the inner judge is silent. It is a place of humility where anger is used positively, prejudice is absent, transgressions are forgiven, and morals and ethics are valued. And it is fostered by a personal commitment – shown by these three generations of Gandhis – to becoming the change we wish to see in all the small details of our lives.

Most of us know this commitment to be necessary and yet it means making time in our busy days to focus on exploring the territory of our inner lives, and questioning ourselves deeply as to what effect our behavior has on others. We can no longer avoid the truth that safe and nourishing homes, schools, and societies are the effect of the belief systems and behavior patterns of those in a position of influence – which includes us! We are each an important presence in the society we are so tempted to blame for our problems, and we have exactly the same potential as saintly Mohandas Gandhi who made a huge difference in the world by simply following his principles with integrity and dedication.

If we truly believe that we are all interconnected and interdependent, then the concept of enemies and allies is impossible to maintain. If we know that we are all related and made of the same substance, playing the same game of life in the best way we know how given the influences we've had, then we will realize, as did Arun, that causing pain to another will ultimately harm us, just as helping others helps us. This wider perspective has no place for racism. It values every colored thread that makes up the whole tapestry, and automatically welcomes difference with interest and curiosity. To call the black thread too black or the white thread too white does not make a jot of sense in this paradigm.

Arun echoes Arn's discovery about anger; it can be used constructively to propel something good into being. I would add that rage can actually help us to survive in extreme conditions and can be a *temporary* savior. It has powerful life force energy, albeit usually fueled by our desire to kill or hurt the enemy and exact revenge. Other emotional reactions such as sadness and depression do not have this same passionate energy to support aliveness and action. Thankfully, Arun shows us the necessity of moving from this desire to "strangulate" to forgiveness and compassion. He puts forgiveness in the realm of common sense by stating the simple choice he was faced with: carrying hate in his heart forever and ruining his life, or forgiving.

Attaining an inner climate of nonviolence and cultivating a deep level of compassion, such as the Gandhis did, may well be a challenge, but there are countless organizations worldwide now specifically set up to help achieve this aim. One way that I highly recommend beginning is to clean up our language so that we say what we mean, mean what we say, and learn to comprehend the unexpressed needs of others behind their words.[24] The most powerful way I have encountered to do this and to see through our labels to the soul of the human being, is by using Marshall Rosenberg's Nonviolent Communication, which he calls "A language of compassion."[25]

Rosalie now takes us further into the quest for the sixth key – cultivating compassion and silencing the judge.

Rosalie Gerut's Story – Meeting on the Bridge

Rosalie Gerut's name was given to me both in the U.S. and England as an extraordinary example of transforming our concept of "the enemy." We finally met in the same quaint Inn in Cambridge, Mass. where Arn had spilled his Cambodian story a few months previously. Dark haired, soft open faced, and strikingly attractive in azure blue, Rosalie sat in an easy chair to gift her story. I remember marveling at the way these traumatic stories kept emerging through people who by their physical appearance I would not dream could have come through hell and back. The most potent remedy in her healing process supports what I heard on the radio news this morning: "A study just released by U.K. police shows that when convicted 'criminals' meet with the victims of their crimes, the expected number of re-offenders is cut by 50 percent because the perpetrators gain a sense of understanding of the effects of their actions."

Rosalie was born to two people who survived one of the worst catastrophes of the 20th century – the Holocaust. Her mother, the daughter of a Rabbi, was from Lodz, Poland. She grew up in a religious, philanthropic family and was leading a normal life when suddenly she found herself herded into a ghetto and forcibly starved. Rosalie's mother told her "I don't know why I was sent to hell. I never did anything bad." She and her younger siblings became slave laborers, scrounged to get food and watched Rosalie's grandfather die so that the rest of the family could have more to eat. Before he died he told his daughter that she had to survive and tell the story. And so she did. One day, Rosalie's mother and a younger sister – there were six altogether – were out looking for food. When they returned, no one was there. Their mother and the other siblings had been taken to Chelmno and gassed.

Eventually the two remaining sisters were taken to Auschwitz concentration camp, which her mother said was better than the Lodz ghetto because they fed you once a day. "My mother was lucky," said Rosalie "because a Schindler-like person came to Auschwitz and took her and twelve other 'beautiful' women to work in his factory in Czechoslovakia making gas masks for the German army. But by then she had suffered from typhoid fever, tuberculosis, and an accident while she worked as a slave laborer, which cut off three of her fingers."

Rosalie's father's life was just as dramatic. He was from Lithuania, a well-loved musician who believed in working for the good of society, not for himself alone. He survived the ghetto, worked with the partisans, got shot, and was taken to Dachau concentration camp. At the end of the war he survived a forced march in the melting snow while the Nazis shot and beat the prisoners around him. At the time of liberation he weighed 75 pounds.

Rosalie revealed her own childhood struggles.

My family life was very, very bleak for the most part – defined by my mother's unending grief and my father's nightmares. Now these holocaust stories are known, but back then I knew of no one else who had such stories in their life. Babies cut out of bellies, thrown up and shot – these tales were part of my childhood. My mother was extremely anxious and ill and was not always able to take care of me. She told me how she wrapped me in blankets, found me blue and had to take me to hospital to rescue me.

She said she didn't know how to feed me, and I imagine that was the beginning of my lifelong struggles with eating disorders. At times I would spontaneously stop breathing and be taken to the hospital by ambulance and left alone in small tent-like structures to help me breathe. My mom would one minute love me, one minute beat me up. I didn't know what was coming next so I decided not to stay close to her. My father was not at home a great deal because of work. I had a brother, but it was a lonely, sad existence and I wasn't allowed friends because my mother feared I would contract polio. That was my life for the first eight years. I didn't go to school consistently until fourth grade.

Teenage years were filled with pain, pain, pain. The theme of my life was dancing between the two extremes of wanting so much to live and so much to die. I fell in love at 16 but my mother broke us up. She was good at taking away things that I loved. I felt it was a re-enactment of the holocaust. Maybe she had to re-enact some of these things in order to process them because there was nobody around to help her psychologically. We were poor and didn't have any financial assistance or extended family to help us. The good part about this was that I grew up in a multi-racial neighborhood and felt very comfortable with people of many cultures and colors.

When I went to college I became increasingly more depressed and gained 40 pounds in the first year. I went to the school psychiatrist and told him, among other things, that my parents had been in the Holocaust. There was no reaction. It was as if I'd never said it. Perhaps there was a conspiracy of silence at that time. Perhaps professionals didn't want to know. It's like the Vietnam War; it takes many, many years before people can face history and its injuries.

Rosalie studied psychology in search of liberation from her dark depression

– pain that felt as if it lived inside her and would always come back. She called it "The Valley of the Shadow of Death." Someone pointed out to her that it's not death; it's the shadow of death. "Maybe death isn't as bad as the shadow of it," said Rosalie.

It struck me, many psychologists later, that our generation had experienced a shadow form of the Holocaust as infants. I used to think there was something desperately wrong with me because I couldn't be normal, but there were darned good reasons. Trauma is thoroughly devastating. It takes a great deal of strength to endure what goes on in the body and not choose to end one's life. Trauma hits people at a biochemical level, affecting brain chemistry, adrenal chemistry, as well as the nervous system. To empower myself I remember that I must be very strong, even though I feel I am falling apart. It still didn't save the many years lost to depression.

My parents' liberation was in 1945, but what about my generation? We don't have numbers on our arms or a dramatic story but we carry their pain; a pain from which they could not be liberated. I think there is a sort of osmosis that passes trauma from one generation to the next and unless we can find a way to stop it, it will go on and on. Some parents didn't talk to their children about the holocaust but the kids still picked up the emotions. We see the same thing with abuse. The cycle needs to be broken and it's not easy to do. I didn't even realize that what my mother did to me was called abuse until I was in my thirties.

Rosalie spoke of how important it is to hold onto any glimmer of hope and to start there: "There is always love somewhere, even in the darkness," she said. She believes that her love of music, people, animals, and nature probably prevented her from dying as a child. She taught herself how to play guitar and sing, and became quite a well known folk singer and now someone who writes music for theater.

Music saved me above all else. When I was a child I pretended I was a great actress and when I was alone I sang and danced and was uplifted by my fantasies. I started out as a folksinger and in the 1980s was asked to sing at Holocaust memorials all over the country. It was very depressing to do one memorial after another, remembering all the dead people. But one afternoon while flying from one city to another I had a dream that was quite amazing. I saw a group of smiling people dressed in black robes coming towards me. I knew they had died in the Holocaust. They said to me, 'Tell the Holocaust survivors to stop mourning. We're not in pain anymore, we love you, we love them. LIVE!' I had always thought my mother's sin was that she spent more time mourning those who had died rather than loving the ones who were alive. And so I used my music to comfort people and try to take them from a dark place to a light, hopeful place. I needed to do this for myself as well. My first album 'We are Here' was inspired by this dream.

Rosalie had another dream in which she was saying, "I want to go down in this life." And a committee asked her if she was sure. Rosalie said "yes" because she thought it would be a great opportunity. But then when she entered she thought... "oh, wait a minute I don't know about this one. The idea is one thing and the reality is another." Rosalie told me, "During hard times I remember that I chose to be here and I'm not ready to die because there's much more I want to do. My belief is there are lessons for the soul in everything we experience, although some of the lessons seem to be much more difficult than we would like them to be."

Then, in February 1993, after a spell of terrible psychic pain, Rosalie came face to face with the most extraordinary healing opportunity that deeply affected her life direction. It began when she saw an advertisement that said, "Children of survivors of the Holocaust wanted to meet with children of Nazis."

It sounded spiritually correct that we should meet, so I went to the Black Forest in Germany and sat in one of the most sacred circles in which I have ever been. It was a circle of descendants of the Third Reich face to face with descendants of Jewish and Christian victims and survivors. We each told our story and we saw that everyone there was in pain. These horrible crimes had not just happened to the victims' side, they also pervaded the psyches of those on the other side because these people felt such horrible feelings of guilt and shame.

During the sharing I sat across from a German man, Otto, who admitted to having been in the Hitler Youth and drafted into the SS as a teenager. I felt terrified. I imagined him as a Nazi in his high black shiny boots, unable to see my kindness and humanity, his rifle ready to annihilate me. I had a dream that night that I was talking with a friend and he came behind her and stabbed her to death. He told me, 'I'm not going to harm you,' and walked on. The next morning we learned that the woman, whose room adjoined his, barricaded her door in fear.

Another woman, Helga, came to turn herself in to the Jews after a recent discovery with which she couldn't live. Her family had told her that her father, who died when she was twelve, had been a very nice man. Later in life she had tried to kill herself, and in the hospital after the suicide attempt they said, 'Maybe you should look into what your father did during the war.' So she looked in the archives and found he had been a mass murderer. Had she somehow known the truth by osmosis? She also uncovered childhood memories of abuse at his hands.

In the room with us was a young man, Alan, who realized that his father's family had been killed by Helga's father. It was earth shattering. Alan said, 'What do I do with her, she's not the one, but her father is.' He couldn't blame her, and he knew that her family had disowned her because she was meeting with us. Alan and Helga hugged and she said to him, 'I have lost a family but I have found a brother.' Alan told her 'You're such a strong inspiration for me and when I look in your eyes I don't see a perpetrator, I see a victim who longs to know the truth. To think that the daughter of my enemy can be my friend is overwhelming.'

Helga is one of the brave people in Germany who bears witness to the realities of the Holocaust and to what her father did. She speaks everywhere. Many Germans don't dare to ask what their family members did during the Nazi times and they have kept things locked up inside. Through our work we have found that when the truth is released we find not only pain but creativity, the ability to speak, write, create and help others.

And so after four days of listening to and telling the untold stories of the Holocaust and the culture of Nazism, and feeling heard, we saw this release start to happen and we felt we had taken our heaviest burdens off our shoulders. Those people did more for me, and I assume we did for them, than years of therapy because they validated our experience. The Germans' apologies set us free: 'I'm so sorry for what my people did to your people' were words that unlocked the vaults of pain for those on the side of the victims. The victims' words 'You are not responsible for what our parents did, only for what you do' unfastened the shackles of those on the perpetrators' side. We experienced a transformation both individually and collectively. And, it was Otto, the one I had feared most, who kissed my forehead and gave me his heartfelt apologies when my turn came to share the tragedies of my family. His sincerity released something in me that had been held shut for a lifetime.

Dr. Viktor Frankl, psychiatrist and author, who had been in Dachau concentration camp with my father, taught me that by giving meaning to suffering, one can change the entire picture. This is one of my favorite quotes from his book *Man's Search for Meaning*.

We must never forget that we may also find meaning in life even when confronted with a hopeless situation, when facing a fate that cannot be changed. For what then matters is to bear witness to the uniquely human potential at its best, which is to transform a personal tragedy into a triumph, to turn one's predicament into a human achievement. When we are no longer able to change a situation...we are challenged to change ourselves.

I gave meaning to my suffering by dedicating myself to making the experience we shared in Germany exist for others. This first meeting had been just a research project for someone else, but I decided this was too important, too sacred, to leave there. Together we created One By One, a nonprofit organization in the U.S. with a chapter in Germany. It was named after Judith Miller's book *One, by One, by One: Facing the Holocaust* in which she tells us that abstraction encourages distance and often indifference. She says 'The Holocaust was not six million. It was one, plus one, plus one.' I had a vision of people joining slowly, one by one, and what they say when they join is: 'I want to live in integrity, I want to share my story and listen to other stories and together we'll help each other transform.' Our task, in part, is to help one another free ourselves of the crippling effects of trauma and interrupt its transfer to the next generation. We use the Dialogue Group as our primary tool and honest, authentic meetings with 'the other side' as an opportunity for transformation.

We have speakers – artists, musicians, writers – who go to schools, community centers, colleges, in the U.S. and in Europe. Those from the perpetrators' side and those from the victims' side stand together, bringing hope and saying, 'Here we are, this is our story. It doesn't have to stay in the darkness, it can be transformed.' We have traveled to Bosnia and were told that great breakthroughs occurred after we spoke. We are joining with people in Poland, Italy and with others who want to work for peace through dialogue. Let's hope that we can, along with the many other groups and individuals that are on this earth, bring ripples of transformation for a planet deeply in need of healing.

I was often taught that things are black or white – that there is right/wrong, perpetrator/victim. I've discovered that this is not true. It's amazing how the perceived dichotomy becomes less pronounced and liberation is found in meeting with 'the enemy' when armed with a desire to understand rather than to seek revenge – if the enemy meets us half way. Restorative justice in Judaism requires that the wrongdoer have a change of heart, acknowledge the truth, approach the victim with a desire to make amends and promise never to do again what was done. Reaching out to the external enemy allows us to befriend the enemy aspects of ourselves that we have put into a dark recess of our psyche. We will see what we need for healing in the other, in the opposite, *if* the encounter is honest, and have the opportunity to become more whole. Let me read from our book, *Journeys of Transformation*,[26] because it will explain the process further.

> *We often see our dialogue process metaphorically as a suspension bridge spanning two sides of a deep chasm. Group members step onto the bridge from opposite sides, each deciding how far they want to approach the person coming toward them. They choose the distance they need between them; if they want they can meet in the middle of the bridge. For the descendants of survivors the chasm is filled with the persecuted, mur-*

dered relatives and memories of their ancestors. While listening to the stories of the other side they may also be hearing an admonition: 'Don't trust the Germans. You are the guardian of our memories. Truth and justice must be served.' For the descendants of the perpetrators, the gulf is filled with national and individual shame, guilt and denial. They may hear the warning: 'Do not be disloyal. Stay with us in our silence. You don't understand what it was like.' With each step the descendants of survivors struggle with feelings of profound grief, anger and fear. The descendants of perpetrators struggle with fear of revenge, with the shame of being German; torn between love and hatred toward the people from whom they come. All these warnings and emotions must be acknowledged, understood, and accepted if members are to meet on the bridge...

Dialogue should not be confounded with forgiveness, the seeking of harmony, or building consensus. Nor is there ever the intention of comparing suffering. Listening to the other side does not mean to cover or blur the difference between the two groups or to eliminate what separates them. For the descendants of the perpetrators in particular, listening to the story of someone from the survivors' side is an attempt to repair the threads of our common humanity that Nazi Germany sought to irrevocably break.

More often than not, however, the gap between the two groups seems to close. When we listen to one another we begin to understand the complexities of our individual lives as opposed to seeing each other as a symbol of a group or nation...Listening connects us...the other's story can become our story, too. We suddenly realize that we could easily have experienced what he or she did if we were born in the other's place. Partners in real dialogue get a glimpse of what Martin Buber calls 'the essential We.'

I believe that part of what happens in One By One is that the anxiety about going to meet with people from the other side brings the person into contact with parts of the self that can be accessed and healed. Meeting with the other side offers a highly charged environment where something can be changed which can't be done when one is alone, meeting with a homogeneous group or with a therapist. People report the healing of things they never thought could be accessed, let alone healed. So there is hope for anyone.

We are often asked if we have forgiven the perpetrators, and we have difficulty with the word forgiveness because it has been interpreted in so many ways. I'll read what Wilma Busse, one of our founding members, says about forgiveness in our book:

In general we feel it is not in our power to forgive on the part of our parents. However, individuals, especially Christian descendants, who view forgiveness as a necessary part of healing, may enter the path of forgiveness to achieve peace in their lives. The notion of forgiveness, however, does not mean to

> *excuse or forget but rather to understand the enemy and move beyond the clutches of revenge and closed-mindedness.*

Sometimes I have thought that my life was meaningless but I have found strength in the Judaic teachings, which tell us that we do have a mission. We're here for a purpose: to bring the broken pieces of light together so we can bring the Big Light once again. If everyone looked for a little bit of light in themselves and others and brought it together in compassionate social action we would soon transform and move beyond the difficult legacies of our past. We call this path 'Tikun Olam'.

Both Rosalie's One By One group and the Gandhis gained compassion, humility, and personal enrichment by actively entering the world of the "untouchables." By opening to hear the stories and feel the suffering of "the enemy", a deeper understanding was gained that dissolved boundaries and labels and highlighted their shared humanity. Ego, personal position, and opinion were put totally aside in order to fully empathize with the other. When this occurs, duality disappears. As Rumi said "the phrase *each other* doesn't make sense any more" and the truism that no one can become fully whole until we are all healed begins to make sense. This unity (which is none other than love) lies between right and wrong, good and bad, and is experienced only when the critical judge is silenced.

The question for me is: do we want to reach this place within ourselves, or is there an unconscious attachment to the concept of "enemies" so that we can keep our own inner enemies from seeing the light of day? We cannot make friends with our external enemies without the inner shift of making friends with our own shadows – and that takes courage. And how do we do that but by truly accepting ourselves, warts and all.

A few months after doing this interview I was invited to breakfast at the house of a dear elder friend of mine, Bina, in the picturesque English village of Dartington. I knew she had a guest staying from Germany who spoke little English. A distinguished looking, gentle-faced man with a white beard like Santa, sat opposite me, twinkling instead of speaking as we drank our tea. His name was Otto. Yes, the same Otto who had stabbed a woman in Rosalie's dream and been a member of Hitler's Youth and the SS! Over that table something happened in me. It was as if, by synchronistic miracle, Otto had been placed before me as a living symbol of wholeness. There, sipping tea and looking at his shining face, allies and enemies merged for me. I was reminded of the Taoist yin/yang symbol with the seed of white in the black and black in the white, and in that moment I gained a deeper realization of my own potential to act out of love or fear. Consequently my critical attitude to my own imperfections began to soften a little and I kept telling myself: I am what I am, and I'm being the best that I can be.

This was sorely tested the following Christmas when I met one of my inner enemies head on at a games party I had arranged at my home. There were children and adults and I had lots of games up my sleeve that I expected to cause much laughter and frivolity. From the first game things did not go according to plan and it felt to me as if everything was going wrong. A man who I had not specifically invited, accompanied a friend of mine. He was in high spirits, which he was expressing by making sexual innuendoes, trying to toss the ball we were playing with down women's tops and suggesting games of strip poker and the like. I had invited two people I had recently met to this party to meet my friends (of whom I'd been speaking very highly) and I was excruciatingly embarrassed by the tone of these happenings. I urgently wanted to make things better and attempted to deal with the situation appropriately by telling the group how uncomfortable I felt, especially with the children present, requesting a change in the focus. Every new game we tried flopped into the atmosphere of unspoken blame and guilt and the party was as flat as a pancake. Finally, given time, it lifted and I laughed hysterically – but for a week or more I cringed with horror at the thought of the first half of that party.

This might seem like a very mundane story following the intensity of the Holocaust, but isn't it often within the ordinary domestic scene that the most insidious enemies show up? My initial reaction was classic. I made the uninvited guest my enemy. I could not see beyond blaming him for destroying my party. He was the culprit and needed to learn a lesson. And, of course, I carried immense dis-ease in this place of inner war and felt off-center and wobbly.

Then I remembered Otto, silenced my critical voice, and began looking for the gift this man brought me that day – the seed of light within the dark. Pandora's box opened with this inquiry, and I realized that, not only have I attempted to hide my physical imperfections all of my life, but also I have been busy trying to hide *everything* about myself that I consider to be unacceptable, because then I'll be safe from disapproval. I have created a wise persona, and a reputation for creating inspirational events, which I needed to maintain to feel good about myself. In my perception, at the party the man's behavior had exposed me as a flustered, red-faced, irritable prude, holding a flop of an event that was supposed to be funny.

But when I dared to open Pandora's box, by looking inwards instead of pointing my finger outwards, I discovered that fully experiencing how it felt to be witnessed in my "weakness" was actually a godsend. My attitude to my guest turned to gratitude for my revelations, although I did not condone his behavior. I could tell that I had finally accepted him because the dis-ease within me had passed. Now I could see how I had been at war with myself, splitting my behavior into "good" and "bad" and presenting only half of my story – just as those German people who have hidden their shame. The energy taken to disguise my shadow has been freed a little more, and I am much more patient and compassionate with who I am – a multifaceted human being who's still learning.

This section has included much about the inner enemy, but what has not been addressed is the archetype of evil. Does such a thing exist that is perhaps the opposite of the archetype of love and if so how does that relate to our shadow selves? After the terrorists attacks of September 11, I conducted a short interview with a Jungian Analyst, Rosalind Winter, most of which is included in the final section, Gathering the Keys from the Ashes of 9/11. Part of that interview I'll include here as it relates directly to the topic of evil.

I worry about the popular view that if we each own our own shadow, evil will be eradicated. It isn't that easy. There is absolute evil. Evil is an archetypal energy. The potential for it exists in the human psyche. And we need to be very careful not to minimize it or put it into a feel good, human potential framework. Let me attempt to explain. Yes, we all project our own rejected aspects or qualities onto other people and then we assume they have them. That's a version of scapegoating, and is core to racism and discrimination of all types. Of course our personal psychological work is to re-collect our projections. But that will not solve the problem of the human potential for evil.

Absolute evil gets expressed through individuals. It's like the difference between what happens in a one-on-one interaction and what happens in a mob. In an individual encounter a person more or less can use his/her ego to relate to the situation. In a mob situation, the individual's ego consciousness is reduced, and they become more vulnerable to archetypal energies. This is part of the nature of the human psyche. Ego consciousness needs to be strong, flexible and resilient if it is to mediate the archetypal energy of absolute evil. As we can see from our collective expressions of evil, it is a fascinating force – just as attractive as the force of good. We need to be conscious of our own pull to the awesome attraction of evil. *And* we need to look at a much bigger picture than that.

We can't mediate the archetypal level unless we have human consciousness. There are two layers of the psyche we need to look at. On the most personal level we have the projection of the shadow onto the other. We need to be aware of our emotions, traits, or methods of defending against vulnerability that we are uncomfortable with and project onto someone else. For example, when we feel vulnerable, how do we protect ourselves? Do we attack, and then do we complain that others attack? In this example we blame others for our own defense behavior. As we mature and get more whole ourselves, we have the capacity to integrate this personal shadow. And to some degree this will make us less likely to enact absolute evil. But there is still the reality of an archetypal absolute evil that is not personal, though our personal circumstances make us more vulnerable to being taken over by it. Absolute evil takes incredibly consistent, ongoing mediation by people with strong egos who have the capacity to reflect on and relate to archetypal energies.

We need to be preventative. For instance, because of some negative experiences with gay Boy Scout leaders, rules were made that prohibited homosexuals from serving as scout leaders. This edict was presented as a method of protecting our children. But, behind the surface of this need to protect children hid the deep instinct to 'annihilate differences,' which is very dangerous. There was a huge uproar in this town because of the deeper issue, but had the parents just been interested in the safety of their children and nothing else, they would have supported the edict. Just fill in the blank, 'In the name of protection we…' It is common and easy to fall unconsciously into projection of the shadow. We don't typically realize we are even doing it. This behavior is both a projection of our personal shadow and a projection of the collective shadow, yet it holds an archetypal energy of safety and survival.

Our psyches are imprinted with various patterns based on instincts, as if they are genetically encoded. They are a substratum in the psyche from which our minds evolve, and these are connected to various energies or drives. They are in all of us, not just in those who had a certain kind of parenting. The archetypal instinct to annihilate I would call evil, whether it's directed against oneself or another. Some call it the death instinct. The collective connects to it, and we individually participate in it. Someone like a Hitler can tap into it.

I would put evil as the opposite to love. Evil involves the misuse of power. It is our ego relationship to all these different pieces of the archetypal realm that helps make up who we are as individuals. Whether we fall into love or evil is in part based on our capacity to integrate our personal shadows and our ego strength to mediate archetypal evil. We, as a collective, need the capacity to be conscious of archetypal evil and relate to it so that we don't become consumed by it in a mob psychology where we unconsciously join the collective.

To complete this theme I'll end with some words from a writer and poet, Mark Nepo, who has been a valuable support to me during the process of writing this book. Each week he sends by email, to me and many others, a carefully chosen page of wisdom from his daybook, *The Book of Awakening*.[27] This one, on how patience promotes compassion for our "enemies", arrived as if on cue.

Fear wants us to act too soon. But patience, which is different from avoiding what needs to be done, helps us outlast our preconceptions. This is how tired soldiers, all out of ammo, can discover, through their inescapable waiting, that they have no reason to hurt each other.

It is the same with tired lovers, and with hurtful and tiresome friends. Given enough time, most of our enemies cease to be enemies, because waiting allows us to see ourselves in them. Patience devastates us with the truth that, in essence, when we fear another, we fear ourselves; when we distrust another, we distrust ourselves; when we hurt another, we hurt ourselves; when we kill another, we kill ourselves.

So, when hurt or afraid or confused, when feeling urgent to find your place on this earth, hard as it is, wait...

and things as you fear them will, more often than not, shrink into the hard irreplaceable beauty of things as they are... of which you have no choice but to be a part.

CULTIVATE COMPASSION: SILENCE THE JUDGE
Questions and Reflections

1. Who do you blame and criticize the most? What kind of things do you say, do or think?

2. After reading this section, assuming you don't have to condone the behavior you dislike, how close do you feel to listening to and seeking to understand the story of the one you criticize?

3. Think of the last time you were in the company of someone who was behaving unacceptably to you. Imagine yourself in his/her shoes for a moment. What do you think was his or her unanswered need?

4. Write down or share with another "My understanding of forgiveness is…"

5. Are there any places of hatred you carry in your heart that you are willing to drop and forgive in the knowledge that if you don't it will affect your life forever?

6. Think of a specific quality that you hate to see in others. Can you think of a time when you exhibited this quality? What does that tell you?

7. What stimulates your compassion? How does compassion feel in your body and how do you express it?

8. Name one thing that would cultivate more compassion in you for others and one way you could be more compassionate toward yourself.

9. Sit silently and non-actively for 3 minutes observing your mental and bodily responses. What was that like? Recall a time when you waited before responding to a challenge. What effect did exercising patience have on this situation?

10. What learning from this section on cultivating compassion and silencing the judge do you foresee being of particular use to you in your life?

The Seventh Key

RECLAIM YOUR HEART AND SPIRIT

I make myself rich by making my wants few.
Thoreau

Reclaim Your Heart and Spirit

We live in a society where consumerism is the name of the game. The size of our bank balance, the level of our IQ, and where we stand on the career ladder are paramount. Reason and logic are deified in this drive for material success, leaving our hearts, spirits and emotional lives to fight for space on the back seat. Do we need something dramatic to occur before we re-order our priorities to allow our hearts and spirits more of a window on the world?

In his interview Arun Gandhi said on this topic:

> We have become so involved in our pursuits of materialism and greed that we will do almost anything for monetary gain. We've got to reverse this trend and put back morals and ethics as things that we value highly. Grandfather said, 'Materialism and morality have an inverse relationship. When one increases the other decreases.' We are going to see more violence occur unless the rich decide they want to share their wealth and technology with the rest of the world. Perhaps that step will take a big catastrophe because, unfortunately, people usually don't learn through the experience of others.

Since he said this, a catastrophe has occurred: the attack on America's largest symbols of power. A salutary lesson – perhaps.

Severe adversity certainly does have the knack of purging the unnecessary things of life by questioning what really matters. And if status, reputation, possessions and money were high on our list before the challenge hit, we may find ourselves struggling to find resources and strength in the foundations of who we are. The seventh key to handling adversity is to begin to discover the power of our inner world – to find out who we are behind what we do and what we have, behind our habitual selves. It is about reinforcing our hearts and spirits and making a shift toward consulting the heart as well as the head, and toward valuing emotional and spiritual intelligence.

There is an abundance of material now being published about heart and spirituality. Not only is emotional intelligence (EQ – the awareness of our own and other people's feelings) now being more widely valued and understood, but also spiritual intelligence is emerging as one of the important human competencies. Danah Zohar and Ian Marshall have co-written a controversial book called *Spiritual Intelligence*[28] that draws together evidence for this "ultimate intelligence" based on a third neural system in the brain. According to Zohar and Marshall, Spiritual Intelligence (SQ) is the intelligence with which we address and solve problems of meaning and value, the intelligence with which we can place our actions and our lives in a wider, richer, meaning-giving context. It is the intelligence that naturally raises its head in crisis asking, "What is the purpose of this mess, of life itself? Why should I go on? What makes life worthwhile? Is there a God?"

This does not mean we need to become religious – many atheists have a high SQ. Most large bookstores have an ever-growing section on Spirituality in addition to the Religion section, saying clearly that you are now not expected to be religious to be spiritual. Author Rachel Naomi Remen says of this, "Religion is a bridge to the spiritual – but the spiritual lies beyond religion. Unfortunately in seeking the spiritual we may become attached to the bridge rather than crossing over it."

She also says, "Spirit is an essential need of human nature." In 1999 a Gallup poll made the encouraging discovery that 82% of people surveyed in the U.S. felt that spirituality and religion were an important part of their lives; and since Sept 11, 2001 these percentages have no doubt risen. Seeking for something deeper than the materialist viewpoint and lifestyle is becoming widely acceptable, if not fashionable – a change that may well have been assisted by the scientists and mystics beginning to agree on the existence of spirit.

At the tail end of his interview, Rick Curwin said:

> You know, maybe life's journey is a series of discoveries of what really matters... Perhaps the need for things blinds us to the true spiritual path of life's deep secrets.

The first story is one where the process of this discovery is unveiled.

Bonnie Kane's Story – The Missing Spirit

Bonnie grew up in the sixties in a small town in Pennsylvania where she led a somewhat sheltered childhood. She told me she has fond memories of hiking and exploring with the few other children who lived nearby. However, things were not as peaceful at home. Her parents married young, and neither of them had seen much of the world before buying a home, settling down and having Bonnie and her younger sister.

Her father suffered from severe depression and drank to ease the pain. "There were two distinct sides to him," said Bonnie "one was charismatic, loving and warm, and the other was dark, moody and angry." She described her father as a reclusive nature-lover, who spent most of the time he wasn't working, out in the sanctuary of the yard or garden. Bonnie's family found it a chore getting him to go anywhere, and most outings and vacations were spent without him. Sometimes he would explode and become verbally abusive. "I was very frightened" confessed Bonnie "and always felt something bad was going to happen."

One night Bonnie's father went out, and very late that night the family got a call that he had been in an accident. His car had been run off the road and had rolled several times down a hill. He was in a critical condition in the hospital, where he remained for a month. He was given the option of surgery but there was the chance of paralysis and he wasn't willing to risk it. So he was in constant pain and no longer able to enjoy the things that made him happy. "His depression worsened" said Bonnie "and the three of us escaped, doing anything to get away from the weighty atmosphere that pervaded our home."

Three years after the accident it was Christmas time and her dad was in even more pain because the weather had been cold and damp for weeks. Bonnie takes up the story.

> It was so scary. He would moan and cry at night and my mother would try and get him to be quiet, but he couldn't help himself. On New Year's Eve my sister and I spent the night at our friend's house, and the next morning my mother called and told us not to come home for a while. It was a very unusual request. After a few hours we decided to head home.
>
> My aunt's van was parked outside and I was excited that she had come for a visit. We ran inside but her face was very serious. My mother took us upstairs and told us that my father had shot himself. She had been downstairs doing laundry and he had called out her name. She went up and found him. He was still alive but would only live for a few more hours. We weren't allowed to see him.
>
> I'm pretty sure I went into denial at the moment my mother told me, beginning with thinking that it wasn't true and yes he was going to make it. My sister began crying and feeling immediately but I went numb and stayed that way for years. I became instantly parentified and took on the role of taking care of my mother and sister. Things got very chaotic from then on.
>
> Mom kind of lost it for a while and made a lot of bad decisions. We didn't go to therapy and we never talked about my dad because suicide was unspeakable in the early seventies. She got rid of all of his things except his wedding ring and his wallet, which we all regretted later. We told people he died in a car accident because it was easier. My mother wanted to move right away, and we moved and moved and moved. I went to four high schools and felt like I was raising myself. My mother offered her friendship and that helped a lot, but I needed a parent. I got very tough and switched into overachiever mode to prove to the world that this wasn't going to get me down. I got so tired of the looks of pity that I became determined to show them all. I enrolled myself in college, took out student loans, and drove myself hard. I had a sales job before I graduated and fell into the yuppie scene.
>
> At the end of the eighties I was 30 years old and I felt proud to have everything I wanted – a 'Fortune 500' job, a beautiful condo, a shiny new Volvo, and a husband who adored me. Things were good but something

wasn't right. I was having chest pains and a gnawing feeling of unhappiness like a dull ache that never went away. I had become something I wasn't, and I wanted more.

After my wedding, which I had choreographed like an MGM movie, my 'perfect' husband and I settled into marriage. But almost immediately things were bad. He had taken a job that wasn't working out and he was angry. He realized that this life we had created was making both of us miserable and so he started to see a therapist. He was dealing with a lot of childhood pain and identity issues, and became both extremely abusive and more distant towards me. He was acting like someone I didn't recognize and I felt scared. I began seeing a therapist myself, unaware that I had any real issues to deal with, but I thought it might help the relationship. Things got worse. We were fighting horribly, he was staying out all night and I was feeling like I was part of a bad dream. I was trying to pretend everything was okay, but it was really bad.

Four days before our second anniversary we were on our way to a party and we stopped for a drink. He had been drinking for several hours and was wasted. I looked him squarely in the face and he looked distorted and crazed. My whole body became flooded with the realization that he was doing drugs. I had partied through high school but after that I was strictly a drinker. For me taking drugs was the unspeakable and he knew it. When I confronted him he denied it but as the night progressed the truth came out that he had been seriously involved with cocaine for at least a year. He was selling it and spending a lot of money on the habit. Everything started to add up – his weird behavior, the times I would hug him and feel his heart pounding extra hard, why we were having money problems. And everyone knew but me. EVERYONE. I felt so foolish, so betrayed. At first I thought I could handle it, but after a few days my pain intensified and I asked him to leave because I didn't trust myself in his presence.

He tried to come back but I stood firm and we didn't talk for a month. In the meantime some very bizarre things happened to me. Okay, your husband lies, happens every day and people move on, right? I was not doing well. Physically my chest was hurting so bad I felt like I was having a constant heart attack. I cried buckets and buckets. The excruciating pain was 20 years worth of unresolved grief. My dad stuff had never been dealt with and I had held a lot of it in my body. I couldn't sleep or eat, and got very thin.

One morning, after a series of fitful nights, I woke up to the strangest sight. The sun was intensely bright and was shining in through my blinds. I looked at the light and felt soothed. As I looked closer I saw that the light was in the distinct shape of a cross. I had been very involved in the church as a youngster but had virtually nothing to do with anything religious or spiritual since my father died. I kept looking at this gleaming, shimmering cross in the middle of my dark blinds and I felt like I was hallucinating.

I realized that I was missing spirit and God in my life, but even bigger than that was a complete understanding of the universe as one, and that the sole purpose for being on earth was to love. I was in some sort of flow with a higher power where I was receiving all kinds of knowledge that I had never even dreamed of thinking about prior to that moment. I remember seeing colors, things were brighter, and from that point forward everything looked different. I had 'woken up.' I had not asked for this. God was the furthest thing from my mind, but when I finally began to 'get it' I was thinking, 'How could I have missed this? It's so obvious!' I was being shown that I was not being true to myself and that we are all here to fulfill our destiny, not to keep up with the status quo.

I got out of bed that morning and ran into my office to look for who knows what. I opened a drawer and there was my grandfather's Bible, which was weird because I don't remember putting it there. I opened it randomly to a page with highlights on it and took it as a message for me.

It was about remembering to live spiritually and not letting ungodly things become a priority. Things began making sense and I felt that through these sorts of events God was communicating with me. I called a friend and began talking non-stop about all of this. He was scared and thought I was losing my mind but then started really listening and was deeply moved. We talked for three hours. It *was* real. I *was* changing, and people were sort of scared but happy for me at the same time.

For the next month I lived each day through things that skeptics might call coincidence, but c'mon, how many synchronistic events can happen to one person? Synchronicities began appearing in my life with such a regularity that I couldn't help but wonder if they had always been there and I just hadn't noticed them. Noticing them and then acting on them seemed to be the next step.

I was in Florida, on a family trip, and I realized I had made a HUGE mistake in going there. There was no one I could talk to, and I was starting to feel rage at all of my family for what I had figured out to be a lot of emotional abuse. I literally felt like I was going crazy. I went for a fast walk and I prayed from the depths of my being, 'God I need someone to talk to or I am gong to lose my mind. Give me someone sane who gets it.' I passed a guy talking on the phone and continued by him, and then much later I saw him again. Still not getting it I criss-crossed in another direction, and up the street he came again. Finally we just stopped and I said, 'Am I supposed to talk to you?' and he said, 'I think so.' We probably stood there about an hour while I told him my entire story. He was a wonderful help and assured me that I was on the right path and that things would get better. I remember walking away saying, 'Thanks God, that helped so much.'

I started really grieving my dad. One night I lay on a bench all night long feeling the agony of my dad's pain, and then had a lot more compassion for him. I woke up my mom that morning and made her watch the sunrise with me while I tried to explain what was happening. I also had the realization that what I needed to do with my life was to become a psychologist. I started studying Buddhism, astrology, and reading a host of other subjects I had previously not been interested in.

Every day the message SLOW DOWN would make itself evident. For example: I drove up to a drive-through window to get something to eat. It worked for the person before me and after me but not for me. I realized I needed to go in, sit down and have some breakfast. It may seem silly, but at that time I was living life in a frenetic, out-of-my-body sort of way. I began to walk slower, to eat slower, and be present. At a more relaxed, present pace I began to notice things, like people's expressions, and nature, and I also remember being really in tune with everyone. I think I was radiating love because people were smiling back at me. But people's facial expressions weren't always good. One day my boss was telling a "racial joke" and as I watched him, his face took on the image of some sort of monster, like a scary mask.

I want to stress that this 'new reality' was a far cry from the way I had been living my life. That year I gave all of my Christmas presents away and didn't go to Christmas dinner with my family. I went to Longwood Gardens to smell the flowers and then I visited my father's grave, which I never went to, and cried for hours. This would have seemed high drama to the person I was before, but I was healing and this was part of the process.

Another realization I had was that the further off your track you are – meaning the further you are away from your true self – the harder the blow or shock has to come to knock you back into what is real. I truly felt as if a train had hit me, mentally and physically. At one point I went for a couple's counseling session with my husband and I felt so nervous and estranged from him. I didn't know how on earth I was going to explain what I had been through. I prayed for help. When we sat down I just opened my mouth and truly cannot remember what I said or for how long I spoke, but when I finished, the therapist was crying. He said, 'You should be a therapist' and I said, 'I know.'

It did not work out with my husband. I moved to a new town and made a new life. I met a man who I knew I could trust, and after telling him my whole story I realized by his response that he had totally understood. I married him!

I could see by now how unimportant material things are, especially when we are surrounded by suffering and the world's destruction. And so I chose to focus on helping individuals who haven't dealt with all of their pain and family issues – people who are in the same state I had been in. I began a Masters program in clinical psychology, and will soon open my own practice. I am currently finishing my dissertation, focusing on survivors of suicide and spiritual emergence.

The change in me is profound. I feel free. I talk about my dad a lot and I still feel shame and guilt, but it's getting better. I do find it difficult to live life in the world while maintaining a spiritual path and a relationship with God, but I will never fall asleep again like I was before. Walking the 'road less traveled' is work, and unless you go at it hard it's easy to stray. My husband works hard with me at keeping it real. Our daughter is my prize. She has opened my heart and shown me immense love. For her, and for all of the things that have happened to me along the way, ugly and discordant as some of them were, I am incredibly grateful.

Dissociation is a defense mechanism that we learn in order to prevent pain. By turning our attention away from a threat, not being fully present to all that we are, we avoid having to deal with a difficult reality. Making materialism all important is a dissociative technique to escape internal feelings. Bonnie's 20-year chase after material security succeeded in numbing the pain of her father's suicide, but she paid the price, being blinded to spirit and to her soul purpose, which she describes as being "to love." Like millions of others, Bonnie thought that she could prove her worth by driving herself hard, obtaining a well paid job and buying happiness through her condo, her shiny new car and the like. Wealth became an addiction – a love substitute that didn't work, because she realized she had become something she was not.

Consumerism is catching and extremely alluring. Stepping out of the status quo is a struggle to say the least. Christmas, for those of us who celebrate it, personifies this issue. How many of us vow each year not to get caught in the madness of Christmas consumerism? But do we manage to actualize that intent, as Bonnie did after her epiphany experience?

Speed and materialism tend to go hand in hand. One of Bonnie's most powerful messages was to slow down. Wayne Muller says in his powerful book, *Sabbath*[29]:

> *In the relentless busyness of modern life, we have lost the rhythm between work and rest…Even when our intentions are noble and our efforts sincere – even when we dedicate our lives to the service of others – the corrosive pressure of frantic activity can cause suffering in ourselves and others…It becomes the standard greeting everywhere: I am so busy.*

I don't know who first coined the phrase "human doing" but I certainly think it is a better description of us as a species than "human being" –

although not a good affirmation. But the good news is that when we stop to rest in the wealth of our own inner being and exude love like Bonnie came to do, that is also catching. People drink in being-ness like travelers in the desert – that is if they can slow down enough to notice the oasis. When we are in emotional pain, the moment that we stop doing anything and just allow ourselves to be with the present, is the moment that the release, processing and integration of the pain can begin to naturally unfold.

Eileen Rockefeller-Growald's Story – A Moonlit Night or a Thousand Dollar Dress

It is my impression that the market wants high impact, concisely packaged stories to fit the quick fix, fast-paced lifestyle of our times. However, the very point of this section is that in order to experience less pain in our lives we need to release our need for such high level stimulation and reclaim the often more gentle note of heart and spirit. The subject of overcoming adversity is likely on the whole to be dramatic, but sometimes wounding is insidious and has built up slowly in the course of living. Also, the more sensitive souls among us will sustain greater hurts than those with a harder shell. Eileen's story is the most gentle one in this book but nonetheless powerful if we are able to slow our pace and open to the gentle wisdom offered.

My first impression on meeting this extraordinary woman was that she is full of heart, generous, open and unassuming. Eileen's story shows her struggle to find her self-worth and to bring the inner wealth of her sensitivity and heart together with her affluent outer life. And her family's history in relation to finance shows how it is perfectly possible to have both morality and money.

Eileen was born in New York City in February 1952. She is the youngest of six children in the prominent Rockefeller family, her name and family riches creating goldfish bowl attention. As she was growing up, her father, David Rockefeller, grandson of John D. Rockefeller who made the money, was finding his way in international circles and coming to the peak of his career. Her father, still healthy and active, is in his eighties and her mother has passed away.

The feeling was that my mother owned everything that was living and my father owned the inanimate things. She owned the relationships; her husband, the children, and the employees, and center stage. My childhood was spent giving her and my father the center stage attention that they needed. I once did a visualization in which I found a silver flashlight, took it apart and realized that the two half empty batteries represented my mother and my father, each half dead in their spirit. But I was expected to shine my light on them, even though they were giving so little energy to me. It was a powerful image.

Eileen's mother had been clinically depressed since before Eileen was born and Eileen felt she needed to be her caretaker in order to survive. She developed highly tuned antennae to read her moods.

> One night when I was about eight, my mother was practicing the piano and I couldn't sleep because I felt empty inside. To help myself I turned my own needs inside out. I went downstairs, knowing she'd been depressed, and said, 'I think you're a wonderful mother and I love you.' It wasn't true in that moment but it was what she wanted to hear and I got what I needed – she melted and I could see her heart. She told me she loved me too and gave me a hug, which helped me to go to sleep. That powerful moment encapsulates my co-dependent relationship with my mother, in which I was too dependent on her and terrified to be myself. I didn't even dare go off and read a book in case I was needed. I had to be alert because there might be a calling.
>
> For a year or two I was the only child living at home, and when my mother got over-tired, which happened fairly often because of all her responsibilities, she could get in very unpleasant black moods. My parents were terribly close but I felt the need to act as a bridge between them, continually injecting the love I needed myself.
>
> My father was always very loving and would sometimes invite me on his lap like a normal father, but he wasn't present often so I didn't have much of a relationship with him at that time. He took on the expectations and responsibilities that were laid on his shoulders with a full heart. My mother, however, was terrified she would never be good enough, and this haunted her, despite excelling in everything she did. She didn't want anyone to know the truth about how afraid she was of not being smart enough, educated enough, and not coming from a similar class as my father. For me the truth is everything, and because she was so uncomfortable with truth, that made our relationship both complicated and painful.
>
> Relationships with my siblings are good now, but in childhood I didn't feel safe with most of them. When my oldest brother, who I had an affinity with, wasn't around I felt very threatened. The other siblings teased me a great deal, and I had a face that showed everything. This incessant teasing had a serious impact on me because I was born so very sensitive. I now see my sensitivity as one of my great strengths, connected to my intuition and openheartedness, but as a child I was criticized for it because it made life difficult for others. I was moody and would fall into deep periods of self-doubt and questioning.
>
> It was very painful to be so excluded. My siblings couldn't get the

attention they needed from our parents who were so busy with the responsibilities of a prominent family, and I think they took that out on me as the smallest one. I felt unwanted and in the way, and like I'd come into the wrong family. They didn't want me there but they couldn't get rid of me, and it made them even madder when I took the role of caregiver. So they tried to push me down and undermined everything I thought I could do. Pretty soon I took on the mantra, 'I can't.'

Going to school was a trauma and I was very frightened. I was unable to think because I believed what my siblings had told me about being stupid. I would be so busy tuning in to what mood the teacher and the kids were in, and what cliques had formed overnight, that by the time I had figured out enough to feel safe to listen, I'd missed half the class. Then, if I did ask a question, I'd discover to my mortification that somebody had just answered that question and I'd engender more ridicule. So I was failing in most of my subjects by the time I was eleven and I'd already tried two of the best schools in New York City.

My father wasn't around enough to understand what was happening, so he was horrified, which led to my ultimate disappointment in myself. It was my mother who had the wisdom and courage to send me to a wonderful boarding school on a farm. North Country School was a community where they taught that it doesn't matter where you begin; just begin. So I began again and at last found hope and the beginnings of belief in myself.

The teachers were very loving and the founder was the father I had not had. He and his wife were there every day. I lived in their house with seven other boys and girls and we romped and studied together. With only 65 children in the school, everybody was part of the community. I made friends, was given multiple opportunities to shine, did farm chores with everyone else and began to feel like a normal human being for the first time in my life.

Though I was only at this school for two years, the success I was able to achieve helped me realize I had something to offer in life. I was devastated to have to graduate after such a short time but as I grew older I saw that it is the quality not the quantity of time that matters. And I saw that this same philosophy could be applied to money too. It is not important whether you have the most amount of money; it's what you do with it or how you live your life that really counts. Although I haven't lived my life on food stamps, and can't say what that's like, I could have spent a lot more. For me, a moonlit night or the smell of fresh grass holds a lot more pleasure than going out and buying a thousand dollar dress.

My mother taught us that it was very important to never act different from other people. We were never to show off we were rich or to make other people feel uncomfortable. By the same token, there was a conflicting message from my father that we really are different and we owe the world a great deal because we've been so fortunate. I felt most comfortable in my old blue jeans and would take particular pride when they got holes in them. I liked it when my car looked dirty. It was reverse snobbism in a way, but I so wanted to be like everybody else, and to be accepted. In college I made sure I had the same amount of money in my bank account as the average person. Then I could tell them, in false honesty, that I had no more money this month. Sure I was Eileen Rockefeller, but a lot of children from wealthy families don't get a lot of money from their families. However, I knew I would come into an inheritance at twenty-one. What I was going to do with it was still to be discovered. In looking back, I see that the groundwork had been laid for turning my wounds into healing for myself and others.

Eileen was moving toward her important work in the field of social and emotional learning, but first she had to learn to give and receive love in a more healthy way. In 1983 she began the Institute for the Advancement of Health (IAH) to further scientific understanding of mind/body interactions in health and disease, which did impact on the acceptance of mind/body practices in mainstream medicine, but Eileen was still exhibiting her co-dependent pattern. The dynamics of the Institute became as dysfunctional as her early family life, and after giving birth to two children in addition to her work, Eileen burnt out, becoming very ill. She moved the Institute on to other hands and became a full-time mother. Eileen knew that her survival and her family's emotional well being depended on her changing these patterns and vowed never to give again without making room to receive.

She believed that emotional literacy would be the work of the future in the mind/body field and, without giving to her own detriment, she supported Daniel Goleman in his research to create the book, *Emotional Intelligence*. Then, in 1994, driven by the impetus to help others develop emotionally, as she had urgently needed in childhood, she cofounded CASEL (The Collaborative for Academic, Social, and Emotional Learning)[30] which promotes social and emotional learning in schools to give children the skills of understanding their own feelings and the feelings of others so as to get along better and to live peaceably together. Eileen spoke about the importance of the heart:

I think I was born with an open heart and, although I didn't know what I was doing when I was younger, I trusted my heart and it never failed me. It was the only thing I trusted because I didn't trust my brain after being brainwashed by my siblings. But I think that trusting the heart is never exclusive of the brain. We just need both. As my grandfather said, 'nothing in excess: everything in moderation.' The heart, to me, is the unseen spiritual leader, and the brain functions as the tool for how to set us on our path. It's a little like going through a dark night without any stars or moon, and needing to feel your way along with your toes. In life your heart somehow feels the energy that is before you. I think most people build shields around their hearts. It takes courage and life-experience to remain open-hearted in a secular and materialistic society.

Eileen told me how useful poetry has been in her healing process. Here's one she wrote about this subject.

Family Jewels

For years I unpacked my heart
at the foot of your bed
Oh noble ones, hoping you would admire
one of my jewels in the light.
But you were distracted
by the Monet on your wall.

I tried becoming the water lilies.
I sold myself for small change.

After years of accommodation
I am not much richer
in your eyes
but now the change is mine
for me to do with it what I will.

I have my own picture.
You have your wall.

Dance also became a powerful healing tool. One evening she felt moved to turn on some music and to express herself through the symbology of animals. She described that important turning point:

First I put on clothes that represented the jaguar and danced, my body becoming a manifestation of the discovery of my own power. Next I put on spider clothes and danced a spider, creating a web. To my surprise, my body became the body of my mother, and I got caught in the web. Then, I became a frog, and the frog swallowed the spider. This was so powerful that I ran into the bathroom and threw up. My body seemed to be saying to me, 'you can no longer swallow for your mother. You cannot let that part of your mother live inside you anymore. You must live for yourself.' The fascinating thing was it was my body not my head that spoke to me. The beauty of dancing is that you are so into your body it becomes like a teacher that has never been used.

I asked, 'what is my true self?' and was given the image of a star. Critical, shaming voices then bombarded me for entertaining the mere thought of being a star. In my family we all had an attraction/resistance relationship to attention, partly because our name placed us in a fish bowl. Anyone who was getting attention was going to be competed with and I had a huge fear of being in that dangerous place of center stage. But, with the courage from the dance of the jaguar I was able to say, 'I'm going to do a star dance, damn it, and see whether I really want to be that Hollywood star you are accusing me of.' So I put on my gold 'star clothes.' As I moved into the image I suddenly burst into tears of relief because I knew that I just wanted to be one of the infinite stars in the universe along with all the others. I wanted to have a twinkle such is due to everyone. And I realized my wish was no different than anyone else's. For the first time, I felt okay in my own body and soul. I had accepted myself.

Despite the personal difficulties Eileen experienced in her life, she considers herself blessed because she has a family with strong values. Her parents role modeled their belief that we are here to do something to make a difference in the world in a positive way. Her mother started two conservation organizations, which are thriving today, and her father made many positive transformations in the world of banking.

He introduced art so that there would be something to feed the spirit as you walked in and dealt with money. When he went overseas to open new branches for the Chase Bank the real substance of his work was the introductions to people in positions of power who had concerns about global or economic issues. Because he treats all human beings in a respectful, confidential manner – from his accountant and chauffeur to the kings and queens – he has become an ambassador of goodwill and civility in this world. Today he probably knows, or has met with, every king, queen, prime minister and president of almost every country in the world.

My great grandfather, John D. Rockefeller, was told by a Baptist minister when he was 13 that it would be very important for him to earn a lot of money in life and to give away a lot of it. He followed that to the letter and earned more than anybody in the world at that time. He truly believed he was a servant of God and was meant to make money so that he could give it away. This is the origin of my philanthropic background. I think that there is meaning in all that is dealt to us in life. It is up to each of us to discover that meaning. In the end we are neither richer nor poorer because of the number of houses that we own. What makes the difference is how full our hearts are. What really feeds the soul is not money, but love.

That last sentence speaks volumes. If the purpose of life is to feed the soul (not the human drives and desires) and the remedy is love, this, fortunately, is a free and limitless resource to us all. Of course we all need sufficient monetary resources to survive, but creating more than sufficiency will not cure our human failings. It seems so obvious that we all have our own specific life challenges – rich or poor – and yet, as Eileen knows so well, there is a popular belief in our culture that money *should* make us happy.

The way Eileen's siblings chose to relate to her sensitivity and open-heartedness – as a weakness to be picked on – is indicative of our society's slowness to recognize the positive values of the feminine. There are two modes that need to operate supportively and in cooperation: 1. The typically feminine mode – heart-full, emotional, receptive, and can wisely intuit the bigger picture. 2. The typically masculine mode that uses logic, facts, and calculation to prove the truth. The longer these stay separated and in opposition, the more struggle we will have dealing with any kind of adversity. We need both.

I'm not saying that men and women are essentially the same, because I know that the sexes have evolved in accordance with the roles we have needed to play and are wired differently.[31] However, I am saying that perhaps our belief systems play a major part in limiting our potentially vast intelligence that includes both "masculine" and "feminine" approaches. We need to value what does come easily to us and to remain open to believing that, even with our physiological limitations, there is a long way yet that we can stretch in order to harness our full human resources.

Eileen can now see that the very qualities that caused her so much trouble are actually her greatest gifts, and has used them to great advantage in her work.

In the past 20 years it has been scientifically validated that the heart and brain are in constant dialogue. The science of neuro-cardiology has shown that 60 to 65% of the cells in the heart are brain cells and that the heart produces hormones that profoundly affect the operation of the brain. The Institute of HeartMath in California is using the language of science to feed into the mainstream academic-scientific community hard data that shows the importance of listening to the messages of the heart.[32]

This next story gives an example of how spirit was (and continues to be) encouraged to enter the field of public education.

Mary Manti's Story (with Linda Lantieri) – A School with Spirit

Mary Manti, whose heart shines through her eyes, was born in Brooklyn, New York, where she has spent much of her adult life as a teacher in public school. She is the kind of teacher I would have adored in my challenging school life. Unfortunately for the children, she has now retired.

Mary Manti and Patrick Daly, whose interwoven story we are about to tell, were two of a dozen people who served together at Public School 15 in Brooklyn throughout their professional careers. Lasting friendships were forged through this commitment to the children and families of the Red Hook neighborhood. At the end of 1992 Pat and Mary had been at P.S.15 for 26 and 25 years respectively. Pat had become principal in 1986 and Mary served as his administrative assistant and acting assistant principal. On December 17, 1992, a child left the school building after being involved in an altercation with another student. As Pat walked through the Red Hook projects in search of the child, he was shot and killed by gunfire being exchanged by warring drug dealers.

In the midst of coming to terms with the fact that Pat had been mortally wounded, Mary felt a very strong conviction that Pat was still in very loving hands and that he just kept walking. She did not feel intrinsically that this was the end of him in any way. Though engulfed in shock and sadness, she never experienced a sense of missing her friend and colleague. Rather she felt as if their relationship had never changed. The feelings of friendship and respect remained constant. Mary shared some of the ways in which the school dealt with the loss of their beloved principal.

> We addressed the tremendous sadness experienced by Patrick Daly's school family as sensitively and carefully as possible. The entire staff joined me in reminding the children of how much Mr. Daly loved them and of how he knew they loved him in return. We spoke of how we were all going to be sad for a long time, and the children knew tissues were available all over the building. If we felt like crying we did. We also told 'Mr. Daly stories' to the children that would bring smiles to their faces. Sharing memories of Pat singing with the children, riding a tricycle in a mini-race in the gymnasium, and falling into a wastebasket after leaning back too far on a wheeled desk chair, etc., soon had the children repeating these stories to each other and adding special memories of their own.
>
> We encouraged them to speak of Mr. Daly, draw pictures, write letters and remember positive things. When P.S.15's official name was changed from the Oliver Wolcott School to the Patrick F. Daly School, each child wrote something either to or about Mr. Daly. These notes were typed out and placed on individual paper doves that became part of a multi-paneled mural of the tree of life that decorated the front of the school during the renaming ceremonies.
>
> We did not try to make Pat come alive in the building. We didn't hang his picture on every wall. Rather we tried to make the spirit of what he stood for come alive in order that we could emulate that spirit.

Pat's death placed a huge responsibility on Mary's shoulders. Being principal required her to make an enormous jump of faith. She knew there would be people with a lot of displaced anger and total sadness.

> I didn't try to walk in Pat's shoes. This sense that he just kept walking reinforced my feeling to do the same. Pat's next step just wasn't here. All I could do was what was placed in front of me, a step at a time, and the big picture would be taken care of by the Director of Life.
>
> In difficult times people have to fall back on the qualities that are developed throughout life such as faith, hope, love, kindness, patience, and courage. These traits connect you with your heart and spirit. I felt the staff exhibited these traits to the best of their ability throughout our time of trial.
>
> There has to be an acceptance of death because ultimately God is in charge. The power that takes people from our lives is the same power that gave them to us in the first place. It took a leap of faith by a lot of members of the school community to believe that things could move on in the school in a positive way. I've heard such a leap compared to a trapeze artist who must let go of the bar with one hand while reaching toward the next with the other hand. There's that second in between when it appears you aren't holding onto anything. We were called on to take that leap, having faith that whatever we needed to sustain us would be there. It was a belief that everything works toward the ultimate good.
>
> After Pat's death, Linda Lantieri asked me what I needed for the school. I asked her to train the teachers in conflict resolution. I think that because of what happened to Pat, the staff more eagerly sought the training. The Resolving Conflict Creatively Program[33] is now at the heart of P.S.15. Everything is built around it. RCCP promotes our goal to address the intellectual, emotional, social, moral, and physical needs of all our children.

Linda Lantieri

My dear friend, Linda Lantieri, is founding director of RCCP. She has been an educator for as long as Pat and Mary, and was closely involved with this story. On the day of Pat's funeral she went to the church but didn't know there would be thousands of people trying to get in. The Chancellor of the Board of Education was in that crowd and when he saw her he told her to get back to the Central Board of Ed. as soon as possible because there were so many principals missing from schools.

We felt like we had to go because any one of us could be a casualty at any time in this war of the drug dealers. Pat's death brought home how close this issue of violence could get and also shed light on the need for peace education in schools. His school was beginning to be a safe haven, and since then it's become a lot safer and very caring.

Here was a person who helped to pioneer peacemaking in schools, helped to give birth to my dream of educating the heart and spirit along with the mind. He was one of three principals who fought for the implementation of RCCP in his school in those early days of initiating this work. He could have died of a heart attack, but he died as a casualty in the epidemic of violence when what he stood for was peace. He used to say he was so happy to be principal of a school that no one knew or cared about. Then someone wrote an article about him and it became a front-page story in the newspapers. They called him 'the angel of Red Hook.' It was so peculiar that all of a sudden, out of nowhere, this little school started getting national attention, and so when he died the whole country was part of his death. In retrospect, all of this seems in preparation for what was to come; everything occurred in line.

Channel 4 featured him, God only knew why, because this was a man who didn't want his picture taken. He said he wanted to give children peace inside school because they had such difficult problems outside. Then, I was called by a television studio that wanted footage about our peacemaking work and I chose Pat to speak about the program. On that news clip he pointed over to where he would be shot and said, 'There's a war going on out here.' That war took his life. We have to show our children another way and use any window of opportunity, such as the desire for peace that increases after violence, to encourage heart and soul to enter the field of education.

Linda's work with the Resolving Conflict Creatively Program began to spread rapidly from that point on and could no longer be contained in New York City. At every public appearance she made for the following year she announced that she was doing it in honor of Patrick Daly. Six months later she was catapulted into doing this work at a national level and now the program is in 400 schools, being disseminated through Educators for Social Responsibility. She spoke specifically of P.S.15 and of how we need to change our understanding of the meaning of education.

Mary Manti's school is a fine example of this work. It is a caring, loving, community that keeps its doors open after hours and has a garden for inner reflection and silence. There is an abundance of children's artwork with positive messages on the walls, group murals, and children's photos. After the death of their principal they adopted the saying 'Peace Begins with Me.' P.S.15 has risen from the ashes. Mary Manti, the students, and teachers are exemplifying a school with spirit.[34]

We need a totally new way of thinking about what being educated means. Most of the shocking violent incidents in our schools of late have been in places where it seems youngsters have too much with too little meaning. This indicates that despite our technical advances, scientific expertise, and academic achievement, we have lost part of our humanity. We need schools to be places that nurture all of who we are – mind, body, heart and spirit. It has now been shown that the work of social, emotional, ethical, and spiritual development enhances academic competence.

Equipped with these competencies we can begin to discover and work with the source of hatred in both our internal and external worlds. It is my hope that each of us will help to make sure that no child's soul is left out and will take responsibility for welcoming every aspect of the human spirit into our homes, communities, and particularly our schools where our children spend most of their time.

Mary's response to Pat's death offers some wonderful role modeling. She was so rock solid in her own resources that this created a safe container for all those around her to grieve in their own way. I could almost feel her energetically holding the school, creating a crucible effect that enabled transformation to take place. It is vital when working with people experiencing trauma to help them find their innate resources, and of course essential that the counselor or therapist is deeply resourced before beginning their work. When we look to Mary's resources we see that from the beginning she was using the qualities she already had – "connecting to my heart and spirit." In fact, what she was modeling was staying in touch with her heart and spirit throughout the experience of external loss – perhaps the ideal scenario.

The resources Mary specifically mentions are the keys that are recurring throughout this book: Trust that the "Director" is in charge of the bigger picture; assigning no blame; acceptance of death: it cannot be controlled; feeling the feelings; seeing it as a gift; bringing happy memories to sit with the sad ones.

Identifying resources is a simple activity, and we all have them. The problem is that we tend to suffer from resource amnesia when in shock. It would be a wonderfully useful tool to simply help another identify the resources they already have and see how they can be applied to the challenge at hand. There are inner and outer resources.[35] Inner resources include spiritual beliefs, connections to one's essential self, good physical health, creative thinking, communication skills, an ability to feel a full range of emotion, a sense of feeling safe in the world, the ability to be in contact with others and maintaining a sense of self. External resources include access to community groups and workshops, spiritual practice, friends, family, having a home, emotional support, access to transport, to the natural world, and to cultural, educational and creative community resources.

Fortunately, one of Mary's school's external resources was the Resolving Conflict Creatively Program that supplied a framework for students and teachers alike to welcome in every aspect of the human spirit.

Trauma expert, Peter Levine,[36] believes that "a substantial percentage of violence-prone children, as well as those diagnosed as hyperactive or having Attention Deficit Disorder, are actually suffering from the effects of unresolved trauma." He suggests that we all need to develop first-aid skills to support those in need, especially the children, to resolve and prevent traumatic reactions. This is the kind of education that we need if we are to help all ages to reclaim the missing parts of themselves and to thrive as whole individuals, both in and out of school.

Seventh Key
RECLAIM YOUR HEART AND SPIRIT
Questions and Reflections

1. How would you describe your relationship to the material world –
    including money, material status, and consumerism?

2. What beliefs do you hold about people who have an abundance of money
    or very little of it? How comfortable are you with these beliefs?
    What do you want to change about them?

3. Make a list of what you treasure most in your life – what would you miss most
    if it weren't there? Spend a few moments feeling gratitude for each treasure.

4. If possible, go and be in nature for a little while (if not, meditate on a place in
    nature that you love). Use all your senses to take in the sounds, sights, smells
    and rhythm of this place. Now imagine a typical day in your life. Are you
    happy with its speed, rhythm, and rest-time? If not, what improvements are
    you willing to make… as from today?

5. Write down or share with someone, "My understanding of 'spirit' is…"

6. How would you describe the balance of your intellect, emotions, heart,
    and spirit? Draw a "pie" that represents that balance.

7. Name two ways that you could help rectify the balance and use more of a
    combination of your IQ, EQ (emotional intelligence) and SQ (spiritual
    intelligence) in your daily communications.

8. How do you already bring your heart and spirit to life? Catch this on paper
    in color or even by dramatic expression such as a song, dance etc.

9. In what way, specifically, could you encourage a child you know to
    value his/her heart and spirit?

10. Referring to the examples at the end of this section, name (with help if
    necessary) six of your most useful resources. How could you apply them
    to a present difficulty?

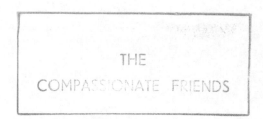

The Eighth Key

FIND
THE HIDDEN
GIFTS

Should you shield the canyons from the windstorms
you would never see the beauty of their carvings.
Elizabeth Kubler-Ross

Find the Hidden Gifts

The French word for wounded is blessé, which is from the same root as blessing. And in Chinese, the symbol for crisis depicts both danger and opportunity. The discovery and constructive use of the blessing/opportunity inherent in a dark night of the soul is the key that runs most consistently through this book. This discovery results from asking the simple down-to-earth question: What can I learn from this? – hardly a new concept, yet how often are we caught in the common mindset that diminishes our ability to see any silver lining to our cloud? How many of us try to wriggle free from the discomfort of pain and yearn for joy, as if it is an illusive quality outside ourselves? The two qualities usually remain separate and mutually exclusive in our minds. In my experience nothing could be further from the truth. I found big, fat pearls of joy and wisdom from the same source as my anguish and became convinced that the further we fall the higher we can climb.

When we finally recognize and accept the hidden gifts presented by our particular challenge (or root them out if they are playing hard to get) the light then joins the shadow, like the Taoist yin yang symbol, and frees us from the see-saw of polarity. Now we can sit in a place of balance. The idea is not to escape or suppress the pain by looking for positives to take its place; it is to accept the cloud of pain while opening our eyes to the silver lining that already exists. By holding the pain and joy, the bitter and the sweet, side-by-side – the two halves make a whole and provide us with a feeling of our own fullness.

Even smiling may seem to be an irreverent possibility at first, which is understandable when all we feel is fiery pain and all we see is darkness. However, there will come a time when the phoenix is ready to stir and then we can either assist or resist its ascension. Our thoughts affect our feelings, which affect our whole system, and no one else can think our thoughts for us. Others can surround us in love, but ultimately we must find and feed ourselves something positive if our life force is to rise again.

What *Mourning Has Broken* shows is that it is not only possible to regain our will to live after the most horrific life hurdles, but also there is the potential to be reborn into an even more enriching life because of the way our eyes have been opened to a more holistic perspective. Mark Nepo depicts this new perspective beautifully in *The Book of Awakening*:

Every crack is also an opening

When in the midst of great change, it is helpful to remember how a chick is born. From the view of the chick, it is a terrifying struggle. Confined and curled in a dark shell, half-formed, the chick eats all its food and stretches to the contours of its shell. It begins to feel hungry and cramped. Eventually, the chick begins to starve and feels suffocated by the ever-shrinking space of its world.

Finally, its own growth begins to crack the shell, and the world as the chick knows it is coming to an end. Its sky is falling. As the chick wriggles through the cracks, it begins to eat its shell. In that moment – growing but fragile, starving and cramped, its world breaking – the chick must feel like it is dying. Yet, once everything it has relied on falls away, the chick is born.

It doesn't die, but falls into the world. The lesson is profound. Transformation always involves the falling away of things we have relied on, and we are left with a feeling that the world as we know it is coming to an end, because it is.

Yet the chick offers us the wisdom that the way to be born while still alive is to eat our own shell. When faced with great change – in self, in relationship, in our sense of calling – we somehow must take in all that has enclosed us, nurtured us, incubated us, so when the new life is upon us, the old is within us.

This section is focused on some of the gifts that can emerge from the pain of facing death, but the concept applies equally to all types of adversity. There are four stories, which, as usual, also show several of the other keys in action. I have purposely placed them back to back without commentary and put my summary of the last key – Find the Hidden Gifts – at the end, because I believe that having done the groundwork, most of the learning is self-evident by now.

Patricia Ellen's Story – Specks of Light in the Darkest Places

Patricia's story has a lot in common with Deborah's story about Linnaea's death presented in the first key. It contains many synchronistic happenings. What struck me most about Patricia is her openness to the grace and opportunity available for her comfort in her darkest hours. It is as if she threw open her arms to receive all that might uplift her broken spirit and was therefore well rewarded.

In 1977 Patricia was a happily married parent of a four-year-old boy named Doug and an eight-year-old girl, Lori. But then, she suddenly found herself separating from her husband and becoming a single parent. She enjoyed her job in charge of education programs in a church, but financial necessity drove her to become a certified public accountant, because they make excellent money. But, interesting as the work was, she felt emptiness in her heart and promised herself that when her kids were grown, she would return to the ministry. Little did she know what was to occur in the meantime that would make her journey back to a fullness of heart and the ministry so poignant.

It was a time of transition in1987, when Lori and Doug were 18 and 14. Their grandfather had died in February, which deeply affected Doug, who was very close to him. Also, the family with whom they had been sharing their house suddenly left, creating pressure of housing costs beyond Patricia's means. Then Patricia, who hadn't been in a relationship for years, started dating. As one is apt to do at the beginning of a new relationship, she became somewhat preoccupied, but the children seemed to be fine.

Doug had enjoyed doing target shooting with his grandfather and had recently asked to buy a hunting rifle. Patricia agreed that he could if he took a safety course first. She continues the story:

> One Tuesday I drove Doug to this course then I attended my journaling group. I felt uneasy, but when I picked him up he seemed particularly settled after class and I began to feel better. Later that evening I spent time with some friends, leaving Doug and Lori at home by themselves. I felt uneasy about going but went anyway.
>
> The next day I spent some time briefly with Lori and Doug, and then I met my new love, Rodney, in town for a movie and a late dinner. We returned about 10pm and Rodney went behind the house to walk his dog. Suddenly the dog started barking. Rodney came in and told me to call an ambulance because there was a problem on the back deck. I turned on the deck light and saw Doug in a chair covered with blood with his gun next to him. My son had shot himself. I screamed, called the ambulance and ran out to the deck. He was still breathing and I took him in my arms saying, 'Doug keep breathing, keep breathing, you can't die.' I kept breathing with him till the ambulance came and took him to hospital. Lori and her friend, Jen, appeared at some point and saw what was happening.
>
> All of us prayed through the long night in the hospital. The surgeon came out and told us that it is very difficult to predict in the case of a brain injury – Doug could get better and return to school, or not. We were grateful that he was alive. While Doug was in intensive care I stayed by his side around the clock and when the heart monitor became erratic I sang lullabies to him and his heartbeat would return to normal. I felt he could hear me although he didn't respond. I belonged to a Unitarian church and Quaker group at the time, and there was always someone in the waiting room to support me, day or night.
>
> After a couple of days Doug was more alert. He was transferred to a room in the hospital and began physical and occupational therapy. He could not speak but pointed to words on a board to show how he was feeling. The doctors told us he wouldn't remember what happened so not to talk to him about the shooting. Thinking we had all the time in the world, we followed their advice. I struggled with deep grief that the son I had known was not visible and grieved for the parts of him we'd lost. I did not understand then how to be present with the essence of a

person, no matter what their state of physical or mental being.

There were tender moments when we found ways to communicate without words. I understood he wanted to see more than his hospital room and was able to walk around with him leaning on me. The doctor's prognosis was that he could be back in school by the spring. A couple of days before he was due to go to a rehabilitation center, Lori, Doug's friend, Dawn, and I were gathered in his room. Someone had given Doug a box of ice-cream sandwiches and as he was eating one, he broke off pieces and gave some to each of us. It was a very special moment – like a communion.

Lori and Dawn left, and I stayed with Doug who fell asleep early. I felt extremely agitated and upset, so I sat by his bed and did a practice I had learned about releasing him. I felt it was time to release him to the rehab center he was going to, which would be near his dad and about four hours away from me. This meant I would only see him when I could make that long trip. I said the words 'I love you unconditionally, I bless you unconditionally, I forgive you unconditionally,' then I imagined cutting the cord that linked the two of us and released him to the next stage on his journey.

I left the hospital and in the car the tears were flowing so hard I could barely see. When I walked in the door of the friend's house I was staying with, the phone was ringing. It was the hospital calling me to tell me that Doug had died. I started screaming, a scream that I thought would never end. Later I would say to Doug, 'I wasn't releasing you to leave this earth!'

Patricia spent the next few days in a blur of funeral arrangements and just trying to be with the agonizing pain she felt. It didn't take long before what she calls "the gifts" started to present themselves. The second night after Doug's death she had a dream about him and awoke with a profound sense of knowing that everything was okay, which sat side by side with her intense feeling of missing him. The following week she had another dream of Doug flying through the air and landing safely on the other side. Again a sense of peacefulness descended.

Images and visions kept coming. One night she was meditating at home and saw a vision of Jesus standing with Doug, who was offering her a round wooden bowl filled with some kind of liquid. This image comforted Patricia and appeared repeatedly in her meditation, nurturing and reassuring her. It reminded her of the old hymn "There is a balm in Gilead that makes the wounded whole." About six months later she was drawn to attend an Egyptian exhibit that had come to a Boston museum, and one of the first things she saw on display was the very bowl that Doug had been offering her. The title on the bowl was "The Resurrection Bowl."

A friend, Joe, gave Patricia another comforting gift. He was raised in a fundamentalist church that taught the "sin of suicide" and he had been having great difficulty with Doug's death. However, he told her about a vision/dream that he had been given of Doug standing with Jesus and there being not judgment but blessing for him. Then she met Carol who had also lost a son through suicide and together they journeyed through much of that first year.

> It was life saving to have someone else living through the same thing to walk with, pray with, and cry with. We gave each other the courage to go on.
>
> One more gift of the divine that carried me through this time was being led to a grief counselor who taught me and Lori an ancient prayer and walked us through each room of the house to cleanse the space. Part of the prayer was – 'May all inappropriateness, disharmony and pain be banished from this space.' I did this cleansing, and also blessed myself, daily for a month.

Shortly after Doug's death, Patricia began to experience a strange heat and sensation in her hands. She knew that it was healing energy and that in some way Doug was going to be there with her in her future healing work. Six months later, at a time she was feeling particularly vulnerable and fragmented, she signed up for a workshop with Ilana Rubenfeld to learn about integrating bodywork and psychology, and during one exercise she experienced this healing energy strongly and felt Doug's presence. Later that weekend Patricia became angry when Ilana kept talking about finding joy. "How could this woman expect a mother who had lost her child only seven months earlier to have joy?" she thought. As if in answer, Illana suggested that Patricia be the "demo client" in the next session.

> I lay on the table and immediately relaxed as Ilana guided me into a light trance. She cradled my head and her touch felt so sacred and safe that I immediately began to cry. Gently she led me into the deep tears and rage that I had been feeling since Doug's death. I experienced Ilana as having no fear as I expressed the deepest pain I have ever known. My tense muscles let go and I felt her being totally present as a witness to my process, enabling me to feel and release much of the trauma my body had been holding.
>
> Ilana asked me to put into words what I was feeling and I talked about my guilt and sense of failure as a mother. Slowly she helped me connect with my nurturing inner voice instead of the critical voice, and I began to discover the self that knows I am a good mother. I heard the voice that knows Doug's suicide wasn't all my responsibility and that I am only a part of the whole picture. This was like salve to a savage

wound. Ilana then had me walk around the room, look people in the eye and tell them 'I am a good mother' and 'I am only part of the whole picture.' With each encounter, the burden of guilt and shame began to lessen.

With the power of the work with Ilana, and her experience of the healing energy and Doug's presence, Patricia knew that the Rubenfeld work was what she wanted to do. Seven months later she began the professional training. Part of the training requirement was to have synergy sessions with many synergists, which she described as "a gift to my soul – each session releasing more of the trauma that I had held in my body." In one session she screamed in rage and sorrow at Doug "How could you have done this to me and to your sister?" while the energy was released up her spine and out of her body. In another session she told Doug how much she missed him and appreciated all they had shared in his time on earth. She told him she didn't want to forget or lose him, and placed him in her heart so she could carry him wherever she went.

On another occasion she worked more deeply with her guilt. Ilana labeled an empty chair "guilt" and Patricia was invited to sit in this chair to *be* the guilt and see what it wanted to say to her. As guilt, she said to the chair representing herself, "You are responsible for the demise of a life. You have no right to go on and be happy. You owe it to Doug to stay miserable. That is the least you can do to make it up to him." Patricia, now back in her own chair, had no response to guilt other than, "I agree." A fourth chair represented Doug. Patricia looked at that chair and spoke to Doug, "I would have done anything to stop you, if only you had let me know how bad you felt." Then she moved to Doug's chair and spoke as Doug, "I didn't want to bother you. I didn't know it was this bad. I thought I could handle it on my own. I kept telling you everything was fine."

As they carried on this dialogue, the realization dawned on Patricia that what Doug had said was exactly what she had always done when upset. She handled difficult feelings by herself, not wanting to bother others, letting out scary feelings a little at a time, then telling people she's fine and putting the lid back on. "Doug had learned from my example, from his father, and maybe even from society," said Patricia. "This was an 'aha' moment, albeit very painful." From this revelation Patricia made a commitment to handle her feelings differently, to learn to feel them and to risk sharing her pain.

Later, at the Kripalu Yoga Center, on a retreat, one of the "monks" suggested that instead of trying to make her feelings go away she commit herself to sitting with them.

This thought was terrifying. I thought I would die from it, but I committed myself to intentionally doing that for a period of time every day, knowing that help was close if I needed it. To my surprise, I not only survived but also began to heal, and as my fear of the feelings diminished, living with them became easier. This is a lesson I carry and share in my teachings and outreaches today. It has allowed me to simply be present with people in deep pain and companion them on their journey.

It is because of Doug that Patricia now uses Rubenfeld Synergy as a vehicle in healing others. She told me of the "mystical sweet union of love" one can experience with a loved one who has died that she has come to know in her connection with Doug. It also helped her to tell Doug "I am happy, I love my work and I have a loving relationship in my life. I no longer get sad every time I look at your picture but I don't want you to think I've forgotten you, I just don't want to be sad anymore."

> I had the sudden knowing that if I were to survive these days I needed to look at something other than the black hole I was feeling all the time. I took time to notice how I had been able to reach across and touch other people's lives. This enabled me to see the tiny specks of light in my deepest, darkest places and to continue to recognize and build the strands of connection between myself and all people. Never again did I take for granted the preciousness of each moment, each sunset, the star light sky, the touch of a friend. This continues to be an extraordinary gift of life from Doug's death.

Since childhood Patricia had talked about going to seminary but held back because she felt the theology of any one church was too narrow for her experience of the divine. However, three years after Doug's death, she began a program to become an interfaith minister. The founder of this seminary, Rabbi Gelberman, had lost all of his family in the Holocaust and had formed the seminary in the hope that as different faiths begin to understand and honor each other, holocausts will be avoided. Patricia was ordained at the Cathedral of St. John the Divine in New York City.

Concluding her sharing she added:

> My life journey continues to draw me ever closer to full aliveness and always with an awareness of the blessing of Doug's spirit that I shared for 14 years on this earth and will share in my heart forever. Today I work with the Center for Grieving Children in Portland, Maine,[37] in their Tender Living Care Program working with families with life threatening illnesses. It is the most rewarding and heart centered work I have ever done. Doug's presence is often with me, especially on outreaches where my lessons from our time together and after his death enhance my teaching.

Hafsat Abiola's Story – Testimony to my Ancestors

Hafsat, not yet out of her twenties, has had more than a lifetime's worth of adversity, and yet she shines with purity and maturity. She herself is an immense gift to the world. In her distinctive, lyrical voice, which sounds like she's almost singing, she shared with me what life has offered her and her close-knit family to date, and revealed her unusual perspective that automatically embraces the gifts of death.

Her roots are in Western Nigeria and her people are the Yoruba people. Her father, Moshood Abiola, was from a very poor home and was the 16th child to be born into that family. The first 15 children died of diseases before they were five. People were beginning to wonder if Hafsat's grandfather, who had several wives, had done something wrong and the spirits were angry with him.

> When my dad turned up, Grandfather looked at him and called out in Yoruba language 'Let us watch him' because he didn't think he would stay. When my father lived beyond his fifth year my grandfather named him a name that means, 'Honor has come into my life' and he began to spend time with him, teaching him the rich tradition and wisdom of the Yoruba.

Hafsat's father and his mother sold firewood so he could go to school. He memorized lessons because he didn't have paper or a pencil, but he ended up being one of the best students and secured a scholarship that took him to Europe. He returned to Nigeria as a chartered accountant, became wealthy, and then became involved in philanthropy. He helped finance Nelson Mandela's National Congress and was at Mandela's inauguration. Then in 1993 he decided that the best way to address the extreme poverty in Nigeria was to run for president in the first democratic presidential election to be held in ten years. He won, with 58% of over 15 million votes. However, the military leaders who were from Northern Nigeria, decided that they weren't ready to turn the country over to a civilian, and certainly not to a civilian from Western Nigeria. So the ruling military council annulled the results and put him in prison, which was devastating for both Hafsat's family and for the country.

The pro-democracy forces remained strong, with some of Hafsat's family again providing crucial leadership.

> My mom, Kudirat, was always happy, always glowing; she thrived on challenges and was incredibly principled. She was not a politician, but when my dad was put in prison she began to mobilize pro-democracy groups to pressure the military to leave power. When she organized an oil worker strike – because the military are dependent on oil – the

government was almost paralyzed and began to attack my family and our businesses.

In was June 1996 when Hafsat's life dramatically changed. She was in Cambridge, U.S. at Harvard University, and her mother was due to come for her graduation. But, two days before that visit she received a call at 4am from one of her mother's friends.

She said she wanted me and my younger sister who was with me, to come right away to Washington DC because there had been an accident in Nigeria. Then one of my father's closest friends in the U.S. called as well and said, 'Have you heard anything?' I said 'No' and he also told me to come to DC. No one would tell me what had happened and I collapsed and started crying. I thought it was my dad because he was in prison in the line of fire, but I also thought that if any member of my family had died (especially my parents because I am so close to them) they would have given me some message and I would have woken up. So I wasn't too worried.

We went to the airport with very little money and no tickets. I said it was a family emergency and we were given cheap tickets. We arrived at Washington and the first thing my mom's friend did was show me an article which had my mom on the front with an interview she'd given about the need to fight for democracy in Nigeria. I thought that was weird because if there was something wrong with my dad, why was she giving me an article about my mom?

I have six siblings. My two young brothers were in Nigeria and the other five of us were in the U.S. for schooling. One sister was still in Philadelphia, but by 11am, the rest of us were gathered in my elder brother's apartment in Washington waiting for news. There were calls coming in from London to say that my mother was in an accident. Then we heard that the BBC had announced that my mom was dead. The Nigerian soldiers had ambushed her car in the streets of Lagos and gunned her down. Riddled with bullets at 44 years old.

Everybody went into shock because there was nothing to prepare us, and our dad was still in prison. I just couldn't understand why I didn't even know before the news came. I am the oldest daughter and if she had spoken to me she would have said, 'Look after your siblings and do things as I would have wanted.' She would have wanted to have someone to step forward and not allow the work she was doing to remain undone, as if the military had won. And so I told my brothers and sisters right then that I was committed to continue my mom's work and fight for the ideals she was killed for, although I didn't know what I was going to do.

We rented a one-bedroom apartment in Arlington, Virginia. All seven of us children were living there because I flew out my two young brothers, who were nine and eleven, within days of mom's death. None of us were working so we had little money because we couldn't get our money out of Nigeria. We had so many things to deal with as well as dealing with our mom's death.

My father had been given the article to tell him that my mom had been killed, and he was still kept in solitary confinement. Then in July 1998, after four years in solitary confinement, he was due to be released. The day before release day we were told that he'd had a heart attack and had died in prison. We believe he was also killed. The country exploded then with riots and demonstrations against the military. The following year there was victory at last and the military were forced to step aside.

My father's death was a shock of course, but you know I didn't have the same trauma to go through as others would because I really don't believe in death. Because I was not aware when my mom or my dad were departing, I don't think death really happens. The trauma that I have is consistent with beginning a new journey. I would have that kind of trauma around any big change or break. I don't feel as if I've lost my mom or dad. They've gone into spirit world where they came from. They are my ancestors now and have completed their circle. It's to be celebrated that they are not here; their spirits are to be honored. In my culture we believe that when they depart they become even more powerful because they are not restricted as we are by the body.

I think about them a lot because they were willing to give their lives to something that could help others. My father was a stutterer and stuttered till the very end. I think it's so beautiful that he struggled to communicate himself to the people and so beautiful how he and my mom played out their lives with all the tests. I'm actually very happy in my heart. They didn't compromise on the challenge of their lives. If they had compromised their truth then I would have been in trauma. I can't wait till I meet up with them to tell them how I lived mine. I believe that because of the struggles in life, the human spirit, whatever colors it starts out with, will become clearer, sharper and brighter. Death is such a wondrous exciting prospect that I'm looking forward to; the body being buried and the spirit being set free.

I wonder if the reason other people go through such trauma around the death of their loved ones is that they are not aware of their story yet. Every human being has a beautiful story and when you see the lessons they learned and the challenges they made it through, you see the beauty. I think how I get through is by discovering the whole story of my parents' lives and making that useful and inspirational to people. Yes, they are not here physically but many lessons from their lives will still be instructive for my children, others, and me.

For me the healing is being aware that in some way I supported my parents and acknowledged their achievements so that when facing death they could be more satisfied and ready to go. I can celebrate their complete lives and focus on what they did, who they were, rather than the loss. So my advice to anyone else is to say, try to be supportive so that when loved ones depart there is nothing to be sorry about.

My parents have completed their work here and I continue in their spirit. The work I do is a legacy from their commitment, but as time passes it becomes my work. I took my mom's name, Kudirat, and created an organization called the Kudirat Initiative for Nigerian Democracy, which is KIND. If my mom had been alive the greatest thing she could have done would be to continue to work to deepen empowerment in marginalized people, especially women and young people, to manifest what is missing in our culture. I want to achieve that work through KIND and I want to enjoy the spirit and voices of those who are presently stifled.

How well I manage to serve myself reflects how well I can serve others. I do totally accept myself the way I am and I listen to my spirit, then I am calm and the spirit leads me. I believe in meditation in action. There's a saying I heard: 'Stillness is not being still. That is false stillness. Stillness is being still in the middle of turmoil.' When I experience this stillness I can feel how we are all interconnected. So many of our problems come from the sense of disconnection.

The people who were responsible for my mother's death were caught recently and are facing the death penalty. I'm really upset about it because I cannot imagine why they would want to kill them. It is not our work to kill them. They killed my mom but that tells me that their struggle in life is that they don't know what to do with people they don't agree with. The response is to help them complete their cycle, their understanding, not to shoot them. Blame, scapegoating, attacking people all the time is the general norm – pointing fingers and deciding who's to blame for the country's problems. It is not a safe space and it stops people bringing their gifts. We all as human beings come with baggage of shadows and light, and the gifts lie in both those aspects of ourselves.

I feel my parents' spirits with me very much and I firmly believe that they are around all the time – more powerful now than they have ever been. I have placed my father's glasses to look over the sitting room – symbolic of him watching over me, and my mother's picture is there too. I go and sit at their graves, which are at our family home, and say thank you. I am stronger now too because of the difficult but wonderful journey that their deaths took me on. I am taking the best of who they were and bringing it through myself in the best way I know how so that I am a walking testimony of the gifts that they gave in life. If I were devastated by their deaths then no one would see their continuation by looking at me.

I know how I must conduct my life so that my death will be a beautiful experience. That is the reward.

Elaine Seiler's Story – The Interweaving Worlds

Elaine is a fascinating person with an extremely unusual perspective on life. When she is not connecting with her four grown children and their families, she is traveling the world listening to inner guidance as to where her next port of call is to be. She is totally dedicated to being a healing channel in whatever place she finds herself. This story takes us full circle, back to the integration of birth and death of which I spoke in Benjaya's story, and concerns her eldest daughter, Elizabeth, and her grandson, Zachariah.

Elaine chose traditional deliveries for all of her four children but Elizabeth, her daughter, had a very different approach. From the moment of conception she took care of herself exceptionally well and intended to give birth naturally at home. She invited her sister, Barbara, and her mother to be present. Then, during later pregnancy, Elizabeth surprised everyone by intuitively making the decision that she needed to be in a hospital where she would still do the birth naturally with the assistance of a doctor and her birthing assistant.

Elaine had changed a great deal since the time her children were born and excitedly anticipated this birth.

When Elizabeth went into labor we were all able to be with her at the hospital, including Shawn, her husband. No problems had been picked up in any of the preliminary examinations and everything seemed fine. We got to the point in the delivery when she really needed to birth the baby but he was not moving. The doctor said, 'you need to have this baby, and soon. There's a muscle spasm in the pelvic floor and I'd like you to have some anesthesia to release it.' Elizabeth said, 'Okay, I want to have the baby now.'

So the doctor went to get the anesthesiologist, meanwhile we did reflexology on Elizabeth's feet and worked on the pelvic floor muscles. The doctor came back in and on the next contraction my tiny grandson was born. He was the most beautiful baby I have ever seen, absolutely gorgeous.

The instant Zachariah came out we all knew there was something wrong. The umbilical cord was around his neck, and his color was very poor. They put him in an incubator and took him to intensive care. Shawn went with Zachariah and didn't leave his side for the next 24 hours, except to take a nap. He sang and talked to him, and massaged his little body, sending him healing energy. It was incredible to watch him with his newborn son.

Elizabeth was very upset, obviously, but somehow on top of the deep distress was this amazing balance. She was moved to a small room off the intensive care unit and after a while, Zachariah, who was hooked up to IV monitors and so forth, and his equipment was moved with the crib into their space. They cleaned out his lungs, put him on antibiotics and on life-support, as he was not breathing on his own. After 24 hours Elizabeth and Shawn made the decision to have him removed from life-support because they didn't want to keep him going this way. They wanted him to decide to live and make it on his own, and the family supported that decision. So they took him off life-support and he started to breathe, which felt miraculous but also really scary. At that point we knew there was going to be some kind of damage – how much was out of our hands.

We referred to Zachariah as 'The sleeping angel' because that's exactly what he looked like. He was in a coma and had not developed any of the normal neurological responses, so he wasn't suckling and had no muscle responses. On the third day Elizabeth and Shawn were learning to feed him with a tube, which was very traumatic for a new mother whose breasts have just filled with milk and who needs to nurse. Barbara and I were at home getting some sleep that night when we received a call to say that Zachariah had stopped breathing and was about to die. We dressed immediately to go to the hospital, but then Elizabeth called and said, 'Relax, come when you're ready. He's breathing again!'

What ensued after that was two days of the most incredible on again, off again, living/dying experience. On the one hand it was absolutely horrid, and on the other it was one of the most magnificent things I have ever experienced. This is very hard to explain. Zachariah would stop breathing for as long as five minutes at a time, and we could all hold him and be with him. We had total access to him in this private room with his parents, who slept with him. He would stop breathing and the nurses and doctors were frantic as they thought he was dying and didn't know how to be with it. Then he would take a huge breath and come back in. You could almost see him go out and come in again. The family began to get accustomed to it, if there is such a state. Finally we reached the fifth day and were all becoming exhausted. I was thinking 'Please God, let this child live and be healthy or let him let go.'

Now, I need to tell you that what I do in the world is to hold energy. That's my work. I'm a kind of a bridge. I work with individuals, with groups and with places, and I hold the energy so that each person, group or place can function at its highest level. Although I was doing this in the hospital, I didn't have the language to describe what I did then. I was exhausted from being there and decided I needed to take a break outside. I stretched out on the grass in front of the hospital, went into a meditative state and talked to Zachariah. I told him, 'We really want you here if you choose to be here, if not we support you to release.' When I came out of the meditative space and looked at my watch – it was ten minutes after two. I went back into the hospital and was greeted at the door by a nurse from the intensive care unit. She looked at me and said, 'Zachariah's gone.' I asked, 'When did he leave?' She said, 'Ten minutes after two.'

There was relief in the letting go. There were tears, grief and empathy for Shawn and Elizabeth, and at the same time there was something else that was so much deeper and so much bigger that there are few words to describe it. I was told that Shawn and Elizabeth, who had been singing to Zachariah before his death, had sung him out with 'Amazing Grace.'

I have a specific metaphysical approach to life, and this experience was for me an excellent opportunity to walk my talk in a way that I never imagined I would be tested to do. And it was from living that way that I could experience Zachariah's death without the hair-tearing and agony that I see around me in the world as it views death. That's not to say I don't mourn this child; somehow they're separate. They go together and they interweave, but they're different and distinct. I am incredibly grateful for my spiritual beliefs because going though this experience without them would have been devastating. It was challenging, it held loss and grief, but it wasn't devastating.

Elizabeth wrote a short piece afterwards in which she talked of what she learned. She said, 'Every moment of his life was a gift and a struggle for one who wanted more than a moment. Zachariah taught me to be focused in the moment; to enjoy it, not be concerned with an hour from now or tomorrow because if I did I might miss the gifts of the present.' She said that when he died the room filled with energy, yet at the same time it was very empty. Her son was there and yet he was gone. Later, when she could separate a little from her situation, she recalled all the people she knew who had 'lost' babies and realized just how many mothers must mourn their children. To remember this gave her comfort.

I believe we come into this life, into the body, to do a job, to learn our lessons and to fulfill a mission or purpose. It's not about coming in to live until you're as old as you can be and have a good time, although hopefully you do enjoy it. It's about fully living the spiritual purpose for which we each came in. I believe that Zachariah had a purpose which he lived fully, completing the whole job in five days when the rest of us need 30, 50 or 90 years to do it. That's not a judgment that anyone is better than another, it's just that they are different.

Zachariah not only profoundly influenced the lives of his family but he also deeply affected the doctors and nurses. I can't completely explain and yet I believe that my grandson brought in a unique kind of healing energetic that he planted somehow in that hospital. We were all influenced by the grace of this experience. Grace really is the word. Not only did he leave on 'Amazing Grace,' but also the grace with which his parents birthed him, held him and released him was truly magnificent. I was in deep respect and awe of the way they did that, and honor their process – which is not to say it did not take many years to heal the loss and wound.

The juxtaposition of the process of birth and death showed me a piece of life that I had not understood before; the incredible similarity of birth and death. I saw the circle of life. It's not that birth is good and death is bad, it's that we're on this circular journey, and somehow, bearing witness to this process in the way I did, left me with the awe and magnificence of it as opposed to the horror. It is very difficult to let go, to be born and come into form, and it is equally difficult to release the form and go back to spirit. To see that process of coming and going in Zachariah was very enlightening.

Given that this coming and going theme had such an impact on Elaine, and knowing that the external world has an uncanny way of mirroring our internal process, I felt moved to ask her whether she had a pattern of coming and going in her own life. She had not thought about this before but admitted,

I have spent most of my life coming and going! As a child I was not comfortable in my body or with my family. The way I dealt with that was to be physically present but emotionally absent. So I came and went all the time. I was pretty out of touch and it took many years and lots of hard work to put me back in touch with my emotions. I was very good at moving my physical body without being emotionally present. This is a fascinating awareness because I had always felt I was totally and completely available for my children to the point where I had abdicated a life of my own, whereas they thought I was 'gone' all the time and that they didn't have me present as a mother.

Elaine went on to add another interpretation of the coming and going which may be difficult for some to understand.

As I've become more in touch with who I am as a spiritual and energetic being, I have come to understand that I do come and go. I'm fully present in the third dimension, but most of me lives most of the time in the fourth. The third dimension is this physical, 3D, tangible, linear, touchable, feelable world; the world that the vast majority of our culture believes is the only world. There have always been a few enlightened beings, primarily in the east, who have spoken of the intangible realms.

But I think that the east and west are beginning to come closer together, to merge. There's much greater awareness now that new quantum physics and science are exploring these realms, opening in people's minds that this realm exists. Another realm interweaves at every moment with the physical world. We acknowledge there's air but we don't talk about the energetics in that void space between us. Most people can go so far as to say they can go into a room and it's so yucky they just want to get out. What they don't know, perhaps, is that there's just been a knock down fight in that room, with cursing and screaming going on. Negativity has an energetic that's palpable if you can acknowledge and open to that level of reality.

I truly believe that my job is to be a bridge between what I'm calling the unseen, fourth dimensional world and the fifth dimension beyond it. The further out dimensionally you go, the less form and individuality it has. And so I do go in and out all the time. What I've learnt to do is to stay conscious and present in my physical and emotional bodies and to bring my awareness back to the third dimensional world to assist people who haven't put on those eyeglasses yet, to help them evolve to that way of seeing, knowing and understanding. I believe that is the path we are all on as a human species.

What I believed was happening with Zachariah was that he was leaving to check out the other side saying, 'Am I down there? Shall I stay? Am I ready to leave? Can I go back?' Then coming back and checking it out here, feeling what that felt like. And yes, we are talking about a five day old infant and I know it will be hard for a lot of people to accept that a soul could be, maybe not even consciously, going through a process of checking out to the point where ultimately he let go.

People who sit with adults who are dying will watch them go out and come in. My experience is that they will leave and be in a sort of coma-like state, talking what appears to be nonsense. They'll talk about relatives who've died and about experiences that don't have any relevance in the physical world around them, and then they'll come back and talk to whoever is there before going back out again. What this says to me is that there is much greater interweaving of the realms than we culturally acknowledge. I think that we are interweaving worlds all the time and we're just not conscious of it.

Back to Elizabeth and Shawn. Elaine told me that Elizabeth became pregnant again and then miscarried which brought the entire grief process back up. (Miscarriage happens to vast numbers women – approximately one in five pregnancies miscarry, and an estimated one in three including the losses of which women are unaware.) Elizabeth and Shawn decided to adopt a child and to try for their own child later. They went off to Russia where they chose a nine-month-old baby, Samara, in an orphanage because she made eye contact with them.

Samara is one of the more extraordinary beings that I have met. She looks just like her adoptive father and not dissimilar from her mother. So what is that all about? I think about the serendipitous, supposedly accidental ways in which our lives unfold and I realize it's phenomenal that the energies of her genetic parents, of her adoptive parents, the energy of her country and the energy here in the U.S., are all interweaving. Each country holds a different energy, and I suspect that Samara's journey has a little to do with healing Russia and America, the two coming together. Maybe one day we'll begin to understand this level. I just came from spending last week with them to celebrate Samara's 'Gotcha Day', the day we 'got ya.' We celebrate that as rigorously as we celebrate her birthday. And so, although today my focus is on my granddaughter, I bless and thank Zachariah for his presence and influence on my family and my life. I don't know if Samara would be in my life today if the sleeping angel had not come and gone when and how he did.

Rob Lehman's Story – The Eternal Moment

Rob, a man with a twinkle in his eye and solid wisdom in his speech, stepped down from his post as president of the Fetzer Institute in Michigan in 1999 when he had an all-consuming encounter with death. The Fetzer Institute is a non-profit foundation specifically interested in exploring the relationship between the inner world of mind and spirit and the outer world of action and service, and this story was first told by Rob to a group of the Fetzer "community" at a meeting called Wisdom of the Heart. I will not interrupt his flow at all.

I thought I knew about death. When I was six, I heard the doctor tell my mother and father just outside my bedroom door that I might not survive the serious case of scarlet fever that I had been unable to break through. I heard my mother crying, no doubt remembering the death of my brother, Dickey, from a heart ailment at age two. I remember walking up to the casket of my grandfather when I was nine, and peering in to see his lifeless face. When I was 50, I held my mother's hand while the doctors disconnected her life-support and she slowly stopped breathing. In the years between these events I have, like all of us, attended many funerals and have been present with dying. It is true that there is nothing sadder than watching a loved one die, nothing more wrenching than to see your child die, or parent or brother or sister or good friend... nothing sadder. At the same time, there is nothing more immediately real than experiencing your own death. And that reality is so powerful, as blinding as the face of God, that one seems initially to have little choice but to close one's eyes to it.

It was 5.15pm on Monday, August 25, 1998 when the surgeon called to tell me the results of a biopsy the previous Friday at the Mayo Clinic in Jacksonville. The call was four hours late and when I reached the nurse after the third hour to ask about the delay she said quietly, 'The doctor wants to call you after he has seen his scheduled patients.'

In the next hour, the hint from the nurse grew into a full foreboding and by the time the phone rang I should have been prepared, but I was not. The doctor said simply, 'Mr. Lehman, I'm sorry to have to tell you that the biopsy shows that you have non-Hodgkin's lymphoma. We will want you to come in to begin a series of tests to see how advanced the cancer is, what stage you are in. I am setting up an appointment with our chief oncologist, Dr. Soleberg, for tomorrow morning.'

After years of taking care of myself, (the total of my running distance over 25 years equals more than the circumference of the earth) after years of meditation and spiritual study, of inner work and close association with mind-body-spirit practices, the first thing that I did after hanging up the phone was not to go for a run or fall to my knees in prayer or begin exhaustive research, but to go out and buy a pack of cigarettes and a six pack of beer and head for the beach. The fact that I was being told in so many words that I might die activated a fear so great that the only thing I could do in those first moments was find a way – any way – to numb my awareness. By the next morning I found myself moving, with a terrific headache, into a reframing state of mind. 'This couldn't be that bad.' 'I'm sure they caught it very early.' 'There won't be a long-term problem.' The sheer panic and deliberate suppression of the night before had been replaced by concrete reasons why the news could not be as bad as it had felt.

I began a week of testing to determine how advanced the lymphoma was. There were CAT-scans, bone marrow tests, x-rays, heart tests, kidney sonograms, and countless blood analyses. Each result brought more bad news, until by the end of the week we had learned that my body, including bone marrow, was filled with lymphoma. Dr. Soleberg was absolutely wonderful, spending a great deal of time with us. When finally we were able to ask him on Friday about the prognosis he answered, 'The statistics say that you have a 30% chance of surviving this, but I think personally you will do better.'

Until that moment my wife, Molly, and I had been in complete denial. Individually we are both optimists, and together we see the glass not just half-full but full and overflowing. Part of our denial was based on the fact that I had not felt sick. I had a small swelling in my groin, which I thought was a pulled muscle from my recent adventures in basketball after nearly 35 years on the bench. Now I was being told that my sports injury was a swollen lymph node and that the malignant cells it contained were spreading throughout my body. My efforts to rationalize the ordeal continued. 'This can't be happening to me; cancer doesn't even run in my family. My grandparents on both sides lived into their nineties. My father is dating at 85. I couldn't possibly die in my fifties!'

I remember asking if the clinic had another Robert Lehman in its computer, suggesting that perhaps there was a mix-up. Soon I learned how common this denial is, and how far-reaching is the repression of the fact of our finite existence throughout our culture.

Psychologists and theologians tell us that many of the attachments to which we cling – from material possessions to psychological scripts to our endless busy-ness – are just props we use to hold us up from the fear of our essential emptiness, of death. Wisdom of the heart tells us that if we want to be truly free from what enslaves us we must learn to face the truth of death. As Joseph Campbell knew, 'The conquest of the fear of death is the recovery of life's joy.' Again, paradoxically, acceptance of death frees us to more fully live. When we fear death we are already suffering from what we fear, yet when the energies of the heart are no longer used to repress this fear they are released for their proper role in true life, in the deep joy that is the other side of suffering. So it is that facing the reality of our own death is the single most important thing we can do to liberate our powers of love and compassion.

That first weekend was important. I walked alone on the beach a lot. I prayed, recited my favorite psalms, and began to realize that in the next months I might die. By then the fear had been replaced by deep sadness. Sadness of not living out what I assumed would be the last third of my life, sadness that the plans Molly and I had made might not come to fruition, sadness about not seeing our children and grandchildren grow and develop. And yet with the sadness of letting go of these external treasures came an unexpected liberation of internal ones. With nothing in outer life to hold on to or to hold me, I began to befriend my inner life and to see with Walt Whitman 'the multitudes contained within' parade before me. And the more I watched this parade the more I realized that the 'I' watching had a very different quality than the participants. They were like temporary guests of the host that is the true center of my personality. The 'I' watching was not leaving after all, not dying, but seemed stronger and healthier than ever for having been recognized.

It is this 'I' that I have come to know through the process of the past eleven months. If asked to distill the essence of this experience, I would offer that, as I began to observe the many dimensions of my personality from the perspective of this Self, I spontaneously began to accept, without judgment, the entirety of my life. I felt in a very tangible way held by a generosity so great that it accepted and loved me in my goodness and badness, in my honesty and dishonesty, in my beauty and ugliness. Love streamed in from everything around me, from trees and grass, birds and animals, and most of all from my family and friends, even from people unknown to me. Everything was okay, and with further surrender I began to feel the center of my personality shift from my personal autonomy to the fullness of the world around me, from my ego, author of my separateness, to a more inclusive locus of love moving through me and through everything.

It has always made sense to me that being with someone who is dying fosters an attitude of love and forgiveness, yet I had never really considered the deeper meaning of this attitude. Now I understand how our fear of death comes out of hiding, and the ego attachments, projections, and other defenses that have grown in the soil of this fear begin to wither and die. The ego – faced with the prospect of its own death – instinctively surrenders to a deeper dimension, to a more inclusive, interdependent experience of itself in the world. In this way the consciousness is expanded, and the internal walls between good and bad, self and other, are dismantled by an unrestricted flow of love that unites the ego with its deepest origins.

With this shift in ego comes a corresponding shift in identity. My identity is not merely the sum total of the many dimensions of my personality. At its most transparent my identity is the integration of all I am with all everyone and everything is, and this integrated whole is held by a mystery of Generous Love. As I allow myself to feel the impact of this shift, I realize that I do not die when I die. I live on in all that is in all that has ever been and ever will be. When we truly accept that we are dying, when we accept that we are not immortal but finite, we become free to experience the reality of wholeness. We begin to experience life as beyond time, as eternal. We notice this eternity in the present moment, as St. Therese explained, in all the small things that we do with great love. We learn that we are not really finite but eternal, and that the present, in all its glory, is the eternal moment.

Letting-go, the transformation of anxious control to the quiet confidence of a deeper order, has been among the most valuable gifts of my acceptance of the possibility of my own death. The essence of dying, I am learning, is the surrender to a larger mystery, to the wholeness of the eternal moment.

Still very much alive two years later in October 2001, Rob spoke to me in his office in Kalamazoo.

I am constantly reminded of my mortality and of the fragility of life as the cancer lymphoma comes in and out of remission. But it's also a reminder of the experience of my mystical oneness with life and with God. I had undervalued my experience of recognizing my sense of one-ness with a tree, a rock, or another person, the wholeness of life. I had relegated it to a religious experience, but I realized that this particular mystical experience of wholeness – meaning recognizing that I am the beauty and the dark – is real, and is the basis for freedom and for living my life in a happy way. When you truly have experienced that wholeness you can free yourself from all the things that hold you back and can liberate love. Crisis can free a deeper vision.

I don't see this kind of experience as esoteric. I think it's very ordinary. We have just not been living on the level of awareness and consciousness to recognize the power that's in a very ordinary space. It's sublime and yet ordinary. We need to democratize religious experience. It's not a religious power; it's something happening in lay spirituality.

I thought that I would become more detached from living an intense life, always having projects, but as I recovered, I found myself very much engaged in life and in projects but in a new way. When I left my position as president of Fetzer, a whole lot of other things opened up for me to do, but if I'm not allowed to do those things it's ok. I might prefer it to be one way but I know that ultimately there is a greater picture that you can't understand that is basically in charge and you have to live your life as best you can.

Each crisis carries its own unique gifts. The list is endless, and yet these stories show that there is common ground. It is this common ground that creates such a depth of rapport between those of us who have been to hell and back. Not only do we have the shared experience of having lived through the fire of grief, but also, if we have allowed those flames to transmute us, we have arrived back with a radically changed perspective on life. Some of us, now that the searing pain has receded, live in a daily state of gratitude knowing that a phoenix has well and truly risen from those flames.

The following gifts to be found in loss have been taken from this section alone, and yet each one will have been witnessed emerging time and time again throughout this book. I feel blessed to have personally known them all.

Gifts to be found in loss

- Discovering how to slow down, let go, and be totally present in each moment with whatever is happening, unconcerned with yesterday or tomorrow.

- Appreciation of the preciousness of life on earth – the sunsets, the star light sky, the touch of a friend, the trees and the rocks.

- Increased gratitude for loved ones and feeling moved to express love more often.

- Compassion and empathy for others in trouble.

- The opportunity to see what needs attention in our own life and to heal what isn't working.

- Awareness of our strengths and the invincibility of the human spirit.

- The desire to serve others and to do something more useful and meaningful in life.

- Increased communication from dreams/visions and other realms.

- Acceptance of the necessary existence of birth and death, pleasure and pain.

- The possibility of experiencing a mystical union – a state of unity in which the concept of death dissolves.

If I were asked what has been the greatest gift from the death of Benjaya, I would definitely say number ten on this list. There has been nothing more powerful than experiencing the conviction I have carried for almost a lifetime – that there is no death. I spoke with Benjaya before he was born and I spoke with him and felt his undeniable presence after his death. Yes, of course there was the awful physical loss to contend with, but the sense of union I have felt with him, with the unseen realms, and with other human beings since he died has been profound beyond words.

The most indelible experience I had of this "oneness" was on the day of his funeral/celebration. I had been up since 4am and had spent the morning with a supportive group of friends, preparing the village hall for the arrival of over a hundred people that afternoon. By lunchtime, back at home, I was wilting and had not a scrap of energy left in me. I was drained, pregnant, nauseous and overwhelmed by the thought of having to do or feel one more thing. I had a morsel to eat then went upstairs to Benjaya's bedroom to put on my funeral clothes. With a sincere and desperate prayer for help to get me through this day, in which I would have to say my final goodbye to my son's body, I stepped into my ivory-white silk outfit and tied the thin black band of velvet around my head. It was at this moment I stepped into the mystical union. I felt an energy of untold power join with mine and I felt myself expand, my aura seeming to reach through the walls and way up above my head. I walked downstairs as if walking on air, feeling as if I could change the world. My parents and Abel sat open-mouthed at the transformation.

I felt totally at one with my son and with life – rock solid in my knowing that ultimately there is no loss. And, as the multitudes poured into the village hall greeting me, I felt their love lifting me still higher. Abel was grief-stricken, but as we sat together at the front facing everyone, I could not help but radiate all that is glorious about death. And when we stood to sing I chose to reign in my joy a little so that it would not be construed as inappropriate. It was at this point that two people saw Benjaya standing behind me.

Patricia felt this oneness after Doug's suicide, Hafsat felt it with her parents, Elaine felt it with Zachariah, and Rob felt it with everything in existence. Judith and the children of war felt it as they danced together in ecstasy, as did Bonnie in her epiphany experience. Given the right conditions, surely this sublime and yet ordinary gift – mystical union – is available to us all.

Eighth Key
FIND THE HIDDEN GIFTS
Questions and Reflections

1. Firstly, remember that place within you that feels totally safe. Then bring to mind a recent crisis. To what extent did you remain present with the feelings and to what extent did you attempt to escape the reality?
   What is your escape strategy?

2. Staying present with that difficulty now, give recognition to the discomfort of the feelings and then see if you can identify any opportunities or blessings offered by this particular event.

3. What have you learnt from your most challenging life experience that could help others? How might you activate this?

4. Since you began reading this book, has your attitude to pleasure and pain changed at all? If so, how? How do you expect that change to affect the way you deal with challenge?

5. In a creative and celebratory fashion, express and honor three of the gifts you have given of yourself in your lifetime (e.g. gave birth and love to two children, took care of sick mother, offered counseling skills for 6 years). Name one other positive influence you intend to have.

6. Sit quietly and bring to mind someone you care about. Think of one way that you could improve this relationship so that when you part you will feel better about yourself.

7. If someone you know has died or is close to death, put their life in perspective by taking a look at their whole life story (or as much as you can). What will you carry forward of them into the future?

8. What, if any, spiritual/uplifting beliefs do you have that could support you in times of trouble, and especially when facing death?
   Think of a way in which you could walk your talk more.

9. How would you describe your true identity? To what extent did the most difficult times in your life shape your understanding of who you are?

10. What are your current beliefs about separateness and the possibility of mystical union? What do you think is preventing you from experiencing such a state of unity?

Gathering the Keys

FROM
THE ASHES OF
SEPTEMBER 11

We have to go beyond grief, anger and fear
to learn something from this.
One of the things we need to learn is to begin to see
what people are enduring, and have endured,
in every part of the world.
Howard Zinn

Gathering the Keys – From the Ashes of September 11

The news hit me like a ton of bricks. Distance seemed irrelevant. We are told that the closer the physical proximity of the event, the more traumatized we are likely to be. Well, I was in my safe, stone walled cottage in a tiny English village when the phone call came and I was knocked sideways with shockwaves for weeks. However, I do have close friends in both New York and Washington and I had been in close proximity not so very long ago. It could have happened the day I had been visiting a friend in her office in the Twin Towers. What had moved her I wonder to spend her September 11th birthday on vacation in Italy? It could have happened three weeks earlier as I was snapping my young son's photograph in front of the towers on his first, long awaited trip to New York City – pictures that had arrived in the post on the morning those towers crumbled. Who does not have a story to tell of where they were on September 11, 2001 and of the impact of the day's unfolding events on their state of equilibrium?

Of course, there are those who passionately point out that ongoing horrors of equal magnitude were being lived around the globe at that very moment. Focusing here on the legacy of learning from this particularly tragic event in the Western world in no way diminishes that fact. On the contrary, I intend that it will raise awareness of the painful plight of human beings the world over.

Terrorism, wherever it strikes, is an act of violence and the resulting trauma experienced by its human targets is described as "violence trauma." Judith A. Swack, an expert on trauma,[38] names the possible effects specific to violence trauma.

My boundaries have been violated or breached.

Feeling of pollution: I (we, our country, our environment) feel contaminated by the evil that was done.

I don't feel safe; I feel vulnerable. I am a victim; I am a target.

People/men/women are dangerous and/or crazy so, I don't trust or I can't receive from anyone.

Power is bad; I am afraid of power (mine and or other people's).

Then, on top of that, if you lost a loved one, physical property, your employment, opportunities, your freedom, there are the possible effects of "loss trauma":

Anxiety about who will take care of me.

People leave me. I can't trust them.

Feeling of emptiness/loss.

Add to that the most common symptoms that can arise in response to both violence and loss trauma (below) and that is a mighty powerful cocktail of inner turbulence to contend with.

Shock, fear, anger or rage, sadness, hurt, and pain.

Irrational feelings of guilt, shame, and blame i.e., what happened is my fault; it is people other than the perpetrator's fault; it is God's fault.

I am helpless and have no control over the situation.

I (we, our country) am:
bad/unlovable/unwanted/undeserving/unworthy.

Anticipatory phobias, the dread that something bad will happen again.

At one point I had a list of six people ready to share their potent personal September 11 stories and was hoping to have examples of how the above symptoms can and have been moved through. However, I suffered a growing concern about how to include so many voices and a discomfort about the possibility of both the storytellers and certain readers being re-traumatized, given that mourning has definitely not completely broken yet for those closely involved. Then came a sharp about-turn. Five of the six interviewees, in an interesting variety of ways changed their minds at the eleventh hour, leaving me with only one – a down-to-earth firefighter by the name of Greg Fagan. Every avenue I followed to obtain more personal stories was blocked, however, two professionals working with those suffering the effects of 9/11 both offered to voice the fruits of their experience. So I decided to focus this section less on the personal angle, much of which the media has covered in depth, and more on a wider angle.

We will enter at the personal level by following the unfolding healing process of our firefighter, whose response echoes countless unnamed others. Next I will include practical wisdom from forensic psychiatrist, Roy Lubit, who has interviewed and worked with many of the survivors of September 11 in New York. Then a Jungian analyst will take us into the profound lessons that emerged for her that day in relation to the place of unknowing. And finally I will expand into what could be called the macrocosmic lessons of this mass crisis, showing how the same eight keys that can be used to handle personal adversity can also be used in a global way to open even bigger doors.

Greg Fagan's Story – Surviving the Valleys of Steel

Carol Patti, a delightfully supportive friend of mine, was so sure that a fireman's voice would be one of the most appropriate for this section of the book that she walked into a fire station near her home in Brooklyn and asked outright who would be willing to talk with me. Greg Fagan answered the call and made an immense effort to ensure he could be with me in a tall office block close to the site of destruction.

On the morning of September 11, I was at home on Long Island in Kings Park, working in my garage. My wife calls me to come and look at the television. They just keep showing that first plane hitting the World Trade Center time and time again. Then, when a plane hits the second tower I know it's a terrorist act and that I have to go back to work. There's havoc in the house because my wife wants me to stay home. She's crying and pleading with me not to go, but she knows I have to go because I'm in Squad Company One. We do confined space, high angle rescue, collapse, trench rescue, and I know the whole squad will be utilized. I say to myself 'Okay, we're going to have our hands full here,' but I don't think the buildings will collapse.

As I'm driving into work on the parkway I'm doing 80 miles an hour, the adrenaline's flowing and you have to get around somebody doing 70 'cause that isn't fast enough! My wife calls me and I ask her to get on the radio stations to ask people to move off the left wing because you can see that firemen and cops going in to work are all doing 80 miles an hour. Then I'm listening to her on the radio. Usually you have to hit people in New York in the head with a stick to listen, but right from the beginning people are moving over.

I arrive in Brooklyn on the other side of the river to the towers. Whoever was off has reported back to work. We gather up our gear and head to the staging area at the bottom of the bridge. The bridge is backed up with fire trucks and you can't get across. We got to get over there and it isn't moving, so a group of us pile into an ambulance and head off over another bridge and get there at the time the second building, Tower One, collapses. We report in to a command post and the chief is overwhelmed with manpower. They want to know exactly who's signed on.

The city's in total chaos. What we're looking at is something you'd never seen nothing like in your life. Devastation! Three to four inches of white muck on the ground, papers all over the place. It looks like a terminator movie. We go down to the Trade Center and enter up by building Seven, which is still standing at this time. Fire trucks and buildings are on fire, cars burnt all over the place. You want to do something so you just keep moving, looking for people. Buildings Five and Six are on fire at the front. One and Two were the towers.

We go into the basement through the parking garage but the place is pretty much empty. The noises, the banging and the sounds the buildings are making are so eerie. We have our fire fighting gear, a couple of flashlights between us and no real tools. When we come across any city agency car we rummage through it to find some equipment. We press on trying to hook up with our guys because we didn't have a clue what really happened until we made it around the block. That's when we saw the towers down all over the street. We find the fire truck for our company and see how tore up it is. The guys write their names on the dust on the rig and that's kind of eerie. Nobody knows where anybody is and the command post has been taken out.

We all look at the pile of metal, like 'what have we got to do here?' There's no viable way of going in. We look through all the piles of steel, climbing up and down valleys of steel, our minds working on rescuing a person out of these piles of mess. We search through any void and keep going down the only part of the towers left standing – a stairwell. It's real precarious, real dangerous but it is the only thing that looks like we might get to the people.

I was involved with pulling two people out of the stairwell, but that was it. It was *very* depressing. We're not used to this. Four thousand people missing; where are they? We figured we'd see them all over the street, all over somewhere, but we didn't see any of them. Even those who had jumped from windows were now under the rubble. In my whole career we always got the job done – Oklahoma or wherever. We'd never seen anything like this or had any concept of this magnitude, and if our guys had weighed all the pros and cons of going into the towers we probably wouldn't have gone in, but our training says you got to get the job done. So, if there was a hole and we could fit into it we climbed in. We went as far as we could.

We stayed there from Tuesday morning until about midnight Wednesday, and then went back to the firehouse to bed for about six hours. We were back by seven the next morning. The next two weeks we worked a lot of hours there and it's hard to remember what we did. They had chairs by World Finance and we all sat down and passed out for an hour or two then got up and went back to work.

What kept us going was hope. I was saying 'people can live for periods of time.' We were looking at these piles of steel and just hoping we would pick it up and there'd be a room full of people. It never happened. We were checking where you caught the train by the World Trade Center where there's a little shopping mall. That in itself was a mission. Everything was collapsed and you had to go through a void where the ceiling had fallen, crawling where you could barely fit. We were working on adrenaline.

We did the best job we could. I don't think we could have done any more or any different as a fire department. We gave 110 percent. Fire fighting is a scary, exciting job. You come out of a building and you're physically exhausted; you gave whatever you had until you could barely walk. Firemen always want to help. They teach you to be a team. If one guy has fallen behind, four guys don't run up and leave the fifth guy back, you all come in together. Now it doesn't matter where you go, they find out you're a New York City fire fighter and they can't do enough for you. That is such a good feeling.

The first couple of days when we were using buckets to move stuff, it was anybody and everybody up on the 'hill.' The firemen stopped and saluted the remains of civilians, not only the firemen, as a mark of respect and that was important to us. News traveled like wild fire on the hill and pretty soon we knew Bin Laden was the guy who caused this grief. We kind of needed somebody to blame, so we released the anger and hate his way and got on with the job. Sometimes I get so enraged. I don't say lynch them; let the courts do what they're going to do with them. What gets me going is that people are already forgetting what's happened.

But the families are still calling the fire department. We've got these ties to the families who lost family members and it's an ongoing thing. This week they just did open heart surgery on this kid who's 16 months old who had a hole in his heart. His father was killed on September 11 and the wife has five kids to look after, so the fire company fills in. The guys have been up in the hospital around the clock. There is a lot of giving happening. The whole country is united now.

You've got to work, got to survive, got to provide for your family but sometimes you get caught up in that. I could say it's a positive thing that I now pay more attention to my family and the things that I've taken for granted. There's like a wake up call here. You might not be here tomorrow. I have three boys: 19-year-old twins at college, and a son of eleven. They were affected this way also. They were scared that I went back in there and when I came home at last, my little guy came running up, and even the twins came up and they were hugging me. That was all positive but life is getting back to normal at home and they're not doing that kind of stuff no more. That's reality. Unfortunately, people are forgetting already.

It is getting easier to a degree. It's a tight group in the firehouse. I have been in the fire department for twelve and a half years and it's like a second family. You work Christmas, New Year and the holidays and you eat together. They're a bunch of kidders who like playing jokes on each other. It's one happy family that's unhappy right now. We got new guys in the firehouse who are doing a good job but it's hard for them because they're not the eleven guys we lost.

Seven months on, the Government assigned counselors to every firehouse that lost people. It lets us get stuff out. I think it's working. It's important to keep talking. Fortunate for us we're a group that talk, we'll open up and talk with each other every work shift, better than with a psychiatrist. If you were say an insurance broker, you wouldn't have what we have. You might be close with your secretary or friends, but we're actually a family and that helped us a lot. Somebody who doesn't have that has got to find it. Find a group of people. That was a big relief. I have an advantage over the other guys because I've been in another fellowship for 15 years. They say 'Hey, how you doing? I say 'I'm doing good' and they say 'you're full of crap.' They call me on my stuff. I have people I have confidence in and I didn't have to build that up.

From the start until now I didn't think I could be where I am today. I didn't know when I was going to get over it but I knew I would eventually. My sister was killed when she was 15 and I was very close to her, so I know that time can heal. At the time I was a wild, crazy guy. My first thought when my sister was killed was that I'd got to kill the guy that killed her. Who could take her away? I knew that if I could survive through that then I could get through this.

We're dreading September coming up again because we are all going to mourn our losses. You know, we don't want to put the uniform on any more. We just wore it too much for death. I don't want to hear bagpipes. That was the highlight of a funeral, sending off our guys with the helicopters above and the bagpipes. I went to a St. Patrick's Day party and the bagpipes were playing. I said 'I'm leaving this second.' It depresses me. I start tapping my feet and I just got to get out of there.

Crying happened to all of us. We just had to. There was a cracking open of the tough guy façade. You just couldn't deal with it all – going from one funeral to another, memorial masses without bodies. The tragedy was so large. Out of the fire department I might have known a hundred of those guys personally. One thing I was aware of going on at the site was that it was easier to just say '3,000 people' because I had enough on my plate. One guy came up and said 'I lost my wife' and I didn't want to put a face to him. It was easier for us not to know the people.

My relationship to other people has changed because there were so many people giving help and support. Candlelight vigils happened outside our firehouse and we knew that the people were behind us in our grief. I was never the most cheery guy around the firehouse so now I make a point of going that extra step – for instance I'm more open now if somebody wants to bring their kid into the firehouse. I feel they were there for us so it's like a pay back.

As a result from the Trade Center tragedy, I'm feeling a bit more open hearted, a little more outgoing, a little more forgiving. Everyone is getting back but it's never going to be the same – there are too many friendships that I'll never have again. It is getting better every day and I do see a change. I'm moving on. Where I'm at is not a bad place most of the time. Keeping busy helps and there's a lot of work to be done.

You've got to have faith – believe in somebody or something. I believe in a higher power, in God. Why did we have the mildest winter in history? Explain to me why. You can say it's coincidence. Maybe. I believe that God was saying 'there's a job that's got to get done.' He couldn't stop the evil but he could make it as pleasant for us as possible so we could work. I believe those that have gone are in heaven. I don't go to church except for weddings and Christmas but I talk to God in my own way. I know he's there because he watched out for us and gave us the strength to go on. Now we're starting to gel and recuperate and I'm fortunate that I'm where I'm at.

Greg's admission that he didn't want to put a face to any of the victims because it was easier to say "3,000 people" is important. It shows us that there is a fine line between protection of our needs and indifference. Greg was filled to capacity with his own grief and genuinely unable to cope with the reality of anyone else's at that time. But that is not always the case when we distance ourselves with abstraction into figures. Just as the holocaust was one by one by one, not six million, so are the wounded of every war one by one by one, not collateral damage. It is up to us to discern and stop this pattern in ourselves when it tips from personal protection into a place that encourages indifference and blocks compassion and helpful action.

What kept Greg going? Hope, adrenaline and a stoic commitment to succeeding in getting the job done. What assisted him in his healing process? Knowing that he had done the best he possibly could; being in a supportive family-like team who could talk; having a track record of success with overcoming grief; releasing his anger (albeit in blame); crying; and having his own connection with a higher power. In what ways has this crisis changed him? His relationships with others have transformed; he is more open-hearted; he cares more for his family; he has negative associations with anything that reminds him of the deaths, such as bagpipes and his uniform (amygdala in action making him want to leave that second); and he is more outgoing, generous and forgiving.

Although Greg is obviously pleased about the move back toward normality he is disturbed by the awareness that people are forgetting. I don't think it is the event that people are forgetting, how could they? I think it is the changes catalyzed in people by the horrific circumstances that are in danger of being forgotten as people fall back into old habits. The British Prime minister, Tony Blair, said on October 2, 2001,

> *This is a moment to seize.*
> *The Kaleidoscope has been shaken.*
> *The pieces are in flux. Soon they will settle again.*
> *Before they do, let us re-order this world around us.*

It is said that it takes six weeks of living a new habit before it becomes integrated. And so we need to be vigilant. All the practical support, the sense of unity, and openhearted sharing that occurred immediately after the terrorists' onslaught (or after any major disaster) needs to be nurtured and continued regularly in order to retain it. And although this attack is not as vividly alive in people as it was, there is still immense need out there for help – both for those directly affected by that day's events and those affected by traumatic events of other days. There were people all around us before the attack who needed help. They are still there. Could it be that now, due to our eyes being opened more fully to suffering, and having experienced a deeper sense of compassion, we have more to give to those in need? I sincerely hope so.

Roy Lubit – Through the Eyes of a Psychiatrist

In his interview Roy speaks of serendipity, which is exactly how we met. I had been bemoaning the lack of an expert voice that could corroborate my findings from the data gathered in this book. Within an hour of my arrival in New York City to conduct the final interview with Greg Fagan, a friend told me that she had met this lovely psychiatrist who specializes in trauma and is doing a research project interviewing World Trade Center survivors to talk about the impact. Within 24 hours, in a state of wonder and gratitude, I was sitting in his office gleaning his generous wisdom. I was delighted to hear him voicing from his research very similar advice to that which has arisen all over this book from the experience of those who have succeeded in personal transformation through crisis.

> I'm a psychiatrist at St Vincent's Hospital in Manhattan, the medical center closest to Ground Zero. I work with both children and adults. On September 11 I wasn't at work. I was taking my 3-year-old to school for the first time. I was in the classroom and a call came through that there had been tremendous explosions at the World Trade Center. I went into the next room and watched it on television. I recall thinking that the world as we knew it would never be the same again. The sense of security that we have had since the Cold War ended would now be gone. There was a sense of shock and worry and wondering what it was going to mean for us and the world my children are going to grow up in. But it wasn't a personal emergency as it was for so many.
>
> From the following day I became a workaholic on overdrive. It was very important for me to *do* something helpful. I spent the next day at a family assistance center helping people see if their missing loved ones were on the list of those hospitalized, with the assumption that if they weren't they were dead. People were not up to talking to mental health professionals then. They wanted to look at the lists of people who had

been hospitalized and, if they were not on the list, go to all the hospitals in the hope that they would find them nonetheless. It was heartbreaking. One couple had moved from Russia three or four years ago to get a better life for their children, and their 21-year-old son was now missing and probably dead.

That weekend I volunteered to work at the family support center set up by a large company that had lost many employees, and over the months since then I have worked with a large number of companies and individuals, some intensively.

A huge number of people continue to have symptoms many months after the tragedy. We're seeing the classic symptoms that people have after life threatening experiences. Both adults and children have difficulty sleeping, nightmares, irritability and are easily startled. Many people have intrusive memories of 9/11. This can involve memories of what happened invading their thoughts and getting in the way of other activities, feeling very upset or physically distressed whenever smells or sights or situations remind them of the disaster, feeling as if it was happening again. Children tend to engage in repetitive play about the disaster. Many people feel numb, are unable to enjoy things and find it difficult to feel close to others. People often avoid conversations or situations that remind them of what occurred. Children tend to become clingy, have sleep problems, develop new fears and sometimes become aggressive. Teenagers often become even more risk prone than usual.

In trauma, painful memories come to dominate our minds. Normally we scan our memories for all sorts of different images. We select what we want to think about. This is often not possible after being traumatized. The painful memories of what occurred keep forcing through into consciousness, pushing aside everything else.

People who lose a loved one generally develop a powerful sense of sadness or another painful emotion, may withdraw from social contact, may lose interest or pleasure in daily activities, and may have somatic/physical symptoms. Those who lose a loved one in a sudden and violent way often develop what we call complicated or traumatic bereavement, with unusually intense or persistent grief, unusual difficulty letting go of their loved one and moving on in life, and a trauma reaction in which they have intrusive memories of the horrible ways in which their loved one died. This can completely prevent them from going through the mourning process and moving on with their lives.

People often don't realize how much children are suffering. Parents and teachers classically don't realize when a child is having problematic levels of anxiety or depression. I've seen children who were suicidal and their parents did not know anything was wrong. An older sibling told me something was wrong and suggested I speak with their younger brother. After a disaster parents are particularly unlikely to be aware that their children are having a hard time since the parents are preoccupied.

One reason that people don't realize how much pain children are in is that they tend to cycle between feeling really badly and playing. Parents see them playing and assume they have gotten over things, but they haven't. People tend to say that children are resilient. They are in the sense that they can step aside from the pain for a few minutes and play. In the long term, however, they are much more vulnerable than adults to disasters. Their personalities are still forming and tragedies can seriously affect them.

Some people, to protect themselves from the painful experience, not only become numb, but also dissociate at the time of the tragedy. They feel as if they are looking at a movie and the world is not real or they are not real. Recent studies indicate that there are physical things happening in their brains that make their experience different from those of people who do not dissociate. The numbness can be protective, and help us to slowly accept the painful new reality that we live in. It can, however, also be very destructive, by getting in the way of rebuilding our lives. The tendency to become numb or dissociate when faced with reminders of a trauma can also be dangerous. It is one pathway by which someone can develop learned helplessness. Dissociation and numbing get in the way of our being able to think clearly and get ourselves out of harm's way. This is why so many people who are victimized become victims again.

Another important issue is that going through a trauma can change how we feel about others and ourselves. After 9/11 many people developed bad feelings about themselves, believing they should have done something differently. I've seen people who behaved bravely and wisely, but feel badly because they did not do something heroic. Some have survivor guilt: 'I survived and you didn't, so I feel badly.'

Many people are struggling to find meaning in what happened and are reassessing what the meaning of life is and what they are doing with their lives. Many people, particularly children, develop a foreshortened sense of the future – the sense that life may end tomorrow. Young people sometimes want to leave school or precipitously get married, or engage in exciting and very risky activities. Sometimes the sense that life is short leads to helpful changes in people's lives as they reevaluate their priorities and how they spend their time. Some adults working hard at their careers say, 'wait a minute; there are other things in life. I want to spend more time with friends and family, be more patient with people.'

The theme I have seen time and time again is that someone whose life was in danger decides to put more emphasis on the present, on enjoying things. One person I worked with has become more assertive. She feels life is short and her time may not come if it doesn't come now.

She sees herself as stronger now that she has survived this terrible incident. I talked with a high-powered businesswoman, whose focus for life had been driving her career and having a good time with her friends. She was very badly shaken up and has been trying to understand what this means and how life can be enjoyed when there's so much pain in it for so many people. Like a lot of people I've seen, now she wants to work in an area in which she can help people. She said that the point of life for her after 9/11 is to feel deeply rather than to just feel good.

It has been said many times: crisis is an opportunity as well as a danger. Some grow from it and some become weakened by it. People are shaken up and forced to rethink their lives. The question is then, which way do they go? Do they fall into despair? Or do they struggle to rethink some of their values and create a more meaningful life? And there's a third option: they get some help and work themselves out of the anxiety and depression to find a path that is more rewarding than the one they were on.

Most people recover from the emotional impact of trauma; but some don't. Almost everyone develops symptoms for a while. One could say that it's failure to recover that is the problem. The people who don't recover are often those with secondary stresses and lack of support. People who maintain a lot of anger or who have negative feelings about themselves after the event also tend not to do well. People who feel that they have some control of their destiny – what psychologists call an internal locus of control – tend to do better than those who feel that they have little control in the world. Other risk factors for not being able to get over the tragedy on one's own are having a dissociative reaction at the time of the event; having been traumatized in the past, and witnessing particularly grotesque things. At Stuyvesant High School, students saw people jumping out of the towers. They learned that you can tell a falling body from debris because debris falls faster than bodies. It's not the sort of image you want on your mind.

During the period immediately after a trauma the most important things are to stop and to contain the damage. I advise people not to re-traumatize themselves by constant reminders of the tragedy. I tell them to turn off the television. People need a comfortable safe place and to limit the uncertainties in their lives: Are their loved ones okay? Where will they live? Will they be financially ruined? Another critical issue is to mobilize your support system. The literature on Post Traumatic Stress Disorder informs us that it is critical for people to mobilize their support system and to avoid secondary stresses. People often need help in doing this, however. After losing a loved one or almost being killed it is often hard for people to think clearly and to act. People often need assistance in remembering what helps to make them feel better. They need encouragement to eat, sleep and take care of any medical problems they have.

The treatment for trauma involves getting past the painful images. For some people this happens in time, by itself, as they share the experience with close ones and go on with life. For many, it is hard to get back to a productive, reasonably enjoyable life. Negative thoughts about themselves and others, irritability, anxiety, and a sense of hopelessness not only fail to heal on their own but also do damage to their relationships and work. The intrusive memories continue. These people need help in processing their memories and thoughts. They need to share the memories in a safe, therapeutic setting in order to move beyond them. We encourage people to replace the painful images with less painful ones. I ask children to draw pictures of that day, of how they see things now, then of how they'd like to see things in the future.

For someone who is filled with an image from fantasy or reality of a mutilated parent, I try to replace that image by asking them to tell me about the good times they had together. You can also suggest that they put a picture of the person in or on their loved one's coffin to try and move their thoughts away from the grotesque way in which their loved one died toward the way they had once shared life together.

It is also critical to talk with them about how the tragedy has affected their images of themselves and the world to resolve the guilt and fear so many feel after tragedies. Cognitive therapists say that thoughts lead to feelings and behaviors, and that you need to evaluate your thoughts because many thoughts are inaccurate or unhelpful. For example, if you're walking down the street and a friend walks by without speaking to you, some people will say 'how dare he', and some will say 'he must be upset.'

Different people have very different emotional reactions depending on which thought the person has. In cognitive therapy you are taught to challenge ideas, ways of thinking about the world, that are unhelpful and cause pain. After a disaster, people often develop a number of thoughts about themselves and the world that cause them pain. People often start feeling that the world is so dangerous that life as they had lived it is no longer possible, that they can't trust others, and that they are weak and possibly to blame. Talking about and evaluating these ideas is crucial for someone to heal.

Another important part of the therapy of trauma is to talk about what occurred, in depth, in a therapeutic setting. The victim needs to learn that the memory of the event can be talked about. The event was dangerous, but the memory of the event is not. They need to see that they can tolerate thinking about it and learn to have the memory come to mind without flooding them. Sharing the memory in a therapeutic environment in which their anxiety level can be modulated serves to detoxify the memories. This may seem to contradict what I said before about not flooding yourself with memories of the disaster. There is a crucial difference between therapeutic exposures and non-therapeutic encounters with traumatic reminders. Finding the line between the two is tricky and often requires the help of a skilled therapist trained in this area. The wrong therapeutic technique can easily do damage.

Once people are doing better I encourage them to take an active role in how they grow and in shaping their future and new life.

Some people can't get through traumatic grief on their own and for them therapy is absolutely vital. They're suffering and trying the best way they know how to deal with the event, which is usually to block it out. But it doesn't work. It needs to be talked about and worked through. This is not analysis that takes years; I usually see people for several weeks.

Unfortunately, the people who are most devastated often do not come for therapy because they believe it will be too painful to talk. Many people sustain tremendous damage to their work and family life as a result of the symptoms that follow tragedies. It is unnecessary and sad. We can't save the nearly 3000 people who died on 9/11. We can, however, help the tens to hundreds of thousands who sustained serious emotional trauma and may be adversely affected for years. The failure of people to get help that is available is another tragedy.

Rosalind Winter's Story – Reflections on 9/11

Rosalind Winter is a much respected and well-loved Jungian analyst and sand play therapist in Montclair, New Jersey and New York City. Her story is a combination of an article called "Reflections on 9/11" that she wrote herself for publication, and a short interview I conducted with her at her home shortly afterward. I'll begin with her article.[39]

On Tuesday, September 11, I was plunged into unknowingness. Unusual circumstances had put me in my car at 10am where I learned about the tragedy over the car radio. Driven by instinct, I found myself parking illegally in front of the local high school. I heard my own voice say: 'Go in.' The principal, in the midst of the chaos, noted my presence, asking, 'Can you do something? I have all the kids whose parents work in the World Trade Center in the library.' Nodding yes, I proceeded more or less unconsciously up the stairs to the library.

The library has double glass doors. From the outside, I saw 60 to 70 kids centered on a television screen: kids who did not know if their parents were alive. The enormity of the situation drew me back into consciousness. I took a deep breath and entered the space of unknowingness. The atmosphere was intense, as though no one was breathing. In a state of contained panic, school administrators were on phones, desperately trying to locate the students' family members. The kids were mostly focused on the television, trying to figure out what was happening. For the next hours, I emotionally and physically held kids, some of whom I had never met before, some of whom I had known since they were four, in a state of not knowing.

A young woman, her second day in the school, having just arrived from Taiwan, sat at a library table alone. When I approached her, Meng-Yee told me that her father worked on the 103rd floor of the first tower that was struck. She was sure that he was dead. In a singsong voice, she told me he would not want her to be sad. We talked about the possibility of not really knowing whether he was dead or alive. Could we wait and see? I suggested. It was easier for her to imagine that he was dead than to tolerate not knowing.

I noticed a group of girls, all cousins, wailing in a corner. They were unable to speak. 'Can you pray?' I offered. Yes. They began praying, saying over and over again that they knew; they just knew their aunt was alive... But?

A 17-year-old boy was sitting alone, agitated, throwing pencils. He looked in the opposite direction as I approached him. He was not going to speak with me. Did anyone know who his friends were? Could they find them? Yes. His sister came into the library hysterical. He pulled himself together for her. When the librarian reached their mother on the phone a few moments later, they walked out hugging.

Then, most terrifying to me, I noticed my son's best friend across the room, rigidly standing in front of the TV. My son appeared. After a quick hug, I asked, 'What's with Alyssa?' 'Her dad's on a plane and there are still five planes unaccounted for.' My heart sank. I held Alyssa as she cried. I struggled to remind her that we did not know, we just did not know yet if her father was alive or dead. In addition, her good friend Linda's aunt was pulled from the rubble dead. How do I hold a differentiated possibility for Alyssa? She was losing it. I had Alyssa call her mother every 15 minutes. It gave her a focus. We held Linda, cried with her and kept phoning mom. Her father was not on a missile plane. He had landed safely in Chicago.

A voice summoned Meng-Yee to the office over the loud speaker. What could this mean? I walked her downstairs. Her mother was standing at the main office hysterical. I had to work with her to find out whether Meng-Yee's Dad was alive or not. He had been getting a cup of coffee on the 30th floor. He was safe. Unknowingness resolved for the moment.

Being able to hold this unbearable tension, the tension of the opposites – of life or death, safe or not safe – and thus staying in unknowingness, was a profound struggle for all of us. A quotation from the I Ching, hexagram number 5, 'Hsii' (Waiting or Nourishment)[40] comes to mind: 'It is only when we have the courage to face things exactly as they are, without any sort of self-deception or illusion, that a light will develop out of events, by which the path to success may be recognized.' In my practice, holding the tension of opposites is a daily work, one in which one waits, with a faith that the transcendent, the 'light' that will illumine, will appear. My practice and training as an analyst had developed my mind and heart to wait, to be in unknowingness, to have the courage to face things exactly as they are, and to trust 'that a light will develop out of events.' Yet never have I felt so put to the test, so pushed to the very edge of my own limits as on September 11, when the opposites were life and death.

At that moment, regardless of our own feelings and of the unbearable tension that we were experiencing, the adults needed to be present, to soothe, to reassure, and to hold the intense anxiety and fear of our children. Within the hour, a few other therapists arrived. Parents appeared; we accepted all help and all need to be helpful. The library became our command center, a place where people could congregate, connect and be of service. I ordered in bottles of water, sandwiches and snacks. I kept remembering and saying to myself, 'water for shock, water for shock.' It was my mantra. We used up all the water in the school building within 45 minutes. Someone got more bottles of water donated immediately. I was amazed at everyone's flexibility and resourcefulness. The school staff was admirable, doing their job and more. The Principal, Elaine Peeler-Davis, was setting a tone of openness and containment. She was holding a tension that provided space for individual initiative and community consciousness.

The television in the library became the campfire that we huddled around. When the teachers checked the latest news, they also could take the opportunity to process their feelings with a therapist. A group of students realized that those 17 or older could give blood. Posters on how to give blood were being made by the dozens. We realized that perhaps more posters than there were 17-year-olds would be created. We offered the kids long rolls of mural paper, markers and crayons. Murals began to appear in the hallways. The library became the hub, the center of activity. There was a place to go, to express oneself. The students stayed in school, at that moment it was a 'safe' a place to be.

As evening approached, a colleague and I organized a meeting for local therapists willing to work in the high school. Between the end of school and the meeting, I checked my email. I remember bursting into tears. There were people on line who were not as exposed as I was, people who were offering help. I downloaded some pieces on how to talk with children about trauma, and a piece on developmental stages and possible reactions to death. I knew the teachers needed support. Something concrete in their hands would help. I took the handouts to the meeting, and they became the basis of a packet of materials that each teacher had in their mailboxes the following morning. Some of those materials were later distributed district wide.

The following day, we worked in the rubble, the rubble of our broken sense of security, in an extreme state of unknowingness. What would happen next? How many students had lost parents? How many had lost aunts, uncles, or friends? How would the students and the faculty members handle themselves, given their own personal as well as the collective levels of fear and grief? Therapists met with classes as requested. Middle Eastern and Indian students were afraid to leave their English-as-a-Second-Language classroom. On the spot intervention was required. Many students were terrified, anxiety was running wild. Mr. Murray, a teacher, chose to deal with the feelings and the content of what was happening as it was happening in his classroom. He used the therapists as resources. And as the unofficial 'Elder,' he served as a role model for the faculty. Through his communication, we were able monitor the emotional state of those students who did not choose to huddle with their peers in the library.

The students felt the need to participate, to be of use. They began working on a candlelight vigil for that evening. Eight hundred plus candles and other supplies were donated from local supermarkets. Arrangements were made for the dignitaries, the mayor and all the city council, police and fire chiefs, and clergy of every religion in town to be present. Approximately 800 people attended a moving evening of student-led poetry reading, singing and speeches. When the young woman singing God Bless America began to cry, the adults on the stage gathered behind her and supported her by continuing the song. That moment served as a metaphor for the day: the adults stepping in, as needed, to be the support our teenagers could count on. As we lit our candles in complete silence a fighter jet flew overhead. It was the first plane we had heard or seen since air space was closed on Tuesday morning. When we sang America the Beautiful it was with renewed determination and pride.

Within two weeks, Roz, who knows the power of working with symbols to access and integrate trauma, had found a way for sand trays to be used as therapeutic aids in schools and in her local Town Hall. Sand trays are simply trays of sand in which miniature objects may be placed for both individual and collective symbol-making experience. People going into the Town Hall for counseling created an ongoing collective expression when they placed a miniature that was symbolic of their experience of 9/11, in relation to the other objects in the tray of sand. The Town Manager reported the success of the sand tray, and said that he and various municipal employees, including the police and fire fighters, used it regularly. Roz told me,

> Frequently used items were lighthouses (standing for the World Trade Centers in their role of orienting points / directions), super heroes (fallen in the sand), broken body parts, buried babies and religious figures. The ugliest evil death images always found their way into the sand.
>
> It is important to understand that during trauma the left side of the brain shuts down. The left side is the linear side of the brain. It is the part that uses logic and verbal expression. Hence, when we are in trauma we are so often speechless. We assimilate traumatic experiences by using the right side of the brain. Our right brain processes images, emotions and bodily sensations. It is non-verbal. In order to work through trauma we need to access the right side of the brain and reconnect to our experiences through images, emotions and physical symptoms.

During the 9/11 experience Roz adapted Sandplay Therapy to the school environment, naming it Symbol Formation. She has trained social workers, psychologists, and school counselors to support students and it is now being used in the Montclair, New Jersey School System and an expanding number of other schools impacted by the crisis.

"Symbol Formation" is a method of accessing and containing the intense emotions, haunting images and physical sensations associated with trauma and its processing. In "Symbol Formation" people select or create a symbol/image that expresses their experience, providing both an opportunity for cathartic relief and a containment of the anxiety or other intense emotions associated with the experience of trauma.

I asked Roz, "As a therapist, what would you most like to convey to others at this point regarding the unnerving events manifesting on our planet?" She spoke about the archetype of evil, which I included under the sixth key as it was even more relevant there, and then she continued with the following:

> I was completely unsettled by Sept 11, but I wasn't surprised. I have nothing in me that can call the terrorists evil because I think that in a state of desperation people will do unimaginable things. Look at our culture and our history: currently hip-hop idealizes violence. But so have other political movements. The sixties were full of revolutionary fever in America. Many were willing to kill and die for freedom. Humans kill to get what they deem unattainable by any other means. I think that if people were aware of their own desperation they would appreciate another's. In my work as an analyst, I am acutely aware of the moment when a new parent finally understands the feelings inherent in hitting a child. Not that they should hit, but the urge is fairly universal. Frustration, feelings of hopelessness and powerlessness are part of all of

our experiences. What we do with them is another thing. Our own unconscious desire to annihilate gets activated; we are pulled to act it out consciously. There is an enemy and it is within us.

In my experience, people who have been directly impacted by the events of Sept 11 have been moved by the power of grief, awed by the collective experience and the sense of being small. They seem less moved by the power of revenge. In my practice, I've been doing intense work to mine the gold the situation inadvertently offered. I told all of my clients that they had a six-week window of opportunity to rework their earliest traumas that were unconsciously re-activated by 9/11. Not only was their own unconscious material now available, collectively there was enormous support for grieving and neediness. You could cry for 24 hours a day and you could be needy and people would understand. People who had suffered severe early trauma were thrown back into the mental states associated with them. But now they had millions of people who could relate to devastating experiences. One woman who lost a parent before the age of six was thrown back into her trauma, this time though, there was a collective acceptance of the unpredictability of the world. She was not the only one who was impacted by circumstances she could not control. Nor was she responsible for what had happened to her; all of the children who lost parents had done nothing that could hold them responsible for the loss of their parents. This was just a part of life.

We can't simply say that, because some have made good use of the terrible situation, life will be different. I want to stress that we need people with strong egos that can mediate the personal and archetypal energies of the psyche. Without strong egos we are thrown about by both personal and collective unconscious forces. I do think that there is a growing sense of an opportunity for peace because of the increased awareness and consciousness of the need to relate to the archetypal power of evil.

The Macrocosmic Lessons

Observing the reaction of people and nations across the globe to the events of September 11, I began to see the same keys emerging generally as had emerged from my individual storytellers.

Key 1. – Find the Bigger Picture

When we lift our eyes from the horror of the thousands of individual crises that began that day, what can be seen? Firstly, the date of this attack was 9/11 or 9-1-1 (the emergency phone number for the U.S.). So was this a distress call – a global call for awakening and action? Eighty nations were affected directly by the terrorist attacks, due to the international usage of the target buildings, which intensified its global impact. There is a call to community on a large scale and the opportunity to experience compassion for all the peoples of the world who live with terrorism or pain in any form. The enormous sacrifice of life has prompted deep questioning. Exactly what do we stand for in life – darkness or light? Do we want freedom, justice, retaliation, revenge, to support life, or cause death? What are the core values of our nation? Do we want global unity and peace?

Synchronicities abound. What a fascinating, and no doubt sobering, research project it would be to discover as many synchronicities, dreams and predictions as possible connected to September 11. This was a foreseen event; by how many we do not know. And that leaves us questioning whether it could have been prevented by heightened security or any other means. Here's one such prediction. Years ago, my friend, Linda, was told in a reading that the time would come when Manhattan, from 14th Street down would never be the same again. There would be a major disaster and she would be spared to continue her work. On September 12, 2001 the BBC news reported, "From 14th Street down has been declared a war zone." Linda was not in her office five blocks from the area the Press named "Ground Zero" that day, and was thankfully spared.

Only the other day, in an English village, I was speaking to an artist, David Cowell, about this book. The subject turned to September 11. "Do you believe in synchronicity?" he asked. When I nodded he told me,

> Three days before September 11, I was out walking and I saw this amazing sight. It was a charred piece of wood that looked like a cross between a crucifix and a human figure. I was so captivated by it that I took photographs and spent the next few days painting a picture from it. I painted flames all around it so that the figure looked as if it was diving out of the fire. It made the hairs stand up on my neck. Then came September 11 and I didn't have the nerve to put it in my forthcoming exhibition as I had intended. Then, in November, out of the blue, I received an email from a gallery in New York asking if I had any response to the events of September 11. Of course I did, except that it was more of a premonition rather than a response!

Key 2. – *Trust and Surrender Control*

One of the things that I have heard and read repeatedly in relation to 9/11 is that this event was particularly traumatic because, added to the momentous loss of life, was the loss of the sense of invincibility of the American security systems. And more than once I read, "What the U.S. needs is to get our sense of control back." I wonder what that meant? Hopefully it meant "power with", for wouldn't any "power over" attitude be sure to cause an escalation of the fury that provoked the terrorist attacks by those who believe, true or not, that they are being controlled by a superpower? If it meant that Americans need to find a sense of balance and inner safety rather than safety dependent solely on military protection, then, in my humble opinion, that would have been good advice.

To trust in a greater plan in this situation is of course a tall order, if not a total impossibility for those who have no such spiritual beliefs. Personally, when I thought of the deaths of all those people, what gave me comfort was to remember what I was told when I thought my second son would die,

> *If you can give your second son fully to his destiny and can sacrifice the security of human attachment, then, and only then will your inner security blossom.*

In a beautifully written article in *Hope Magazine*[41] by author and resilience expert, Derrick Jenson, he said,

> *It is possible to look back on one's history, no matter how horrible. And find places of relative safety, where fear was never allowed to enter. Those places can teach us, if we let them, that as well as knowing fear we can know safety and peace.*

What occurred to me on reading this was that the U.S. has a recent history of feeling safe, and although that makes the contrast of losing that feeling all the more pronounced, it also means that there is a national resource in those remembered places of safety. Many other countries have no recent track record of peace and little faith that they will ever find safety.

Key 3. – Share Your Pain and Choose Life

The catastrophic events of 9/11 gave a vivid example of the kind of energy that can be released when pain is shared. Grief was not hidden. It was spilled in public and was fully heard by many allies, creating connection and compassion beyond compare. Forums for collective grief such as candlelight vigils, the funerals attended by thousands, Union Square in New York with its giant roll of paper that was filled in a half-hour with expressions of inner feelings, and fences plastered with memorial items and condolences, all helped make visible the authentic state of the people. Marks of respect, minutes of silence around the globe and personal stories in the media about those whose lives were lost gave recognition to the reality of the pain. And because of the sharing, love and prayers were sent in great waves to New York, Washington, Pennsylvania and to those who were suffering the loss. (There were those who also sent love and prayers to Afghanistan, where hundreds of thousands of Afghan refugees in a habitual state of terror were amassing to flee their country.)

Rob Lehman, who told us earlier about his cancer experience, spoke to me of the power of being a witness, "In the New Testament there is something about a cloud of witnesses and it was so much like that. We were all witnesses to this and it makes an enormous difference. We all had some form of oneness experience."

The communal sharing of pain seemed to spark a spirit that was admirable and created in many the determination not only to survive, but to thrive. The multitude of positive actions by professionals and civilians, including simple acts like the giving blood, baking cookies for workers at Ground Zero, or the selling of lemonade on street corners by children for the relief fund, were ways of choosing life and mobilizing the spirit in the midst of chaos. These were examples of the survivor mission mentioned earlier – taking the pain and using it to help others.

This quote by Howard Zinn[42] says eloquently all I would wish to say about choosing life when surrounded by destruction.

> To be hopeful in bad times is not just foolishly romantic. It is based on the fact that human history is a history not only of cruelty, but also of compassion, sacrifice, courage and kindness. What we choose to emphasize in this complex history will determine our lives. If we see only the worst, it destroys our capacity to do something. If we remember those times and places – and there are so many – where people have behaved magnificently, this gives us the energy to act, and at least the possibility of sending this spinning top of a world in a different direction. And if we do act, in however small a way, we don't have to wait for some grand utopian future. The future is an infinite succession of presents, and to live now as we think human beings should live, in defiance of all that is bad around us, is itself a marvelous victory.

Key 4. – Reassess Relationships

Millions of people's relationships to self, others, objects, and countries changed dramatically overnight. One New York man said, "Before Sept 11th I had never told another man I loved him. Now I put my arms around whoever, and tell them I love them." A worker at Ground Zero told how he was making his way home after a harrowing stint of service when a man in a garbage truck pulled over and said, "Hey, buddy, jump on I'll take you wherever you are going." New York Magazine reported that people that week were not going to bars or clubs to drink or dance but to embrace "strangers." One woman, shortly after the attacks, said, "On Monday I was an African American; on Tuesday I became an American." At the other extreme, innocent Muslims became targets for misplaced anger – enemies overnight. And now that the knee jerk reactions to the crisis have been observed and felt unfolding in relationships, we have the opportunity to become conscious and choose what patterns we want to nourish or reject.

The last steel girder to be removed from the Ground Zero site in May

2002 was wrapped in a flag and lowered with as much respect as if it had been a body – steel turned to sacred symbol. And an empty stretcher was ceremoniously carried from the site to represent the carrying out of the 1,700 people whose bodies were not recovered. This attack brought to the consciousness of millions the power of symbolic objects to help in rituals of release and what American's call "closure."

In order to maximize good global relationships, all nations would surely benefit from a regular reassessment of their relationship with and policies that affect each other. Just as one wounded person can affect the entire family dynamic, so can one needy or greedy country prevent the rest truly living in peace. Wounded nations require help. Until they are healed, we are all sick.

Key 5. – Identify and Release Lifelong Patterns

September 11 first shocked us to the core, and left millions feeling as if the "wrong" of terrorism was coming up to meet us everywhere. Then, slowly, it dawned that wrongs closer to home were coming up to meet us. It was inevitable, in espousing the belief that those responsible for perpetrating violence should be held accountable, that any violence in our own national history was brought into the spotlight, begging the question: Will we repeat our ineffective patterns or seek a new way of approaching the problem?

Nothing can remain under the carpet. It is as if our past – personal, national, and global – if not dealt with in an appropriate manner will come back to haunt us. Any areas of numbness, places we have frozen over in our attempt to hide from the difficult reality of what we have done or experienced, will begin to melt if the fire is hot enough. Whatever our sins (an archery term for off-center), the time of crisis offers the opportunity to pinpoint and change behavior that has in the past undermined our personal and global wellbeing.

Remember that Rosalind Winter told most of her clients after September 11 that they had a window of opportunity to access their earliest traumas with the collective support that they had never had before to rework them to another level. Windows of opportunity of this immensity are short-lived, but that does not mean that the past cannot be dealt with now when that communal support has waned. We can be thankful that it has helped us identify the challenges in need of attention and commit to finding specific support to release these long held patterns once and for all.

Key 6. – Cultivate Compassion: Silence the Judge

In the aftermath of the crisis I was bombarded with emails from around the world sent by those who knew I was writing this book and would be including wisdom stemming from the events of that day. This key, the necessity to cultivate compassion and calm the voice of revenge, was the most urgent and the most emphasized message.

The edited piece below[43] by psychiatrist, James Garbarino, (also Co-Director, Family Life Development Center) and E. L. Vincent (Professor of Human Development, Cornell University) summarizes the central message of them all.

> *Tibet's Dalai Lama is a world leader in teaching about compassion. One of his most important lessons is that 'true compassion is not just an emotional response, but a firm commitment founded on reason.' It is easy to feel sympathy for the victims of violence – human decency demands it. But it is much more difficult to feel true compassion – unshakeable understanding of how violence and rage arise in human beings…*
>
> *It is one thing to talk in public about 'bringing the perpetrators to justice,' quite another to speak of exacting our revenge. It is one thing to understand the origins of terrorism, another to portray the struggle as simply one of 'evil versus good.'*
>
> *Terrorists typically are caught up in their own scenarios of revenge and retaliation… For them, the acts they commit are not 'unprovoked assaults,' but rather their own version of 'bringing the perpetrators to justice.'*
>
> *All this is not to excuse the terrorist. No one of good faith or sensitive heart could or would do so. But if we are to do more than continue to escalate the cycle of violence we must do more than feel outrage and practice more than retaliation. We must seek a deeper understanding… It is more than a matter of our good and their evil. Each individual has a story to tell, a human story. Even as we oppose and block the terrorists we should remember this. Perhaps we can even understand something about the conditions abroad that give rise to this fanatical hatred of America.*

Family members of victims of September 11, who launched the project Peaceful Tomorrows[44] on Valentine's Day 2002, have been demonstrating in action what true compassion really means. They have been campaigning relentlessly to promote a discussion about better solutions to the tragedy – ones based on justice, not vengeance. A delegation of four traveled to Afghanistan and met with family members of Afghan civilians who had died as a result of the U.S. bombing campaign, in order to understand and to highlight their plight. Kelly Campbell, sister-in-law of Craig Amundson, who died in the Pentagon, told reporters, "We met many Afghan families who lost loved ones due to the U.S. bombing because they happened to be in the wrong place at the wrong time, just like our loved ones were on September 11."

And Phyllis Rodriguez, who lost her son, Greg, at the World Trade Center, said, when delivering a valentine letter to President Bush asking for help to set up a fund for innocent Afghan victims, "By helping others who are suffering from the effects of violence and war, we honor the memory of our lost loved ones in a positive way."

Key 7. – Reclaim Heart and Spirit

A few months before the September attacks, Native American Chief Arvol Looking Horse, 19th Generation Keeper of the Sacred White Buffalo Calf Pipe, wrote an article from which I quote:

> For the past six years, my work has concentrated on an effort on uniting the global community, through a message from our sacred ceremonies in recognizing a day of World Peace and Prayer on June 21st as a time to unite spiritually, each in our own ways of beliefs in the Creator… In our Prophecies it is told that we are now at the Crossroads, either unite Spiritually as a Global Nation, or be faced with chaos, disasters, diseases and tears from our relatives' eyes… In times of disasters it is sad to say that it is the only time that we unite spiritually… This new millennium will usher in an age of harmony or it will bring the end of life as we know it. Starvation, war and toxic waste have been the hallmark of the Great Myth of Progress and Development that ruled the last millennium. To us, as caretakers of the heart of Mother Earth, falls the responsibility of turning back the powers of destruction… The fate of future generations rests in our hands. We must understand the two ways we are free to follow, as we choose – the positive way or the negative way; the spiritual way or the material way. It's our own choice – each of ours and all of ours.

This is almost identical to the warning given by Arun Gandhi, "We are going to see more violence occur unless the rich decide they want to share their wealth with the rest of the world… Perhaps that step will take a big catastrophe."

The media has said time and again that symbolically the terrorists attacked the heart and soul of America. What does that mean? I think the truth is that they attacked what they perceived as America's heart – the biggest symbols of power and money, which are the terrorists' symbols of powerlessness. Yes, they murdered thousands of innocent people and consequently broke countless hearts, but their intent was undoubtedly to strike at the security of the nation – security based in wealth and military might.

At first, countless voices – the same voices that the terrorists sought to silence – defiantly called for bigger, better replacements for the magnificent twin towers, maybe believing that rebuilding these symbols of wealth would show America's strength of resolve, will and power. I think not. Not the power that matters anyway. Compare those voices with the voice that was heard a few months later suggesting light at the site of terror to mark the sixth month anniversary. How much more powerful a message could you ask for than the two beams of light that reached way higher than the concrete towers and stirred our emotions, our hearts, and our spirits with their dramatic symbology?

Someone said to me that they had heard that the towers could be seen in the light. Quite what they meant I don't know, but the image I was left with was of the material concrete world that includes money, possessions, our bodies and our five physical senses, being flooded and infused with the lighter energies of love, intuition, and the source of spirituality. Most certainly the image of those light beams blazing from Ground Zero spelt hope that the American people, in the wake of their loss, would intensify their expression of heart and spirit.

Interestingly, those who died in the attacks were of almost every color, culture and religion of the world – a microcosm of the world's people. The consequence of that was that every public ceremony or ritual that was conducted in their memory was called to represent the core truth of all religions. Spirituality and inter-faith wisdom were the order of the day. And this is exactly what Chief Arvol Looking Horse said was such an urgent need, "…to unite spiritually, each in our own ways of beliefs in the Creator." Maybe the reordering that British Prime minister, Tony Blair, spoke of could include creating inter-faith places of worship where we can rebuild our connection to the source of who we are and celebrate the unity beyond our diversity.

The images from Sept 11 are so powerful. Here's a comforting one about love noticed by Rob Lehman.

> I can't help but imagine the phone calls from so many people who could only say, 'I love you' while the terrorists attacked. It was as if those words almost transported the person into eternity. I think the words were carrying their souls as they said them. And the terrorists crashing into the top of the Twin Towers and dying in hatred while firemen and others rushed into the bottom sacrificing their lives out of love.

Key 8. – Find the Hidden Gifts

Each person will have their own personal silver lining to the black clouds of September 11, even if they are not yet seen. But what are the most evident macrocosmic gifts, the gifts to the human race? Most of these have already been covered because they are the opportunities offered by the keys. So, let me summarize these, firstly recognizing that these gifts are to be found in the bigger picture and that their discovery relies on the ability to look up from the personal angle and to include a wider perspective.

- The multitude of questions that have arisen calling us to consciousness as a species. What are you doing? What do you believe in?

- What will you do to change what doesn't work?

- The opportunity to explore where true safety resides and how to obtain it for ourselves, our nations, and the world without feeling controlled or being controlling.

- The experience of a kind of unity through shared pain that can be accessed and used as a resource in the future.

- The chance to give, to serve and to enhance community, both local and global.

- The clear reflection of international relationships at this time and the call to integrity in all dealings with others.

- Light being shone on past "mistakes" and a renewed impetus toward learning from them and releasing ineffective patterns.

- The awakening of mass compassion that can then be extended to all who are in pain, whatever "side" they are on.

- The challenge to keep our hearts open wide rather than contracting in fear.

- The emergence of a shared spirituality and inter-faith worship.

I deliberated whether I should include the next piece, channeled writing by author and spiritual teacher David Spangler, (who helped create the Findhorn spiritual community), for it is a little out of the ordinary. Then I remembered something very similar my mother impressed on me when my grandma died: how she was totally convinced, because she felt it, that on death a kind of package of energy had been released. This energy she was sure was an inheritance that she could use in her life. I received this piece three times as it made its rounds on email in September 2001. See whether it resonates as truth for you.

> What has taken place is an act of sacrifice and a gift given by the Soul of America to the world at large... Whenever a death occurs, an energy of spirit is released. An incarnational portal is opened, just as it is at birth. This energy is unformed. It is a gift that flows between the worlds. What is shaped from this gift is up to those who receive it, as well as by the one whose death has released it...
>
> Think of this energy as a kind of inheritance... Not all inheritances are spent wisely or well, not all gifts are used with grace and blessing, but the gift itself is there nonetheless. The giving of this gift is an act of soul and is automatic... a result of crossing the boundary. To release this energy and to give this gift is not a conscious decision, but someone who dies in a mindful and loving way will greatly add to this gift and turn it from an unconscious energy into a consciously positive one. Also, if love is present in the last moments of physical life, even if the death is violent or as a result of hateful acts, this gift can emerge untainted by the hate that may have caused the killing. Many of those who died in this event did so with thoughts of love and courage... and the importance of this cannot be underestimated...

There are energies of hatred and violence circling your world, so to speak, looking to land, and all nations, including your own, are contributing to this simply because people contribute to it in millions of small and mindless ways. That this particular energy landed in your nation in this way was partly a matter of consequences returning for certain patterns and actions you have set into motion. You cannot avoid paying a price for your own acts of violence in the world. But in spite of what many may say about America's responsibility, this action was not primarily one of paying a price. It was an act of sacrifice, a deliberate taking on of a portion of the world's hatred and suffering, because the soul of America has the capacity to receive this hatred and transmute it... The soul of this country took it on, knowing it could absorb this blow. An energy of love and courage has been released into the world. There will be changes and there will be blessings.

The gift of this sacrifice can be received in many ways by people. For those who can receive it in a way that takes them into the deepest places of love and the celebration of the common spirit of humanity, and whose hearts can be opened to forgive, let them be grateful, but they should not condemn those who will receive this gift in different ways. If your heart is broken and opened to love, this is a grace for you to embody, not a club for you to hold over your brother's or sister's heart.

...In the opening of the portal so powerfully by the deaths of so many, this gift of life from death, even though initiated by the hatred of a few, became a channel for an outpouring of the love that is at the heart of America. It is, I know, a painful gift, but it is a gift nonetheless. It is for you who remain to take that precious gift and reshape your world with it.

Powerful, thought-provoking words. I often think of death as a kind of sacred sacrifice because of the profound wave of teaching that it offers, and I guess that the teaching potential alone could be seen as a kind of package of possibility to be grasped and shaped to our benefit. I wonder if this, and the potential for using the event of death as a destructive tool, is contained in this invisible energetic form mentioned. Life is so full of mystery.

It feels fitting to complete our journey together in the Church of Love – an ancient vision of a landscape of united "worship" showing us that although there is certain progression as humanity evolves, wisdom is timeless.

The Church of Love

It has no fabric, only understanding.
It has no membership, save those who know they belong.
It has no rivals because it is non-competitive.
It has no ambition because it seeks only to serve.
It knows no boundaries for nationalisms are unloving.
It is not of itself because it seeks to enrich all groups and religions.
It acknowledges all great teachers of all the ages who have shown the truth of Love.
Those who participate practice the art of Love in all their beings.
There is no walk of life or nationality that is a barrier. Those who are know.
It seeks not to teach but to be, and by being, enrich.
It recognizes that the way we are may be the way of those around us
because we are that way.
It recognizes the whole planet as a Being of which we are a part.

It recognizes that the time has come for the supreme transmutation, the ultimate
alchemical act of conscious change of the ego into a voluntary return to the whole.

It does not proclaim itself with a loud voice but in the subtle realms of loving.
It salutes all those in the past who have blazoned the path but have paid the price.

It admits no hierarchy or structure, for no one is greater than another.

Its members shall know each other by their deeds and being and by their eyes and
by no other outward sign save an embrace.
Each one will dedicate their life to the silent loving of their neighbor and environment
and the planet, while carrying out their task, however exalted or humble.
It recognizes the supremacy of the great idea that may only be accomplished
if the human race practices the supremacy of Love.
It has no reward to offer either here or in the hereafter save that of the
ineffable joy of being and loving.
Each shall seek to advance the cause of understanding, doing good by stealth
and teaching only by example.
They shall heal their neighbor, their community and our Planet.
It has no secret and no initiation save that of true understanding of the power of Love
and knows that, if we want it to be so,
the world will change but only if we change ourselves first.

All those who belong, belong. They belong to the church of love.

Attributed to be a Cathar prophesy of 1244 AD
Translator unknown.

NOTES

1   A. Strauss & J.Corbin: *Basics of Qualitative Research* (Sage Publications, Ca. 1990).

2   M'haletta and Carmella B'Hahn: *Benjaya's Gifts* (Hazelwood Press,1996). See www.carmellaB.freeuk.com or www.amazon.co.uk.

3   Ted Andrews: *Animal-Speak* (Llewellyn Publications, St. Paul, 1999).

4   This specific information about trauma and the work of James Garbarino came from a conversation with Linda Lantieri, following a study she has done on the subject.

5   James Garbarino and Claire Bedard: *Parents Under Siege* (The Free Press, 2001), p.42

6   *Parents Under Siege,* p.36

7   James Garbarino: *Raising Children in a Socially Toxic Environment* (Jossey-Bass Publishers, San Francisco, 1995), pp 158-62

8   It is suggested that *Mourning Has Broken* is used for study groups of this subject matter by reading one section, or key, per week and working through the Questions and Reflections for that key at each meeting. This offers an eight-week long course in exploring and transforming your personal relationship to adversity. The questions can be approached individually, in pairs, or small groups but it is important to always feed back the learning into the whole group. It is advisable that one person takes responsibility for reading through the questions and deciding in advance how they would best be approached in this particular group setting. A minimum of 2 hours will be needed for each session. Colored pens/crayons and journals will be required.

9   Adapted slightly from the work of Mircea Eliade.

10 Daniel Goleman: *Emotional Intelligence* (Bantam Books, 1995)

11 Peter Levine: *Waking the Tiger, Healing Trauma* (North Atlantic Books, 1997)

12 Dean Radin: *The Conscious Universe: the Scientific Truth of Psychic Phenomena* (HarperEdge, 1997)

13 Ellen Bass and Laura Davis: From *The Courage to Heal* (Vermillion, London, 2002).

14 Linda Lantieri and Janet Patti: *Waging Peace in our Schools* (Beacon Press, Boston, 1996).

15 Mark Josephs-Serra: *Sex, Spirit and Community* (Jon Carpenter Publishing, 2000)

16 Elizabeth Lesser: *The New American Spirituality* (Random House, New York, 1999)

17 Explained further in *Emotional Intelligence* by Daniel Goleman (Bantam Books, 1995)

18 Judith Lewis Herman: *Trauma and Recovery* (Basic Books, New York, 1992)

19 Karl Slaikeu and Steve Lawhead: *The Phoenix Factor — Surviving and Growing though Personal Crisis* (Houghton Mifflin, 1985).

20 Jack Kornfield: *After the Ecstasy, The Laundry* (Rider, 2000)

21 Hakomi Somatics Institute, P.O. Box 19438, Boulder, CO 90308, U.S.A.; www.hakomisomatics.com

22 Peter Levine: *Waking the Tiger, Healing Trauma* (North Atlantic Books, 1997)

23 Patricia Hentz: "The Body Remembers: Grieving and a Circle of Time" in *Qualitative Health Research,* Vol.12 No 2, February 2002 (Sage Publications), pp161-172

24 For more information on how to clean our language *see* www.cleanlanguage.co.uk

25 Center for Non-violent Communication Address: CNVC, P.O. Box 2662, Sherman, Texas 75091 email: CNVC@compuserve.com Website: www.cnvc.org Marshall Rosenberg, PhD.: *Non-violent Communication: A Language of Compassion* (PuddleDancer Press, 1999)

26 *Journeys of Transformation* (One By One, Inc. P.O.Box 1709, Brookline, MA 02446, U.S.A.)

27 Mark Nepo: *The Book of Awakening* (Conari Press)

28 Danah Zohar and Ian Marshall: *Spiritual Intelligence: The Ultimate Intelligence* (Bloomsbury, London, 2000)

29 Wayne Muller: *Sabbath* (Bantam Books, 1999)

30 The Collaborative for Academic, Social, and Emotional Learning website is: www.casel.org

31 For more information read Allan and Barbara Pease: *Why Men Don't Listen and Women Can't Read Maps* (Pease Training International, 1998)

32 Institute of HeartMath, 14700 West Park Avenue, Boulder Creek, CA 95006, U.S.A. Website: www.heartmath.com.

33 For further information on the Resolving Conflict Creatively Program see www.esrnational.org. Linda is also connected to the Collaborative for Academic, Social, and Emotional Learning (CASEL) www.casel.org.

34 Linda Lantieri: *Schools with Spirit* (Beacon Press, 2001)

35 From an article by Pat Ogden in the Hakomi Somatics Training Manual (Hakomi Somatics Institute).

36 Peter Levine website: www.traumatichealing.com

37 Center for Grieving Children, PO Box 1438, Portland, Maine 04104, U.S.A. Tel: 207-775-5216 Website:www.cgcmaine.org, Patricia's e-mail at the center: patricia@cgcmaine.org.

38 Lists of symptoms of trauma taken from Judith A. Swack's paper: "Antidote for the Psychological Effects of Terrorism: A Rapid Biological Technique for Healing Trauma from mind and body." Website: www.jaswack.com

³⁹ First published in the *Journal of Jungian Theory and Practice,* Fall 2001, vol. 3, NY, C.G. Jung Institute of New York.

⁴⁰ Richard Wilhelm: *The I Ching, or Book of Changes.* (Rendered into English by C. Baynes. Princeton: Princeton University Press, 1950)

41 Hope Magazine, May/June 2002.

⁴² Howard Zinn: *You Can't Be Neutral on a Moving Train: a Personal History of our Times* (Beacon Press, 1994)

⁴³ From an email entitled: "The Attack on America: What Can It Teach Children About Understanding and Revenge" by James Garbarino and E. L. Vincent.

⁴⁴ www.peacefultomorrows.com

The author's website is
www.carmellaB.freeuk.com

*For personal counseling and
requests to run workshops/talks
she may be contacted at*
carmella@macunlimited.net